AF788711

To: William Stokes.

From: David M. Hollingsworth

The Rise, the Fall, and the Recovery of Southeast Asia's Minidragons

The Rise, the Fall, and the Recovery of Southeast Asia's Minidragons

How Can Their History Be Lessons We Shall Learn during the Twenty-first Century and Beyond?

David Anthony Hollingsworth

LEXINGTON BOOKS

A division of
ROWMAN & LITTLEFIELD PUBLISHERS, INC.
Lanham • Boulder • New York • Toronto • Plymouth, UK

LEXINGTON BOOKS

A division of Rowman & Littlefield Publishers, Inc.
A wholly owned subsidiary of The Rowman & Littlefield Publishing Group, Inc.
4501 Forbes Boulevard, Suite 200
Lanham, MD 20706

Estover Road
Plymouth PL6 7PY
United Kingdom

Copyright © 2007 by Lexington Books

All rights reserved. No part of this publication may be reproduced, stored in a retrieval system, or transmitted in any form or by any means, electronic, mechanical, photocopying, recording, or otherwise, without the prior permission of the publisher.

British Library Cataloguing in Publication Information Available

Library of Congress Cataloging-in-Publication Data

Hollingsworth, David Anthony, 1970–
The rise, the fall, and the recovery of Southeast Asia's minidragons : how can their history be lessons we shall learn during the twenty-first century and beyond? / David Anthony Hollingsworth.
p. cm.
Includes bibliographical references and index.
ISBN-13: 978-0-7391-1981-5 (cloth : alk. paper)
ISBN-10: 0-7391-1981-8 (cloth : alk. paper)
1. Southeast Asia—Economic conditions—20th century. 2. Southeast Asia—Economic policy. I. Title.
HC441.H65 2007
330.959—dc22 2006100865

Printed in the United States of America

™ The paper used in this publication meets the minimum requirements of American National Standard for Information Sciences—Permanence of Paper for Printed Library Materials, ANSI/NISO Z39.48–1992.

In Loving Memory of

My Grandmother, Imogene Scott.

My guiding light and my shining star! The woman who took all that life had to offer and unselfishly gave so much of it to those around her.

My Eternal Love for her that shall remain Eternal.

In Lasting Memory of

My Grandfather Edwin Cooper, whose love and gracefulness is never forgotten.

In Fond Memory of

Karl Williams, a father figure who sacrificed a lot and who played a huge part in showing me what the world was like.

This Literature is Dedicated

~To my mother Audrey Cooper, who never gave up on me and who is keeping hope alive.

~To my Grandfather, Constantine Scott, who remains endearing and special to me.

~To my uncle Winston O.B. Smith, my aunt Paulette Smith, and to my wonderful cousins Kaunda and Keisha.

~To my family, who never lost faith in me.

~To my landlord and friend Charles Fields, who saved my life in more ways than one.

~To St. Raymond's High School and SUNY at Buffalo, the sources of the most defining moment of my life.

~To my professor Dr. Ronald E. Muller, who reminded me of the essence of being a better, more direct writer.

~To my professor Dr. C Randall Henning, who have never doubted me.

~To my professor Dr. John Richardson, who kindly gave me advice of how to present my book and who taught me a thing or two about the publishing business.

~To my friends Gunninand Persaud, Ian Plant, and Michael Zwibel, three of the most generous souls who never stopped caring.

~To all my friends, colleagues, and peers, who continue to give me advice along the way and who still believe that I have a chance to make a difference.

Thank You and God Bless!

The Table of Contents

List of Figures

List of Tables

Abbreviations and Acronyms

ACC	Anti-Corruption Commissions (Indonesia)
ACU	Asian Currency Unit
ADB	Asian Development Bank
ADO	Asian Development Outlook (annual report from the Asian Development Bank)
AMC	Asset Management Corporation (Thailand)
AMCs	Asset Management Companies (Taiwan)
AMU	Asset Management Unit
AOT	The Airport Authority (Thailand)
APEC	Asia-Pacific Economic Cooperation
ASEAN	Association of Southeast Asian Nations
BAPEPAM	Capital Market Supervisory Agency
BAPPENAS	National Development Planning Agency
BBC	Bangkok Bank of Commerce
BBC	British Broadcasting Corporation
BCA	Bank Central Asia
BIBF	Bangkok International Banking Facility
BIS	Bank of International Settlement
BNM	Bank Negara Malaysia
BOT	Bank of Thailand
BTN	Bank Tabungan Negara
CAR	Capital Assets Ratios
CBC	The Central Bank of China
CGI	Consultative Group on Indonesia
CIECD	Council of International Economic Cooperation and Development
CNN	Cable News Network (of the United States)
CPF	The Central Provident Fund (Singapore)
CPI	Consumer Price Index
DBS	Development Bank of Singapore
EDB	Economic Development Board (Singapore)
EGAT	State electricity generation authority (Thai land)
EOI	Export-Oriented Industrialization
EPB	Entrepreneurs Promotion Board (Thailand)
EPU	Economic Planning Unit
EPZs	Export Processing Zones (Taiwan)
ERC	Economic Review Committee (Singapore)
ERSO	Electronics Research and Service Organization
ESB	Economic Stabilization Board

FDI	Foreign Direct Investment
FIDF	Financial Institutions Development Fund
FMP	Fourth Malaysian Plan
FRA	Financial Restructuring Agency
GDP	Gross Domestic Products
GLCs	Government-linked corporations (Malaysia)
GNP	Gross National Products
GOLKAR	Golangan Karya (Functional Group) -Military run political party of Indonesia
HPAEs	High Performance Asian Economies
IBRA	Indonesia Bank Restructuring Agency
IBRD	The International Banking for Reconstruction and Development (of the World Bank)
ICA	Industrial Coordination Act (Malaysia)
ICG	International Crisis Group (headquartered: Brussels)
ICTs	Information and communications technologies
IECDF	International Economic Corporation Development Fund
IGGI	Inter Governmental Group on Indonesia
IMF	International Monetary Fund
ISCAP	Institutional Securities Custodian Programme (Malaysia)
ISI	Import-Substitution Industrialization
IT	Information Technology
ITRI	Industrial Technology Research Institution
KBE	Knowledge-based economy
KLSE	Kuala Lumpur Stock Exchange
KMT	Kuomintang Party (Taiwan)
LTCM	Long Term Capital Management
LTOs	Large Tax Payers Offices (Indonesia)
MAS	Monetary Authority of Singapore
MBS	Mortgage-backed securities
MFN	Most-favored nation (of GATT/WTO)
MIDA	Malaysian Industrial Development Board
MIER	Malaysian Institute of Economic Research
MITI	Ministry of International Trade and Industry
MNCs ***OR***	Multinational Corporations ***OR***
MNFs	Multinational Fims
MTI	Ministry of Trade and Industry (Singapore)
NAP	New Aspiration Party (of Thailand)
NBFIs	Non-bank Financial Institutions

NCDs	Negotiable Certificates of Deposits
NDP	New Development Policy
NEAC	National Economic Action Council
NEP	New Economic Policy
NGO(s)	Non-governmental Organization(s)
NICs ***OR***	Newly Industrialized Countries ***OR***
NIEs	Newly Industrialized Economies
NOPs	Net Open Positions
NPB	National Productivity Board
NPL	Non-performing loan
NT	New Taiwanese dollar
ODA	Official Development Assistance
OECD	Organization for Economic Cooperation and Development
OTC	Over-the-counter (an option)
PAN	National Mandate Party (Indonesia)
PAP	People's Action Party (Singapore)
PDI	Partai Demokrasi Indonesia (Indonesian Democratic Party)
PDI-P	Partai Demokrasi Indonesia-Perjuangan
PKB	The National Awakening Party (Indonesia)
PKI	The Communist Party of Indonesia
POSBank	Post Office Savings Bank
PPATK	Center for Financial Transaction Analysis
PS	Peso (Philippines' currency)
PTAs	Preferential Trade Agreements
PTT	State Petroleum Company (Thailand)
RG	Ringgit (Malaysia's currency)
RP	Rupiah (Indonesia's currency)
S	Singapore dollar
SAR	Severe Acute Respiratory Illness
SBI	Sertifikat Bank Indonesia
SBPU	Surat Berharga Pasar Uang
SDR	Special Drawing Right
SET	Stock Exchange of Thailand
SFC	Securities and Futures Exchange Commission
SFIs	Specialized Financial Institutions (Thailand)
SMEs ***OR***	Small and medium-sized enterprises ***OR***
SMBs	Small and medium-sized businesses
SOEs	State-owned Enterprises
TAFI	Total Assets of all types of Financial Institutions
TDB	Trade Development Board (Singapore)

TSMC	Taiwan Semiconductor
UMC	United Microelectronics
UMNO	United Malay National Organization
UNCITRAL	United Nations Commission of International Trade Law
UNDP	United Nations Development Programme
WTO	World Trade Organization

The Preface

> The East Asian tigers were simply the best investment opportunities in the late 1980s and 1990s: disciplined work forces, low wages, pliable yet reliable governments, and no need to worry about inadequate internal markets to buy goods destined for export the better. These were countries where, when crisis hit, ordinary citizens carried gifts of family gold to Korean banks to help the banks meet foreign payments and thereby "shaming" the nation. Truly a lender's dream (Hahnel, 1999: p. 46).

This phenomenal growth was made possible because of the governments', leaders' and the people's visionary stance towards economic growth, sustainability, and prosperity. A social contract was created between leaders and the population to make economic growth and prosperity possible; the contract that cherished the mechanisms for such a growth, but at the same time, involved the population as much as possible. That was what happened since the late 1950s in East Asia, beginning with Japan. There were plenty of protectionism, but that was accompanied by fixing up health care, education, income disparities, and infrastructure. While people were encouraged to save, they were given opportunities to work and invest. Labor poolings (or labor recruitments and trainings) were done efficiently and with that aforementioned visionary stance. That stance did not occur only in Asia, but also in parts of the Americas, Europe, and Africa.

Other than the social contract, there was an economic dimension of this phenomenal growth that resulted not only from the contract per se, but from the daring yet realistic subsequential shift from the region's inwardness to essentially global participation (to what most today would call globalization). The end results of this shift, from the protectionist ladened import-substitution industrialization (ISI) to export-orientation industrialization yielded a rather long-standing and influential economic prosperity. This was complemented by capital and investment inflows, technological transfers, and developmental aid from countries like Japan, the United States, and of Europe. The policies countries of the region initiated assured their respective economic growths and sustainabilities.

But matters went much astrayed after the early 1980s, which culminated to the Asian Financial Crisis of 1997-1998. Policies started to divert from that social contract, that visionary stance, as governments leaned more towards liberalization and favoritism. Liberalization per se was not a cause of the financial mishaps of the 1990s (in Taiwan and Singapore, it worked quite well). It was the matter of how it was used. In many cases, countries engaged in liberalization in the midst of huge capital inflows while supervision of the financial sector was lacking. Furthermore, what made matters worse was that governments began to engage in moral hazard behavior and crony capitalism, which became among the prominent trepidations in the Pacific-rim region and beyond: that is, the series of ill-advised economic endeavors and policy makings undertaken by much of the global community including Southeast Asia became paramount. Much of the end results from the series of mismanagements and ill-conceived policies (and politics) were not intentional. But then again, remedies to reverse them were met by corruption, favoritism, lack of prudence, and promises to reform that were either short-lived or never really reached fruition. Once the Crisis hit, it was too late, and the responses to the crises like in Asia by the governments and the international community including the IMF, yielded no easy answers.

It must be pointed out in haste that the imbalances of policies were not uniquely Asian. The aforementioned set of developments that led to the financial mishaps of the 1990s went beyond Asia and into Latin America (Mexico, Argentina, Brazil), Europe (in Russia for instance), and much elsewhere. The Asian Financial Crisis of 1997-1998 happened to be one of the major crises in this past decade alone that represented the watershed of what were going on before and essentially revealed, and starkly so, how unstable and vulnerable the global financial system actually was. As Peter Beinart puts it:

> ...the East Asian financial crisis had exposed the frightening fragility of a world economic system in which capital was so mobile that it could bankrupt whole nations virtually overnight. Blair proposed a new financial architecture to stabilize the global economy, just as the Allied powers did at Bretton Woods in the final days of World War II. He urged a new push for free trade and for relief of third world debt, to promote global economic development (Beinart, 2006: p. 84).

Prime Minister Tony Blair's proposal was anything but new or original. But at least he represented a growing consensus of those who continues to argue that the global financial restructuring is of critical importance. But for Thomas Friedman, something much more involving and far-seeing shall commence in the post-Crisis era, that something that goes beyond the surface matters. A new, contemporary look at the social bargain is needed to resume the economic growth of East Asia and abroad. However, what is needed more than anything is what I call vision, the road map that would give the population a clear picture where we are and where we shall go a generation from now. It goes hand in hand with the social bargain argument and it is that vision which is implicit in Thomas Friedman's eloquent statement:

> A politics of sustainable globalization needs more than just the correct picture of what is happening in the world. It also needs the right balance of policies. Specifically, it demands a new social bargain between workers, financiers, and governments that will make for sustainable globalization. What is needed instead of either of these extremes is a new social compact that embraces free

> markets but also ensures that they benefit, and are tolerable for, as many people as possible. You stabilize globalization by democratizing globalization-by making it work for more and more people all the time (Friedman, 2000: p. 424).

This book will explain Southeast Asia's phenomenal growth, its eventual downfall, the responses to the downfall by the countries of the region as well as by the international community including the IMF, and the current state of the countries' economies in the Post-Crisis recovery era. Recommendations and prescriptions towards continual recovery are included throughout this book. After a lengthy introduction, which paints the overall picture from growth, to the Crisis, and to the recovery, five of the Southeast Asian countries (namely Taiwan, Singapore, Malaysia, Thailand, and Indonesia), will be case studies and are the empirical basis for this literature. While countries like Korea, Hong Kong, and the Philippines, also enjoyed economic prosperity after the 1960s, they will merely be referenced throughout in regards to the region's overall picture of the economic growth, sustainability, and the eventual downfall. The final chapters will be as broad as the first in using the Asian experience in the global perspectives of proper policies that ensured growth and sustainability and the improper policies that yielded the misfortunes in recent memory.

Chapter One is that introduction and it accomplishes the aforementioned objectives in broad terms, namely, analyzing Southeast Asia and East Asia roads and mechanisms for economic development and sustainability. The chapter does so by: 1) explaining the prerequisites for economic growth, including investments toward education and health as well as policies toward land reform and income distribution, 2) explaining the importance of import-substitution industrialization (ISI) as a necessary economic strategy for export-oriented industrialization (EOI), 3) explaining the importance of foreign direct investment and portfolio (indirect) investment, and 4) explaining the success of Southeast Asia after shifting from ISI to EOI.

However, the chapter concludes by painting the overall picture of the financial crisis that plagued the Asia-Pacific region. This will be done by: 1) examining the short-term and long term causes of the Asian Financial Crisis that plagued the Asia-Pacific region, 2) explaining the reactions of the international community to the Crisis, and 3) outlining the possible solutions formulated by the international community in reversing the Crisis and to prevent the re-occurrence of another (or at least of the severity of a crisis of that calibre).

Chapter Two examines Taiwan's economic growth and development, economic sustainability, and its success in weathering the adverse effects of the Financial Crisis. What made Taiwan unique from Singapore and Malaysia was that its efforts towards economic growth were accompanied almost from the onset by FDI and economic aid-based development assistance chiefly from the United States. The United States, primarily instrumental in the development of

Taiwan, helped to accelerate economic development from ISI to export-oriented strategies. Through the Four and Six-Year Plans that led to industrial and financial liberalization from 1953 through the 1990s, Taiwan became among the major trading partners of the Pacific region.

The government's decisive economic and financial policies and actions propelled Taiwan through the Asian Financial Crisis relatively unscathed. Before the Crisis, Taiwan was able to maintain good economic fundamentals, such as expansive foreign reserves, minimal or no foreign debt, current account surpluses, relatively strong banking systems, and sound monetary and fiscal policies. It successfully maintained current account surpluses through saving rates, which were higher than investment levels. Therefore, short-term and unhedged debts did little harm to Taiwan during the Asian Financial Crisis of 1997-1998. More importantly, it was the Taiwanese government's prudent budgeting and active management that ultimately prevented the Taiwanese markets from the emergence of the Asian Financial Crisis (Noble and Ravenhill, 2000: p. 104).

The chapter will conclude by assessing Taiwan in the Post-Crisis Era. Although Taiwan did not suffer the severity of the Crisis as did, for example, Indonesia, it took steps in initiating a series of financial reforms including the "Symposium on the Current Economic Problems and Resolution Schemes" of 1999. A brief recession occurred in 2001 through 2002 notwithstanding the reforms. However, Taiwan's monetary policy remained flexible and trading performances improved, thanks in large part to China's Central Bank in its role in stimulating the Taiwanese economy.

Chapter Three explains Singapore's economic growth and development, economic sustainability, and its capacity to weather the Asian Financial Crisis. The uniqueness of Singapore rested in the fact that it continues to be a compact urban society, with neither an agricultural base nor the natural resources to build upon and tap in order to generate wealth. However, after Singapore separated itself from the Malaysian Federation in 1965, it engaged in a series of policies and deregulation efforts toward a predominant laissez-faire government. Furthermore, Japanese FDI proved to be instrumental in the continual economic emergence of the country. Consequently, Singapore became a successful financial center, and a major trading partner in the region.

Singapore, like Taiwan, Malaysia, and Hong Kong, exercised successful economic fundamentals since the late 1960s. However, its failure to escape the Asian Financial Crisis of 1997-1998 was not due to governmental policies per se. Instead, the Asian Financial Crisis had an indirect impact on the Singaporean economy, primarily because Singapore had large trade and investment links with other countries of Southeast Asia and East Asia. As investment and trade decreased rapidly before and during the Crisis, Singapore's economy and stock market consequentially declined.

Singapore, like Taiwan however, underwent a brief recessionary period in 2001 through 2002. Even before the recession, notwithstanding Singapore's sound economic performances in 2000, it began to witness a rise in unemployment, lower wages, property depression, as well as general decreases in trade of non-oil products. A considerable drop of global demand for high-valued products was the main reason for this brief economic slide. However, the government's resilient response to the recession was swift, efficient, and flexible, bringing forth a variety of stimulus packages that aided Singapore in overcoming the recession by the Spring of 2002. The packages were not well received, however, for Singapore remains among the most trade dependent nations in the world. However, the recovery, modest in nature in 2002 and more so in 2003, continues to give hope of a more fuller recovery phase for Singapore in 2004 and beyond, especially since the government demonstrated in the past how well it adapted to the ebbs and flows of the global market. Singapore exceeded that hope in 2004 and 2005.

Chapter Four evaluates Malaysia's economic growth and development, sustainability, and its ability to react to the Asian Financial Crisis of 1997-1998. Through governmental policies towards financial and industrial liberalizations, Malaysia enjoyed high economic growth and low inflation for three decades. Prime Minister Dr. Mahathir's "Look East" policies of 1981 collectively paved the way for the recipience of Japanese FDI and technological transfers. However, Malaysia was plagued by governmental indecisiveness during the outbreak of the Financial Crisis, and, its currency, the ringgit, devalued by over 30 percent in late 1997, resulting in an economic recession. In 1998, when the Malaysian government became more decisive in the reflation efforts (such as capital controls and expansionary macroeconomic policy), it effectively reversed the effects of the regional financial panic and gave Malaysia a growth rate of 4.7 percent by 1999 (Perkins and Woo, 2000: p. 242). The growth rate persists quite strongly since then.

However, this literature will also discuss the financial downturn and managerial crisis of Malaysia. After Malaysia enjoyed its economic success of the 1980s, thanks in part to its financial liberalization policies, Malaysia began to be succumbed to the Financial Crisis of 1997-1998. What made Malaysia unique was that it succumbed to the Crisis with only a little foreign debt exposure of its banking system. Therefore, it was successful in sorting itself through the Crisis without an IMF sponsored rescue package. But, Malaysia was plagued with severe slippages of the stock market and the exchange rate, partially due to political indecisiveness and unorthodox attacks made by Prime Minister Dr. Mahathir on currency speculators and currency traders. The financial sector was highly vulnerable due to non-performing loans, huge capital flights, and crony capitalism. By 1998, however, political and economic efforts became more decisive and coherent, which turn Malaysia around towards recovery. That recovery was made even more possible by the government's move towards capital controls as well as expansionary macroeconomic policies (including stimulating tax measures and adjustments in investment allowances and depreciation).

However, Malaysia has ways to go towards full recovery. Among the areas Malaysia must continue to work on is enhancing its competitiveness and labor productivity. In addition, issues such as protectionism, fiscal balancing, and China's economic boom and its growing influence especially in East Asia, are continuing to challenge the country, particularly with an historic change of leadership in October 2003 when Abdullah Badawi took over as leader after Dr. Mahathir.

Chapter Five explores Thailand's economic growth, its economic downfall, and its strong recovery since the Crisis. Thailand's economic growth was, at least to an extent, unique, because of the level of uncertainty and doubts expressed on the country's potential for economic development and prosperity. From the standpoint of many, Sarit's dictatorship and heavily politicized sectors were impediments to investment as well as to commercial activities. However, the Sarit administration proved quite the opposite by not only limiting the power of technocrats, but by attracting new investors and clients through expanding entrepreneurial opportunities. During its ISI phase, Thailand initiated a variety of investment incentives despite the protectionism it held rather tightly; the protectionism that remained during its exporting phase. The incentives, as well as the financial liberalization policies of the 1980s, propelled Thailand's economic growth.

However, it was the same liberalization policies that served as critical factors in Thailand's economic downfall. In discussing the origins of the Crisis, this chapter will point out a variety of policy errors that fueled the severity of the Crisis even more profoundly, including Thailand's financial liberalization efforts. Furthermore, political confrontations especially during the Chavalit and Leekpai administrations will be explained in evaluating the political and electoral weaknesses of Thailand. After discussing the nature of the Crisis and policy responses towards it, this chapter will discuss how Thailand rebounded strongly after this economic catastrophe (for instance, its GDP in 2003 was 6.7 percent and 4.5 percent two years later). But Thailand is not without problems. Along with high global oil prices that has some adverse effects in Thailand's economic performance, there's a current political uncertainty due to a serious rift with Thaksin Shinawatra and his administration since early 2006 (his Shin Corp deal fueled the political conflict). On a more promising note, however, is that among the policy recommendations Thailand has successfully met include lowering unemployment, being accommodating in its monetary and fiscal policies, stimulating credit expansion, as well as generating greater financial and fiscal transparency.

Chapter Six discusses Indonesia's rise to commercial power before being plagued by political and economic instabilities by the early-1990s. Achieving independence and a complete, stable governing body, was hard-earned, and was marred by political unrest after the Second World War. Sukarno's *economic nationalism*, the principle that argued for economic autarky and isolationism, placed Indonesian economy further in doubt. It was not until Suharto's arrival to power that Indonesia's economic evolution began to take flight. He achieved that through the principle of *economic rationalism,* the principle that emphasizes the achievement of economic efficiency. Consequently, the GDP growth rate for Indonesia was no less than five percent for the next twenty-seven years (1970-1997).

Although Indonesia enjoyed economic prosperity due to financial liberalization and the series of deregulation packages since the 1980s, it became plagued with economic and financial crisis of unprecedented severity. As this chapter will explain, among the reasons for the financial crisis was the unstable political climate under the leadership of Suharto. Moral hazard and crony capitalism were "the norms of the land" and led to increasing vulnerability in the financial sector and further political confrontations which eventually became violent. Although the rescue packages of the International Monetary Fund (IMF) were made with good intentions, they deepened the severity of the Crisis by not directly attacking the sources of Indonesia's macroeconomic and financial woes. Indonesia's recovery from the Crisis was slow and precarious at first. The economy contracted by 16 percent during the peak of the Crisis in 1998 through 1999. Although the GDP grew by over 5 percent in the fourth quarter on 1999, Indonesia witnessed a surge of unemployment and poverty by 2000. From 2000 through 2002, the GDP growth remained modest in nature due to declining investment as well as limited advances in overcoming the underlying impediments to investor confidence. However, the government remained active in generating initiatives and reforms for the ongoing recovery phase, including the introduction of the "White Paper," a program which comprises a number of economic measures. The measures includes maintaining macroeconomic stability, restructuring and reforming the bank and non-bank financial sectors, and increasing the level of investment, exports, as well as employment by improving the overall business and investment climates. Although credibility and crony capitalism remain, the recent election of Susilo Bambang Yudhoyono offers at least some optimism that Indonesia will become a more ideal participant in the global trading community.

Chapter Seven serves as a comprehensive summary of this literature. Other than dealing with the overall picture of the Asian experience, this chapter conjures up lessons to be drawn from Asia's economic growth, to its dealing with the Crisis, and to its Recovery phase. The lessons surround both: 1) economic growth and sustainability, and 2) the factors leading up to the Asian Financial Crisis of 1997-1998. This chapter is a recapitulation of why the Southeast Asian region achieved such phenomenal economic success after the mid-1960s, why this region became adversely affected by the Crisis in scope both unprecedented and unforeseen, and the steps the region has taken (and in some instances, ought to take) to reverse the lingering effects of the Crisis as well as to prevent the severity of this previous one that essentially shook and shocked our global community. Also, because both China and India are becoming more influential in regional and global economic affairs, they will be examined briefly in this chapter.

However, what makes *Chapter Eight* stand out as the most unique and far-reaching of the chapters is because it goes beyond the history, the numbers, and the mechanics that made and ultimately break the countries of Southeast Asia and beyond. The issue of social contract is to me the most pressing for not only did it provide the very seed to the idea of economic development and sustainability, but it encompassed the decision makings and policies that were right, and those that, quite frankly, went ultimately wrong. Thomas Friedman quote surrounding the social bargain emerges in this chapter as it does in this preface. The reason for the decision is because the social bargain captured the idealism and the immense scope of building for the long-run since the late 1950s in East Asia, the Americas, Europe, and to some extent, Africa. It was the idealism that had within the promises, the excitement, and the hope that was expressed by leaders and peoples from a variety of spectrums, whether by President Kennedy and President Johnson, Reverend Martin Luther King, Jr., or even Japan's MITI. The key behind the bargain was the creation of a better society through the provisions of opportunities as well as through propelling a nation to achieve new heights in economic development through investments, training, and optimism.

As mentioned before, matters unfortunately went astrayed since the 1980s when long-term building of nations was replaced by issues of immediacy and greed. The visions of the past lost much of their illumination and inspiration by then and a series of ill-policy makings gave way to a series of financial crises throughout the Americas, Europe, Asia, and parts elsewhere throughout the world. However, as seen in the recent presidential election in Indonesia, there is now recognition that the focus must be on a rebuilding of a nation that will yield the same, if not, better prosperity for sake of the present and succeeding generations. The recognition is not as uniformed or pervasive enough to bring about more sweeping changes in the societal, economical, and financial aspects of nations and the world overall. However, with current changes in leadership in various countries (particularly in Asia) along with a growing awakening of what's happening and what shall be done in response, there's a greater sense that all must be done to correct and ultimately prevent the mistakes and misguided policies that continues to plague this global community over the past decade. Only time, will, focus, commitment, vision, and a sense of urgency of the people and our leaders will tell.

Chapter One
The Rise and Fall of Southeast Asia as a Regional Economic Predominant: Some General Evaluations

I.
In Brevity: The Pre-requisites for Economic Growth

Since 1960, Asia and Southeast Asia, which is the largest and the most populous of the continents, has become richer, faster than any other region in the world. In terms of the GDP, the economic growth in the Philippines grew at roughly 2 percent per year.[1] The average growth rates in Indonesia, Japan, Malaysia, and Thailand were 3 to 5 percent. However, Hong Kong, Singapore, Taiwan, and South Korea experienced growth rates of no less than 6 percent (Sarel, 1998: pp. 408).

The accumulation of labor and capital in the 1960s, during and after import substitution industrialization (ISI), was among the main reasons behind this phenomenal growth. However, the initial impetus for economic growth included strong investments towards education and health. At the same time, governmental policies engaged in land reform that did much to decrease the levels of inequality among members of the population, and to increase the marginal propensity to save.[2] While the Asian countries were poor in the 1960s, their primary education systems were good, fertility rates were low, life expectancy was high, and the equality in both land and income was improving (Sarel, 1998: pp. 418-419).

Between 1950 and 1974, it was found that there was no systematic relationship between growth and inequality. Inequality increased in about as many growth situations as it decreased (Weaver, Rock, and Kusterer, 1997: pp. 41-42). Economic growth included both highly equal and highly unequal societies (as in the cases of Southeast Asia and the West respectively). Secondly, poverty tended to decrease with economic growth in most, though not in all, cases. Finally, there was no clear relationship between the growth rate and either the degree of inequality at any point in time, or the trend in inequality over time (Weaver, Rock, and Kusterer, 1997: pp. 41-42). Improvements in both poverty and human welfare continue to be related in part to the rate, and the kind, of growth. And it is this kind of growth that led to the fastest reductions in poverty which included an emphasis on improving an equal distribution of education, and an equal distribution in the ownership of land. Essentially, such an emphasis became a growth strategy that increased the demand for these "broadly owned income-producing assets" (Weaver, Rock, and Kusterer, 1997: pp. 41-42).

Generally speaking, the power of landed elites was broken in Asia by the 1960s. In every instance, the heavy investments in agricultural modernization that followed the development of smallholder agriculture proved to be politically stabilizing (Weaver, Rock, and Kusterer, 1997: p. 51). The emphasis on education and savings played a role in the engagements of heavy investments that served as a stabilizing force to further improve both economic and political development and sustainability. East Asia is also more culturally, linguistically, and ethnically homogeneous; which made state building, and a focus on economic development, more feasible and easier (Weaver, Rock, and Kusterer, 1997: p. 51). Additionally, Southeast Asian countries were instrumental in involving large numbers of people in political affairs, thus doing away (at least for the most part) with traditional hierarchical patterns of rule. It was, as Neher puts it, "a fundamental innovation" (Neher, 1991; p. 21).

Since the East Asia resource base was less rich in comparison to Latin America, countries in that region, until the late 1980s, had never experienced the political, social, and economical distortions of resource-based export-oriented policies in the presence of highly unequal distributions of land and natural resources. Consequently, countries in that region (including Japan, Taiwan, and South Korea) established a state-dominated neo-mercantilist incentive structure to promote ISI in its first stage. As the returns to the ISI strategies slowed, the countries in Southeast Asia, along with Japan and eventually China, shifted to an incentive structure that promoted the export of labor and, later, capital-intensive manufactures after the mid-1960s (Weaver, Rock, and Kusterer, 1997: p. 51).

In essence, what made Southeast Asia's phenomenal economic growth possible was the *social bargain* between the governments, the workers, and the business leaders that was needed for sustainable economic development and globalization. The governments realized the need to embrace free markets while understanding, and foresightedly so, the need to deal with the issues that confronted the general population, such as education, health care, income and income distribution, as well as infrastructure. It was this requirement for effective leadership that was not only unprecedented, but it was "an indigenous inspired change from the centralized policies that had pervaded the region for centuries" (Neher, 1991; 21). The governments of much of globe democratized globalization by making sure that economic growth and social prosperity benefited as many people as possible. Japan led the way, investing heavily on infant industries before embracing free trade. Other countries, particularly in Asia and Latin America, followed suit, and with relatively huge success. It was only later that globalization began to lose much of that democratization as political and economical mismanagements became commonplace. But that per se (and what it led to) will be explored throughout the latter half of this chapter and beyond.

II.
The Arguable Importance of Import Substitution Industrialization and the Shift to Export-Oriented Industrialization

A. Import-Substitution Industrialization

Figure 1.1: The Learning Curves

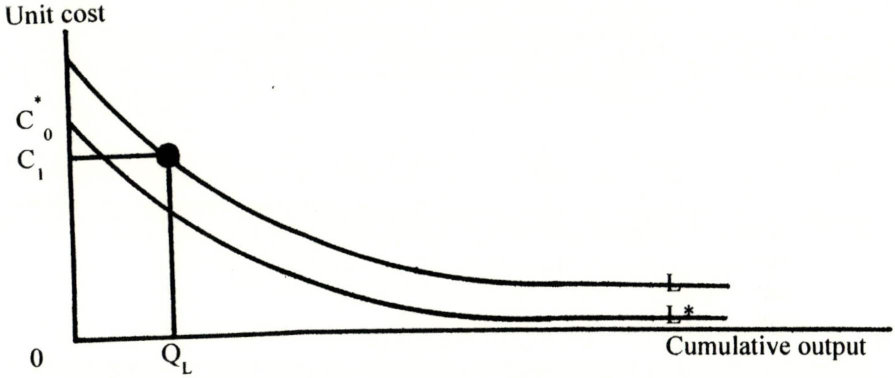

Source: Krugman, Paul R. and Maurice Obstfeld. *International Economics: Theory and Policy*. Fifth Edition. New York: Addision-Wesley, 2000: p. 153.

Figure 1.1 illustrates the learning curves between a country having an initial advantage, or a head start, in an industry, and a country having less production experience. The learning curve is a curve describing how the cost of production declines as cumulative output increases over time: the relationship between unit cost to cumulative output (Stiglitz, 1997: p. 417). In Figure 1.1, the learning curve (L) is that of a country that pioneered an industry, and has an extensive experience in such an industry. Consequently, it may have lower unit costs than another country with little or no experience, even if the other country's learning curve (L*) is lower due to, for example, lower wages. In contrast, the learning curve (L*) is that of another country that has lower input costs (for instance, wages), and less production experience. The experienced country has a sufficiently large head start in an industry. However, because the inexperienced country has potentially lower input costs, it still may not enter the market. For instance, suppose the experienced country has a cumulative output of Q_L units, giving it unit costs of C_1, while, on the contrary, the inexperienced country has never produced the good. Therefore, that country will have its' initial start-up costs (C^*_0) that is higher than the current unit costs, C_1, of an established industry (Krugman and Obstfeld, 2000: p. 153). This is because not only does it lacks production experience, it produces goods that are not competitive in the global market. Therefore, the country might increase its long-term welfare either by encouraging the production of the good through subsidies, or by protecting it from foreign competition during the ISI stage until the industry becomes self-sufficient (Krugman and Obstfeld, 2000: p. 153). The goal of the inexperienced country is to eventually duplicate the production experience and the rewards of the first country, therefore moving away from ISI towards export-oriented industrialization (EOI).

Southeast Asian countries, the eventual newly-industrialized economies (NIEs) after the 1970s, faced the same scenario as the "inexperienced country" previously discussed.[3] These countries did not have much production experience compared to the West (Europe and the United States), and the initial start-up costs for these countries in Southeast Asia were comparatively higher than those of their Western counterparts because of protectionist policies on the input goods that were not competitive in the global markets. The firms producing these low value-added goods were bestowed with "temporary protection" during the ISI stage while they gained further production experience.[4] Initially, the emerging markets in Southeast Asia had desires to produce low value-added goods because the costs of exports were higher from developing countries: in other words, the tariff rates on raw materials were lower than those on finished goods.

After the governmental initiatives towards land reform, political stability, education, and equalized income distribution, ISI became the next strategy towards economic development. Countries which have exercised import substitution policies looked at two variables of interests: trade policies and economic growth. The goal of the "inexperienced" countries of Southeast Asia since the 1950s was to move past the critical point (point Q_L). It was after this point that the governments of these countries sought to cluster industrial sectors where labor pooling, knowledge spillover, and improvement of infrastructure could take place and institute a transition from unskilled to skilled labor. Essentially, the importance of import substitution rested on the fact that it provided the countries of Southeast Asia with the incentives to use their natural resources as efficiently as possible in order to develop skilled labor, knowledge spillover, capital, human capital, and technology.[5] In short, the incentives paved the way for the *learning by doing* concept that was crucial for export-oriented industrialization. *Learning by doing* is a technological change characterized by the firms' decrease in their production costs as they gain experience from their production, resulting in self-sufficiency and competitiveness in the global market (Stiglitz, 1997: p. 417).

However, the criticisms against ISI are not wholly without merit. Protecting industries through tariffs and quotas does not necessarily mean that efficiency in production and knowledge spillover will occur. Furthermore, a period of protection will not create a competitive manufacturing sector if there are fundamental reasons why a country lacks comparative advantage in manufacturing, or the manufacturing sector that lacks the entrepreneurial drive to be competitive. Furthermore, protectionist policies of many less-developed countries tend to distort governmental incentives (Krugman and Obstfeld, 2000: p. 260).

Through ISI, there is a well-known tendency of import restrictions to promote production at an inefficiently small scale, especially in smaller economic environments. Quite often, the entire domestic market is not large enough to allow an efficient large-scale production facility. Therefore, should this market be protected, a single firm entering the market can earn monopolistic profits, which can lead other firms to enter the market that is already small and congested. Consequently, production is carried out on a highly inefficient scale. In addition, import substitution industrialization policies create capital-intensive factories that can generate little employment. Therefore, most people tend to be left out of the modern industrial sector, and consequently, seek their livelihood in the informal sector (where earnings tend to be low) (Weaver, Rock, and Kusterer, 1997: pp. 61-62).

Lastly, import substitution policies tend to generate corruption and favoritism to certain industries and firms. Preferential access to foreign exchange, credit, and import quotas was usually granted on the basis of patronage, rather than for the sake of economic efficiency. Therefore, economic growth became slower while income inequality worsened. This situation promoted the development of "crony capitalism," which was a chief feature in Indonesia and the Philippines and among the main contributors to the Asian Financial Crisis of 1997-1998 (Weaver, Rock, and Kusterer, 1997: pp. 61-62).[6]

These arguments against ISI are compelling since they remind us that the quality of intervention (via the policies) is what matters, not the intervention per se. *However, the importance of ISI was that not only did it necessitate the use of resources at the highest level of efficiency possible; it also gave each country the need to develop an industrial base* (Tan, 2000: p. 19). The type of policies employed by governments of developing countries would influence the state of their economic performances after the ISI stage. The goals of Singapore and Malaysia from the 1950s through the 1980s have been interventionist in nature, with the direction of their economies very involving and detailed in character. After the 1990s, however, Singapore became a country whose economy is virtually laissez-faire. In contrast, Taiwan's economy remained dominated by small, family-run companies with considerable governmental interference and guidance (Krugman and Obstfeld, 2000: pp. 269-270). Furthermore, these Southeast Asian countries (except Singapore) had a comparative advantage in natural resources that many advanced nations were lacking. Although Singapore was not blessed with natural resources, its labor-pooling was a just compensation for that agricultural void (Neher, 1991: pp. 3 and 127-129).

After the demise of ISI, the Southeast Asian countries experienced phenomenal economic growth by the early 1970s. However, to be seen in section five of this chapter, the Asian Financial Crisis reminds us that remnants of ISI remained. The governments' involvement and incentives in the industrial and financial sectors became increasingly distorted after the 1980s in regards to capital controls, liberalization, industrial and financial protectionism, and macroeconomic policies.

B. Export-Oriented Industrialization

After establishing an industrial base, agricultural reforms, and the more efficient uses of resources, each of the Southeast Asian countries entered the export-oriented industrialization (EOI). The EOI involved the dismantling of import barriers (such as tariffs), and the encouragement of export-oriented manufacturing industries.[7] As will be further elaborated throughout this manuscript, such an encouragement of export-oriented manufacturing industries came in a form of various financial incentives.[8] Industrial estates were established to provide subsidized factory space and public utility supplies in order to lessen the costs of export-oriented firms. Product and factory markets were deregulated to allow relative prices to be determined by both domestic and foreign markets. As EOI was well underway after the 1970s, liberalization of the banking sector began to take place and included the admittance of foreign banks into the domestic markets of Southeast Asian countries and the deregulation of interest rates in order to encourage savings (Tan, 2000: pp. 19-20).

ISI, with the manufacturing of labor-intensive consumer goods (such as textiles, clothing, and footwear) became less economically viable in the developing Southeast Asian countries by the early 1970s. With export-oriented industrialization, FDI and portfolio investment began to pour into Southeast Asia. As a result, the Asia-Pacific region began to manufacture high value-added goods (such as electronics components and products). The manufacturing of electronic goods was responsible for much of the export-oriented industrial success of the eventual newly-industrialized countries (NICs) (Tan, 2000: p. 21). The success of export-oriented industrialization in Southeast Asia was reflected in the rapid growth of exports, as shown in Table 1.1.

During the 1960s and 1970s, labor-intensive goods (especially textiles, clothing, and footwear) dominated the exports of the Asian NICs as ISI itself was being dismantled.[9] These goods accounted for between 30 to 44 percent of their total exports while electronics accounted for 25 percent of their total exports during this period (Tan, 2000: p. 24). This rapid growth resulted not only in increased employment, but also in persistent balance of trade surpluses for over three decades and the accumulation of high levels of foreign reserves per capita. However, South Korea was plagued with chronic current account deficits, which were due to its dependency on foreign loans as means of financing its EOI strategy, its high dependency on imports, and the low profit margins of its export-oriented industries (Tan, 2000: p. 24).

Table 1.1
Growth rates of exports (% per annum)

Countries	1960-1970	1970-1980	1980-1990
Hong Kong	12.3	14.5	22.4
South Korea	11.6	38.6	37.2
Singapore	7.3	3.3	28.2
Taiwan	12.1	18.1	14.1

Source: Tan, Gerald. *The Asian Currency Crisis.* Singapore: Times Academic Press, 2000: p. 23.

III.
The Importance of Foreign Direct Investment and Portfolio (Indirect) Investment

Foreign direct investment (FDI) is an important part of the international capital movement. FDI consists of the international capital flows a firm in one country creates or expands a subsidiary in another country and is typically a multinational corporation (MNC). The distinctive feature of a FDI is that "it involves not only a transfer of resources but also the acquisition of control. That is, the subsidiary does not simply have a financial obligation to the parent company; it is part of the same organizational structure" (Krugman and Obstfeld, 2000: pp. 169-171). In other words, FDI is "any flow of lending to, or purchases of ownership in, a foreign enterprise that is largely owned by residents (usually firms) of the investing country" (Pugel and Lindert, 2000: p. 628). Direct investment consists of any investment where the investing firm owns ten percent or more of the foreign firm (Pugel and Lindert, 2000: p. 628). However, *Portfolio investment* is an indirect investment in a bond or a stock, which indicates that the investor's home country does not own a large share of the enterprise being invested in, but is simply investing as a part of a diversified portfolio (Pugel and Lindert, 2000: p. 330).

FDI, especially from the United States and Japan, has been crucially important in the development of Southeast Asia. Even though most of Southeast Asia, with the exception of Hong Kong, exercised some levels of economic management in trade through tariffs, import quotas, and export subsidies, their high trade ratios had much to do with the phenomenal economic growth of the region. The high volume in trade after 1965, particularly with Japan and the United States, was responsible for FDI to start pouring into the Southeast Asian countries. *It shall be noted, however, that FDI, especially from Japan and the United States, did not "jump-start" economic development in Southeast Asian* countries.

Instead, FDI inflows *accelerated* economic growth for Southeast Asia, most especially after the shift from import-substitution to export-orientation strategies. In other words, the change in the mix of output towards more industrial products so characteristic of Southeast Asia was facilitated by a higher level of investment (Solomon, 1999: p. 34).

The roles of Japan and the United States in investment and technological transfers coincided with the Southeast Asian countries' efforts to engage in economic development and industrialization, as was exemplary in Singapore's economic growth and stability. Investments coming from the United States occurred after countries such as Taiwan and Korea began to engage in economic policies geared towards economic growth and free-market orientation. *It shall also be acknowledged that trade with countries like Japan and the United States was the necessary prerequisite for FDI to start pouring into the countries of the Association of Southeast Asian Nations (ASEAN) and the eventual NICs.*[10] This was because Southeast Asian countries such as Thailand, Singapore, and Malaysia were among the favorite sites of production for the multinational corporations. These MNCs directly generated most of the new exports made from raw materials imported from Southeast Asia (Krugman and Obstfeld, 2000: p. 268). Offshore production by multinational corporations "was facilitated in the 1960s by both the reductions in transport costs and the reductions in the costs of communications" (Tan, 2000: pp. 20-21).

Large inflows of foreign capital were important in that they relieved large export-import gaps of Southeast Asian countries, particularly Indonesia and Malaysia. For instance, Indonesia's current account deficit was -$7.7 billion by 1996, which was roughly four percent of its GDP. Similarly, Malaysia's current account deficit was -$5 billion, which was about six percent of its GDP (Tan, 2000: p. 68). By the mid-1990s, these current account deficits were being financed by enormous inflows of short-term foreign portfolio investment and loans.[11] Such inflows were facilitated after the mid-1980s by reforms in the banking and foreign exchange control implementation. In 1995, foreign portfolio investment in Indonesia amounted to $7.1 billion, over 1.5 times higher than FDI (which was $4.4 billion). In Malaysia, on the other hand, foreign direct investment of $5.8 billion was, in actuality, higher than $4.5 billion in portfolio investment (Tan, 2000: p. 68). Most of the Southeast Asian countries, such as Taiwan, Malaysia, Korea, and Singapore began to make relatively small portfolio investment abroad after the mid-1960s, as illustrated in Table 1.2. Let it be noted that by the mid-1990s, Southeast Asia accumulated up to thirty percent of the total global portfolio equity flows at a more steady pace (Grenville, 2000: p. 37).

Table 1.2a
Portfolio Investment in and by the Asia-Pacific economies (in U.S.$ million), 1965-1986

Countries	1965	1970	1975	1980	1985	1986
Korea	0.0	0.0	0.0	40.0	982.0	301.0
Taiwan	-	-	-	45.0	-46.0	69.0
Hong Kong	-	-	-	-	-	-
Singapore	0.0	0.0	-2.0	13.0	175.0	-549.0
Indonesia	0.0	0.0	0.0	46.0	-35.0	268.0
Malaysia	88.0	-28.0	268.0	-11.0	1942.0	30.0
Thailand	0.0	13.0	1.0	96.0	895.0	-29.0

Source: Das, Dilip K. "An Introduction to the Regional Economy." *Emerging Growth Pole: The Asia-Pacific Economy.* Dilip K. Das, editor. London: Prentice Hall, 1997: p. 44.

Table 1.2b
Portfolio Investment in and by the Asia-Pacific economies (in U.S.$ million), 1987-1991

Countries	1987	1988	1989	1990	1991
Korea	-113.0	-482.0	-29.0	811.0	-
Taiwan	-371.0	-1711.0	-902.0	-1006.0	45.0
Hong Kong	-	-	-	-	-
Singapore	252.0	-293.0	324.0	287.0	232.0
Indonesia	-88.0	-98.0	-173.0	0.0	0.0
Malaysia	140.0	-448.0	-107.0	-255.0	170.0
Thailand	346.0	530.0	1486.0	-38.0	-

Source: Das, Dilip K. "An Introduction to the Regional Economy." *Emerging Growth Pole: The Asia-Pacific Economy.* Dilip K. Das, editor. London: Prentice Hall, 1997: p. 44.

IV.
The Consequent Economic Success of Southeast Asia

After the countries in the Pacific-Rim region moved from ISI to EOI stages, they began to reap the benefits of FDI and portfolio investment. With capital investments, foreign firms (primarily MNCs) not only bestowed the countries with the much needed capital, but they also introduced to them new technology and ready-made foreign markets, as well as management and administrative skills. As a result, the manufacturing of electronic components, among the key ingredients in the success of Southeast Asia, became standardized. The standardization of electronic products meant that they could be manufactured by relatively unskilled workers. Miniaturization also meant that with lower transport costs per unit of output and the development of container ports, offshore production was often encouraged by MNCs. For example, by 1974, there were fifty-one major electronics component manufacturing firms in Southeast Asia and East Asia, employing over 77,000 workers (Tan, 2000: p. 21).[12] By the 1980s, Southeast Asian countries (such as Korea, Taiwan, and Singapore) began to challenge Japanese and Western MNCs in the production of electronic goods and components.

The achievements of Southeast Asia were reflected in the substantial growth of GDP, per capita incomes, employment, and manufactured exports. The GDP growth rates for the four selected countries are illustrated in Table 1.3 below.

Table 1.3
Growth Rates of Real GDP (% per annum)

Countries	1960-1970	1970-1980	1980-1990
Hong Kong	10.1	9.8	7.1
Singapore	9.2	9.3	7.3
South Korea	9.5	8.2	9.9
Taiwan	9.6	9.7	8.5

Source: Tan, Gerald. *The Asian Currency Crisis*. Singapore: Times Academic Press, 2000: p. 22

Taiwan, for example, has maintained its unemployment rate of no greater than 3 percent since 1968. Although the Oil Shocks of 1973 and 1978 caused recessions in the Taiwanese economy, the employment growth rebounded to over eight percent in a relatively short period of time. However, as with other Southeast Asian countries, the employment growth in Taiwan has been slightly downward, since wages were generally increased due to shortages in labor. Therefore, the earnings or wages in the manufacturing sector were increasing by 8 percent per annum. These increases in earnings made the sector unable to support labor-intensive industries, and these industries, therefore, moved offshore as a result (Tan, 2000: p. 25).

The high performance Asian economies (HPAEs) successfully maintained macroeconomic stability, low and stable inflation rates, low internal and external debts, and positive and relatively stable real interest rates.[13] Also, as pointed out before, these countries invested immensely towards education and training in order to maximize their capacities for new technology. Hence, the financial sector was secured, and savings were encouraged. Because the HPAEs engaged in further trade liberalizations, the inflows of FDI and portfolio investment enabled them to increase their efficiency and their competitiveness in the global markets (Tan, 2000: pp. 43-45).

Trade liberalizations during the 1980s and the early 1990s were largely aided by the Asia-Pacific Economic Cooperation (APEC). Established in 1989, APEC helps to foster further economic growth and prosperity in the region (its hallmark is open regionalism). The key to its policies continues to be free and open trade and APEC works, since its inception, to reduce tariffs as well as other trade barriers, creating efficient domestic economies, and dramatically increasing exports (APEC.org, 2004: p. 1). Cooperation, investment, economic growth, and trade are all of the goals APEC seeks to maintain for further prosperity of the region. This forum now has twenty-one members: Australia, Brunei Darussalam, Canada, Chile, China, Hong Kong, Indonesia, Japan, Malaysia, Mexico, New Zealand, Papua New Guinea, Peru, The Philippines, The Federation of Russia, Singapore, South Korea, Taiwan, Thailand, the United States, and Vietnam (APEC.org, 2004: p. 1).

The governments' intervention in the domestic markets before the Asian Financial Crisis was to a large extent well crafted and successful (Krugman and Obstfeld, 2000: pp. 267-271). On the eve of the Crisis, however, the governments' involvement and incentives in macroeconomic and financial policies were plagued by severe distortions, and an increasing lack of decisive policy making and enforcement.

V.

The Asian Financial Crisis: Why the Mini Dragons Lost Their Fire?

A. The Unforeseen Nature of the Crisis

In recalling the success of Southeast Asia after its shift from ISI to EOI, the severity of the Asian Financial Crisis was for the most part unforeseeable. This was because by 1997, most of the East Asian countries enjoyed high investment rates, high savings, robust growth, and moderate inflation for over three decades. Furthermore, domestic saving and investment rates averaged more than thirty-percent of the GDP between 1986 and 1996 in Thailand, Indonesia, Korea, and Malaysia, and over twenty percent in the Philippines (Glick, 1999: pp. 33-36). The average GDP growth in these countries averaged close to eight percent over this period. Furthermore, it was widely contended that *international market conditions were favorable before the onset of the Asian Financial Crisis;* the United States' interest rates were low, growth in the industrial countries (with the exception of Japan) was strong, and world commodity market prices were relatively stable (Glick, 1999: pp. 33-36).

B. The Spark Behind the Asian Financial Crisis

The spark of the Asian Financial Crisis was the devaluation of the baht (Thailand's currency) by mid-July of 1997. Thailand, among the most successful countries in Southeast Asia, experienced a massive outflow of its foreign investment capital.[14] Furthermore, Thailand's currency, which for many years had been pegged to the U.S. dollar at the official rate of exchange at 25 baht per dollar, was devalued under sustained international pressures by speculators, bankers, corporate treasurers, and mutual fund managers Thereafter, the baht had been experiencing a steady decline in its value against the U.S. dollar. By mid-December of 1997, the exchange rate was roughly 42 baht per dollar: it increased to 54.75 baht per dollar by January of 1998 (Tran Van Hoa, 2000: p. 12).

The series of currency devaluations was due to the decreased confidence of both domestic and foreign investors in Thailand's economy. The loss of confidence resulted in the plunging currency value, rising interest rates, and the depressed economy. As the currency devalued, coupled with the lack of strong domestic economy, companies, banks, and households began to experience financial problems (including honoring outstanding debts). The result of this predicament was the continued lack of confidence in Thailand's economic stability, which resulted in the *"Vicious Circle of the Financial Crisis"* (Krugman, 2000: p. 94).

The consequences of the aforementioned debacle were a series of economic, political, and social upheavals in Thailand. Initially, the devaluation of the baht led to the closure of roughly one-third of Thailand's banking and financial institutions. Furthermore, Thailand received a sum of $17 billion of the International Monetary Fund's bail-out plan of its financial system, as well as from a number of foreign countries (such as Australia, which contributed $1 billion of the overall $17 billion) (Tran Van Hoa, 2000: p. 12).

C. The Contagion Effects of the Asian Financial Crisis

According to Robert Blecker, contagion effects occur when,

> in a aftermath of a currency crisis in one country, speculators look around for countries in similar circumstances that may be vulnerable to a speculative assault, but where the inconsistencies in the fundamentals were not severe enough to induce a speculative attack on their own. After the successful attack on the Thai baht in July 1997, speculators attacked several other currencies in rapid fire-succession, including the Malaysian ringgit, the Indonesian

rupiah, the Philippine peso, and the Korean won. In each case, speculators found problems to exploit, from weak banks in South Korea to "crony capitalism" in Suharto's Indonesia. *But in none of these cases was a currency crisis expected based on the country's own internal policies and external situation prior to the Thai crisis* (Blecker, 1999: p. 73).

The financial woes of other Southeast Asian countries followed suit by late 1997, as the vicious circle of the Financial Crisis became more pervasive. Malaysia experienced the devaluation of its currency, the ringgit (RG), of more than 30 percent.[15] This devaluation led to, as Tran Van Hoa states, "an outcry by the Malaysian government at the possibility of an international conspiracy by 'marauding currency speculators' to damage its economy and growth" (Tran Van Hoa, 2000: p. 12).

Indonesia's currency and financial crises were the most serious, however. The rupiah underwent devaluation and fell below the critical 10,000 rupiah level of 10,700 rupiah per dollar by January of 1998, notwithstanding the level of closure of Indonesia's banks, as well as a $38 billion bail-out program courtesy of the IMF. The failing health of President Suharto and political instability did not help in stopping the depreciation of the currency (Tran Van Hoa, 2000: pp. 12-13).

South Korea also suffered a huge devaluation after 1997 and became the recipient of the largest bail-out program of the IMF, in the amount of $57 billion. While the Philippines' peso devalued to 46.5PS per dollar, the currencies of Singapore, Taiwan, Vietnam and Hong Kong did not experience severe devaluation after 1997. In fact, the devaluation on Vietnam's currency (the dong) was mild, for it never exceeded 20 percent of its slide in the stock market (Tran Van Hoa, 2000: p. 13). Table 1.4 shows the currency depreciation in the worst affected countries by December, 1996.

Table 1.4
Currency depreciation in the worst affected countries

Countries	$value (Dec. 31, 1996)	$value (Dec. 19, 1997)	% change
Thailand	25.63 baht	44.85 baht	-42.9
Malaysia	2.5264 ringgit	3.815 ringgit	-33.8
Indonesia	2362.25 rupiah	5100.00 rupiah	-53.7
Philippines	26.30 peso	39.65 peso	-33.7
South Korea	844.5 won	1557.0 won	-45.8

Source: Robins, Fred. "Asia's 1997 Crash: Its Character, Causes, and Consequences." *The East Asian Development Model: Economic Growth, Institutional Failure, and the Aftermath of the Crisis.* Frank-Jurgen Richter editor. London: MacMillan Press, Ltd., 2000: pp. 17-52.

The responses to the Asian Crisis by both Singapore and Hong Kong are noteworthy in their own rights. The Crisis of 1997-1998 caused a sharp decline in demand for their exports in the rest of the Asia-Pacific region: no doubt an external shock never quite witnessed beforehand of this magnitude. Malaysia, Indonesia, and Thailand were among the countries with sharp decreases in exports, as shown in table 1.5.

Table 1.5
Annual Export Growth (percentage of U.S.$ values)

Countries	1994	1995	1996
Malaysia	25	26	6
Thailand	23	25	-1
Indonesia	9	13	10

Source: Robins, Fred. "Asia's 1997 Crash: Its Character, Causes, and Consequences." *The East Asian Development Model: Economic Growth, Institutional Failure, and the Aftermath of the Crisis.* Frank-Jurgen Richter editor. London: MacMillan Press, Ltd., 2000: pp. 17-52.

To be explained in *Chapter Three*, Singapore countered this shock by allowing its currency to depreciate. Meanwhile, Hong Kong decided to maintain a fixed exchange rate with the U.S. dollar, a rate that has been stable since 1984 (Sachs and Larrain, 1999: pp. 88-89). However, the end results of their responses to the Crisis were startling. Singapore, like Taiwan, escaped recession in 1998 through 1999. Hong Kong, meanwhile, had experienced the sharpest decline in output in recent history: its real GDP dropped by 8 percent from its peak during the period up to the mid-1990s (Sachs and Larrain, 1999: pp. 88-89).

D. The Long-Term Causes for the Southeast and East Asian Financial Downturns

1. Indecisive Policy Initiatives

The real issue facing East Asia and Southeast Asia is not whether to reform, but how to reform and at what pace while maintaining financial stability. The Southeast Asian countries, like Malaysia (in the beginning), were guilty of not instituting more decisive and coherent reforms to offset the deleterious effects of the Crisis. Taiwan, Singapore, Hong Kong (and eventually Malaysia) were the only countries in the region with decisive and practical financial and economic reforms. Although Taiwan and Singapore were indirectly affected by the Crisis due to the overall decreases in trade and investment in the region, their domestic economies and the financial sectors went through the Crisis largely unscathed.

Nevertheless, the reforms in other countries of the region were met with chronic confrontations between and among economists and political leaders. Leadership failed to be strong and harmonious and was affected by the IMF, which over-loaded the reform agenda. As Stijn Claessens and Thomas Glaessner point out, "in a world that is increasingly integrated financially, East Asia can no longer postpone difficult choices-the penalty of maintaining a fragile, underdeveloped banking system are too severe" (Claessens and Glaessner, 1997: p. 13).

2. The Microeconomic Fundamentals in the Asia Crisis

If anything, the causes of the Asian Financial Crisis could be explained by the weaknesses in the financial sector including relationship-based lending practices, excessive risk taking, and inadequate financial supervision and regulation. *The following trends of Southeast Asian economy became causes for concerns:*

First, the real exchange rates appreciated precipitously between December of 1994 and early 1997 by 15 percent or more in Thailand, Malaysia, the Philippines, and Indonesia. The cumulative rate of real appreciation in these countries was greater than 25 percent between 1990 and 1997.[16] *Secondly,* the Pacific-rim region began to experience the decline of exports. In 1996, Thailand's exports in dollar terms fell by one percent, notwithstanding its previous two-year period of growth above twenty percent (Glick, 1998: p. 36). Although Korea's exports grew by four percent, it was down from a 30 percent growth in 1995. Meanwhile, Malaysia's export growth of six percent in 1996 was down from 26 percent a year earlier. Only the Philippines registered a significant export growth of almost 20 percent in 1996. *Lastly,* the current account deficits in Thailand, Indonesia, and Korea increased by merely one to two percent of their GDPs during the 1995-1996 period. In 1996, the Philippines, Korea, and Thailand ran current account deficits of 4.5 percent of the GDP, whereas Indonesia and Malaysia ran deficits at roughly 3.5 percent (Glick, 1998: p. 36).

There were additional factors that contributed to the decline in exports, to the increase in the current account deficits, and to the over-evaluation that continued to plague Southeast Asia's financial and industrial sectors. *First,* the sharp appreciation of the U.S. dollar relative to the yen and the European currencies between mid-1995 and mid-1997 led to the worsening of cost-competitiveness in those Asian countries whose currencies were pegged effectively to the U.S. dollar (Glick, 1999: p. 37). *Secondly,* the Japanese economy became stagnated by 1990, which led to a significant slowdown in the growth of Asian exports to Japan as well as massive problems with bad loans which proved disastrous to the banking system. Furthermore, Japan ceased being the leading provider of foreign direct investment into Southeast Asia after 1990. Whereas Japan was instrumental in the growth of Southeast Asian countries in the 1970s and the 1980s, the role of Japan in the 1990s was severely curtailed. The consumption, and consequently, the decline in Japanese economic activity aborted the gradual economic recovery of 1996 (Glick, 1999: p. 37).

Third, the default of Russia's ruble (R) essentially harmed investors, who collectively lost at least $33 billion. Also, the loan default by the Russian government on $40 billion of ruble bonds, despite over $40 billion given by the IMF, was without a doubt a severe blow. Due to the default, 1) the Long Term Capital Management (LTCM), among the world's most prominent hedge funds, announced technical bankruptcy, and 2) American banks and hedge funds lost at least $8 billion (Robins, 2000: pp. 23-24).[17] The effective collapse of the LTCM "starkly highlighted the systematic risk to the global financial system resulting from the extremely high levels of leverage enjoyed by hedge funds and others" (Robins, 2000: p. 24). *The collapse was a warning sign that highly leveraged institutions proved harmful not only to individual economies, but to the stability of the entire global financial system* (Robins, 2000: p. 24). The financial crises in Latin America, especially in Mexico and Brazil, were also instrumental in alerting the individual economies and the global markets against speculative attacks and against leveraged institutions. Indeed, the numerous leveraged institutions in Southeast Asia were avoided especially after the baht collapsed.

Fourth, sector-specific shocks caused by over-production in industries, such as semi-conductors, resulted in the decline in export growth[18] (Glick, 1999: p.37). *Fifth,* global attention has been shifted towards China, the emerging country that is continuing to compete against other firms in the region in electronics, apparel, and textiles. In addition, the devaluation of the yuan in 1994 fueled competitive pressures in the region and abroad. *Finally,* the real appreciation was related to the upward pressure on domestic non-tradables prices from large capital inflows (Glick, 1999: p. 37).

3. The Fundamental Financial Causes of the Asia Crisis

Distortions and weaknesses played crucial roles in the Southeast Asian Financial Crisis as well. Asian countries tended to lean towards centralization, and behind-the-scenes relationships between financial institutions, businesses, and government for the intermediation and allocation of capital. For example, in Indonesia and Thailand, a large share of lending and investment decisions were made as the results of *personal relationships or governmental influence, not as a result of decentralized open market transactions.*[19] There were cases in which banks were controlled (directly or indirectly) by the government or by "Minister's nephews," and directed credit to politically favored firms, sectors, and investment projects (Glick, 1999: p. 38). These kinds of practices hindered the efficiency of credit allocation, as "clientelism" became something of the norm in these transactions and beyond.[20]

In addition to the behind-the scenes relationships and transactions that were commonplace in Southeast Asian countries, *financial institutions and their agents had lacked the desire to manage risk effectively and to bear the full costs of failures.* Banks in particular ran the habit of lending to excessively risky projects. Because bank depositors were offered implicit or explicit deposit insurance, they felt little need to monitor the lending decisions of those banks. Meanwhile, the banks themselves were generally given implicit guarantees of a government bailout should adverse widespread financial conditions emerge (Glick, 1999: pp. 38-39).[21]

Most Southeast Asian countries *were plagued by inadequate financial supervision and regulation.* For example, there was minimal enforcement on capital adequacy ratios and lending limits to individual borrowers or sectors. Furthermore, transparency in the banking system likewise raised concerns. For instance, state-owned banks in Indonesia and Korea were allowed to break many prudential regulations on a regular basis without penalties issued. What's more, disclosure requirements were limited and assets classification systems lacked adequacy and definitions, which maintained at least a sense of murkiness in the language in terms of what could be included in capital, and ultimately disguised the extent of non-performing loan problems (Glick, 1999: p. 39). Therefore, bank officials and investors had difficulties in determining whether bank balance sheets were healthy and whether loans were sound. Barry Eichengreen puts it yet in another way in avowing that:

> As banks are in the business of building a capacity to gather and analyze information about their customers, they will find it hard to raise liquidity by selling assets in times of crises, given the difficulty this information asymmetry poses for third-party evaluation of loans. Combine this with the fact that banks provide liquidity-transformation services, and it is clear that banks are susceptible to self-fulfilling runs in which investors, uncertain of their access to deposits, scrambled to get their money out. To be sure, this problem is most severe when, as in Asia, banks fail to use recognized accounting standards or to rely on reputable international accounting firms to audit their books, leaving their creditors unable to distinguish good banks from bad ones and permitting isolated runs to become systemic banking panics (Eichengreen, 1999: pp. 81-82).

Likewise, the incentives for risk-taking mounted due to the issue of financial supervision irregularities (Glick, 1999: p. 39). There was too much foreign capital chasing too few sound investments capable of earning foreign exchanges sufficient enough to service both the principal, and the interest, on the debt. To make matters worse, banks, in response to this predicament, opted not to exercise restraints, but to re-lend monies borrowed abroad to speculative investments in real estate (which earned no foreign exchange), or to protected and non-competitive enterprises such as steel and petrochemicals (Jackson, 1999: pp. 5-6).

Moral hazard in many ways went hand-in-hand with the excessive borrowing from domestic and foreign firms as well as the lack of financial discipline that were proved pervasive and prevalent among Asian banks as discussed above. Moral hazard is defined as the *increase in recklessness* that takes place when people are protected against the consequences of their risky behavior. It is essentially the readiness of the governments and international institutions to provide bail-outs in times of emerging market financial crises. *Whereas bailouts constitute one element of moral hazard, the fixed exchange rate regime comprises another.* The fixed exchange rates can indeed serve as an implicit *guarantee* that a government will protect the value of its currency, thus keeping investments safe as well (Hausmann, 1999: p. 66).

Moral hazard makes an economy vulnerable, especially because investors become less vigilant in weighing the risks involved in investing. Furthermore, the moral hazard that resulted from a combination of perceived government guarantees and weak regulation of the guaranteed institution has helped fuel excessively speculative investment in many economies (Krugman and Obstfeld, 2000: p. 694). As in the case of the IMF and World Bank, excessive lending with no effective follow-up conditionalities constitutes moral hazard and damaged the credibility of the multi-lending financial institutions. As Morris Goldstein puts it:

> In practice, however, inadequacies of information and moral hazard problems associated with official explicit and implicit safety nets (that is, guarantees and bailouts) can either blunt the impact of market discipline or cause it to operate in a delayed and draconian way. If market participants cannot obtain timely and comprehensive information on the borrower's creditworthiness, they will not be able to price the borrower's obligations correctly. And if borrowers know that certain kinds of financial information do not have to be disclosed publicly, they will be more likely to hide their problems under those statistics (Goldstein, 1999: pp. 58-59).

Here is one example of the moral hazard, particularly in regards to the banking practices of Thailand, which will be explored in greater depth later in this literature. The Bank of Thailand detected irregularities in the Bangkok Bank of Commerce (BBC) in 1991. It was determined that 27 percent of BBC's total assets were non-performing. This predicament did not get better in the next two years and the government agreed to purchase a huge stake of the bank through the Financial Institutions Development Fund (FIDF), though in absence of any write-down of shareholder capital or replacement of management. A total of $7 billion were spent to keep the BBC afloat and the fact that the BBC mismanagement became publicized prompted the Bank of Thailand to take formal control of the institution. The consequence was dire, for the bailout set a dangerous precedent and severely damaged the credibility of the Bank of Thailand (Haggard, 2000: p. 25).

Arguably, *excessive borrowing abroad, primarily by the private sector, was one of the hallmarks of the Asian Financial Crisis.* Even if an exchange rate of a particular country is not so fixed, problems can still occur when poor public and private debt management are accompanied by inadequate liquidity defenses against shocks. This is especially true when a country engages in the buildup of short-term, un-hedged, foreign currency debt by banks and/or by their corporate customers. This very habit formed, according to Morris Goldstein, the very heart of the Asian Crisis and this was compounded by currency exposure to those external shocks and inadequate control leverage (Goldstein, 1999: pp. 48-50). In the five years prior to the 1997-1998 Crisis, banks' and non-banks' borrowings in the affected country grew at a rapid pace. Banks in each country rapidly increased their net foreign liabilities by large percentages during this period. By the time the Crisis hit the region by mid-July of 1997, the total indebtedness had reached large proportions, exceeding fifty percent of GDP in Thailand, the Philippines, and Indonesia (Jackson, 1999: p. 3). There were several instances where large amounts of short-term borrowing took place such as in Korea, Indonesia, and Thailand: their short-term loans equaled 13 percent, 14 percent, and 22 percent of their respective GDPs (Jackson, 1999: p. 4).

The markets in real estate, steel, automobiles, petrochemicals, and semiconductors became glutted to the point of decline in earnings, which resulted in the fall of foreign confidence. Domestic investors became unable to meet payments to domestic bank creditors on stalled or non-profitable projects, and began to pull capital out of local stock markets. Due to the apparent deep-seated weakness in the financial sector, and the consequent lower confidence, *capital flights became prevalent especially in the Philippines, Thailand, Indonesia, Malaysia, and Korea* (Jackson, 1999: p. 6).

Southeast Asia had profited from massive amounts of domestic and foreign direct investments, and portfolio investments during the late 1970s through the early 1990s. The governments in this region were instrumental and effective in *maintaining the fixed exchange rates that minimized foreign exchange risk for domestic borrowers and foreign investors.* Furthermore, local banks borrowed offshore at low, short-term rates, and lent money for long-term investments at a substantial premium to manufacturers and real estate developers (Jackson, 1999: pp. 5-6).

On the debit side, however, *inexpensive capital became abundant, and local bank loans based on personal relationships did not help alleviate the lending problems.* These flows not only became large, but also short term, and this move towards large, yet short-term, capital flows, increased the risks of collapse should those flows reverse, as was the case in the latter half of 1997 (Hanna, 2000: p. 49). For example, banks that reported to the Bank for International Settlement (BIS) saw their external claims on Asia rose from \$141 billion in 1984 to \$372 billion in 1994. From 1995 through mid-1997, these banks received \$203.2 billion worth of capital flows. However, during the onset of the Crisis,

$63.2 billion left East Asia and Southeast Asia by the latter half of 1997. By 1998 through the first half of 1999, another $270.5 billion of capital flows exited the region (Hanna, 2000: p. 49).

In addition, *the banks of Southeast and East Asia built-up foreign liabilities by borrowing at low foreign rates, and then re-lending at higher rates.* This was true especially since local interest rates in these Asian economies were typically higher that those abroad. Countries with pegged exchange rates increased the vulnerability of their financial sectors by not hedging foreign currency borrowings. The absence of hedging not only significantly lowered the cost of funds in the short run, but it also created a significant heavy exposure of foreign currency loans "to the effects of possible exchange rate changes as well as the refusal of creditors to roll over these loans" (Glick, 1999: p. 47). The short-term maturity of capital inflows also accentuated the *mismatch* between short-term liabilities and long-term assets of the financial institutions of the region. Consequently, these institutions faced greater difficulties in making appropriate risk assessments (Glick, 1999: p. 47).

Widespread misallocation of capital into speculative and noncompetitive sectors and enterprises resulted, and returns on investments fell steadily in Korea, Indonesia, and Thailand. The fall was profound to an extent that large number of projects could no longer generate enough income to meet both principal and interest payments. Investments became poorly conceived, and non-performing loans resulted (Glick, 1999: p. 40). The principal disadvantage of non-performing loans was that these loans curtailed of the banking systems' ability to maintain the economic expansion through continued lending. Non-performing loans, which essentially signified deteriorating loan quality, constituted 15-20 percent of the total loan portfolio of many banks and finance companies in Thailand, Korea, Indonesia, Malaysia, and 14 percent in the Philippines (Glick, 1999: p. 40). Essentially, most of the banks in Asia were technically insolvent before the baht collapsed in mid-1997 (Jackson, 1999: p. 8).

Along with weak national banking and financial systems, *financial liberalizations, more prominent during and after the 1980s, were in some cases premature and poorly supervised,* as in the case of Thailand and Indonesia. As to be reiterated later in this book (especially in its seventh chapter), financial liberalization by itself is not bad, dangerous, or even undesirable. It's the matter of how it is implemented. Liberalization can work, as it did quite well in Taiwan and Singapore. However, there is a risk of such a policy especially in emerging economies if it's not under prudent policy guidelines and enforcement. When liberalization, in the presence of heavy capital inflows (like FDI), becomes a source of vulnerability, it can happen "if it is implemented in a way and/or at a pace that outstrips the domestic capacity to supervise the financial sector and to build a credit culture" (Goldstein, 1999: p. 46).

E. The Interpretations of Michel Camdessus and Alan Greenspan Surrounding the Asia Crisis

Michel Camdessus, the then Managing Director of the IMF, argued compellingly that the most important causes of the Asian Financial Crisis were the loss of confidence and faith of domestic corporations in the perceived stability of the local currencies and the rush to buy foreign exchange instead. Furthermore, Camdessus argued that while the difference between hedging and speculation is blurred, it would be erroneous to blame the hedge funds for the Asian Financial Crisis (Tran Van Hoa, 2000: pp. 15 and 17). Camdessus' arguments are not without credibility. The blurred visions upon the differences between hedging and speculation as well as the lost of faith on the part of domestic corporations were due to financial and industrial mismanagements so much pervasive in much of Southeast Asian countries, as explained above. As Tran Van Hoa states:

> This is an addition to the presence of nepotism or favoritism in many Asian countries under which investment and loans were given to people or companies with close connections to government officials or the ruling class. The nepotism is more pronounced in Indonesia, where monopolies even for staple foods or commodities have been created for the benefits of the elitist and highly connected business people (Tran Van Hoa, 2000: p. 17).

Greenspan expanded Camdessus' contentions, arguing that the banking structure in many Asian countries inevitably had led to the investment excesses and errors to which all similar endeavors seem prone, such as unprofitable expansions and loan defaults. Greenspan believed that Asia's financial system can return to prosperity, only if the region's governments reform their troubled banking systems (Tran Van Hoa, 2000: p. 19). Ultimately, better disclosure and discipline among banks are of crucial importance. As Eichengreen contends:

> ...better information, secured by adherence to internationally recognized auditing and accounting standards and strengthened prudential supervision, can help to ameliorate the panic problem. However, if asymmetric information is why most economies continue to rely on banks for intermediation services, bank fragility is unavoidable. The advocates of information-related initiatives mislead when they assume the problem away (Eichengreen, 1999: pp. 81-82).

VI.
The Reactions Toward the East Asian Financial Crisis: Remedies Sought

A meeting in Manila (the capital of the Philippines) took place on November 19th, 1997 in order to adopt a number of principles in solving the Asian Financial Crisis. These principles were endorsed by the Southeast Asian finance ministers in December of that year in Kuala Lumpur (in Malaysia) to develop plans for improved surveillance of their economies to avoid the recurrences of the Crisis. The principles were also created in order to set up an early warning system to spot problems before they reach a crisis level, to call on the IMF to speed up plans for increasing its revenues, and to establish a "new quick disbursing short-term facility" (Tran Van Hoa, 2000: p. 18).

Michel Camdessus praised the idea of a surveillance body under the auspices of the Manila-based Asian Development Bank. To Camdessus, this idea was a good sign of solving the Crisis which he diplomatically ventures was a short-term in nature. Earlier, Dr. Stanley Fischer, First Deputy Director of the IMF from 1994 to 2001, contended that the emphasis should be placed on surveillance, noting that Thailand's neighbors had been reluctant to exert pressure for corrective policies. Dr. Alan Greenspan himself was no stranger to the consensus of the need for intra-regional efforts to reverse the effects of the Asian Financial Crisis. Greenspan acknowledged that although the necessary adjustments may be difficult, reforming the banking systems that were based on politically-driven lending in many of the Asian countries would have crucial, worldwide benefits. Furthermore, Greenspan contended that to avoid a global financial market fallout, developed countries should offer temporary loans through the IMF, provided that the loans would be accompanied with reforms (Tran Van Hoa, 2000: p. 19).

Ian Macfarlane, the Governor of Australia's Reserve Bank from 1996 to September 17th, 2006, challenged the IMF solutions, however. To Macfarlane, the solutions were macroeconomic in nature when the Asian economies were facing a financial crisis, the type of crisis that required a proper remedy in the form of improved policies directed at financial system stability (Tran Van Hoa, 2000: pp. 19-20). Macfarlane's contentions are compelling for three reasons. *First,* much of the increasing foreign debt of Asian countries was short-term. By the mid-1997, the share of short-term foreign debt in total liabilities was more than 50 percent in all Asian-5 countries.[22] This implied an increasing dependency on creditors' willingness to roll-over short-term liabilities (Glick, 1999: p. 42). *Second,* by mid-1994, the ratio of short-term foreign borrowing to official foreign exchange reserves was well over 100 percent for Indonesia, Thailand, and Korea, though below 100 percent for Malaysia. That ratio over 100 percent is not sufficient to trigger a crisis per se, because it can be sustained as long as foreign creditors are willing to roll-over their loans. However, the ratio does indicate vulnerability to a crisis, for foreign creditors has the incentive to demand repayment immediately once a withdrawal of foreign capital occur (Glick, 1999: p. 43). *Finally,* the M2/foreign reserves ratio was 400 percent or higher in all five crisis countries, including Malaysia and the Philippines.[23] Simply put, *the rising imbalances between short-term foreign liabilities and official reserves suggest an increasing exposure of Asian 5-countries to shift confidence fostering a financial panic* (Glick, 1999: p. 43).

The following solutions to strengthen the financial systems are currently under general consensus, and, with the assistance of the IMF, the Basle Committee, and the World Bank, those solutions are being adopted by policy-makers in the Asia-Pacific region. The solutions include: 1) tighter prudential and securities regulations, 2) limiting connected lending, 3) ensuring that banks meet capital requirements, 4) providing for bad loans, 5) publishing informative financial information, not excluding disclosure provisions, and 6) ensuring that insolvent institutions are dealt with promptly (Tran Van Hoa, 2000: p. 20-22). The meeting in Malaysia during the week of April 1st, 2001 to discuss currency swaps further supports the notions of coordinated efforts towards regional recovery from the Crisis. To be discussed at Chapter Seven, the proposed agreement for currency swaps is called the *Chiang Mai Initiative.*

VII.
Conclusion

The countries in Southeast Asia have proven that there were additional avenues toward economic development rather than through creating industrial bases by substituting domestic manufactured goods for imports. For one thing, these countries strove for more equal income distribution, more equal land distribution, and political stability. The HPAEs made heavy investments towards education, job training, and health. After the 1960s, these emerging countries used a bottom-up approach while improving their infrastructures.[24] Furthermore, with the encouragement of higher rates in savings, investments, and productivity, negative externalities decreased.

Although the countries of the region created industrial bases by the substitution of domestic manufactured goods during ISI, they went further in creating an additional path towards industrialization and growth through exports of these goods primarily to economically advanced nations. In effect, these countries demonstrated that economic growth involved a multi-step process. *First,* a developing country must establish both political and social stabilities characterized by the emphasis on more equal income and land distributions, as well as sound educational and health obtainabilities. *Secondly,* a developing country shall employ proper industrial protectionism accompanied by knowledge spillover, well-organized and efficient use of resources, and labor-pooling. *Finally,* a developing country must engage in export-oriented industrialization with industries having sound production experience and the consequent capacity to compete beyond their national borders.

To put it in another way, economic growth and sustainability of a country involve three stages. *The first stage* is the capacity of a country to maintain profitability in existing industrial and financial sectors, notwithstanding cyclical economic changes and the plethora of domestic or global markets. *The second stage* is the ability of a country to engage in structural changes through diversification by transferring resources to new sectors, industries, or products (Doner and Ramsay, 1999: pp. 171-172). Such diversification includes a wide range of structural shifts. These shifts are characterized as: 1) the movement from a mono-cultural, ISI based economy, to an economy based on the cultivation and export of several commodities, 2) the movement from cultivation and export of raw materials to their processing and export, 3) the movement from agriculture and mining to manufacturing, 4) the movement from simple assembly of finished goods to manufacture of high value-added and immediate goods, 5) the movement from one or a few industrial sectors to several or many sectors, 6) the movement from manufacture for domestic consumers to production for exports, and 7) the movement from exporting finished commodities to one market to exporting such commodities to a wider range of markets (Doner and Ramsay, 1999: pp. 171-172). These shifts exemplify the movement from import-substitution industrialization to export-oriented industrialization.

Therefore, *the third stage* for a country's economic growth and sustainability is that country's capacity to develop global competitiveness in new and higher value-added activities, even if remnants of ISI remained, such as tariffs and industrial protectionism. The objective is not merely to move into and expand exports into new sectors, but to increase local capacity for production (Doner and Ramsay, 1999: pp. 171-172). Thus, *the learning by doing* concept props up whenever a sector not only gains knowledge and experience in production, but also gains the ability to compete among global markets.

After the countries engaged in efforts towards global economic integration through trade and financial liberalizations, foreign MNCs bestowed them with FDI and portfolio investments. These investments accelerated the economic growth of Southeast and East Asia after the mid-1960s. Consequently, their GDPs grew on the average of 5 to 9 percent. Furthermore, until the Asian Financial Crisis of 1997-1998, the HPAEs successfully maintained macroeconomic stability, low and stable inflation rates, low internal and external debts, and positive and relatively stable real interest rates. With the goals firmly established by the mid-1960s, these HPAEs were able to maximize their capacity for new technology, which was critical to their ability to trade, and consequently, to attract FDI. The financial sector was secured and savings were encouraged. As the HPAEs engaged in further trade liberalizations, the inflows of FDI and portfolio investments enabled them to increase their efficiency and their competitiveness in the global markets.

However, although the Southeast Asian governments were highly instrumental in the phenomenal growth in the region, they were also highly instrumental in their respective countries' financial and economic downfalls. With significant exceptions of Taiwan, Hong Kong, and Singapore, countries in Southeast Asia were plagued by the lack of political coherence and decisiveness as previously explained. They failed to achieve sound macroeconomic fundamentals: sufficient foreign reserves, little or no foreign debt, current account surpluses, relatively strong banking systems, and "sound" monetary and fiscal policies. Although Singapore and Taiwan were bestowed with sound macroeconomic fundamentals, they were indirectly affected by the Crisis through the overall decrease in both trade and investment. The key word is *indirectly*, because regardless of the adverse effects brought on by the Crisis, such as speculation and currency depreciation, their economies remained strong.

VIII.
Notes

1. Beside the GDP, other measurements for economic growth include the unemployment rate, the consumer price index (CPI), and the inflation rate.
2. The marginal propensity to save is the higher level of savings which stems from an extra currency of income.
3. The NIEs include Korea, Taiwan, Hong Kong, and Singapore.
4. Although such temporary protectionism was lowered after the ISI stage, it still existed especially in forms of import barriers such as tariffs.
5. Singapore was somewhat of the exception of the Import-substitution argument for it never fully engaged in Import-substitution policies. That was due to its small domestic market (as a compact urban society, it lacks the agriculture base and natural resources from which to generate wealth). Instead, it started with labor-intensive manufacturing onto export-orientation (Neher, 1991: pp. 127-129).
6. Crony capitalism is an economic phenomenon that occurs whenever and wherever there are absences in prudent financial or economic regulations or reforms (such as transparency in financial reporting). The collapse of Enron, once one of the world's largest electricity and natural gas traders, is a proven case in point. Its former leaders, Kenneth L. Lay and Jeffrey K. Skilling were found guilty on May 25th, 2006 of fraud and conspiracy. Corruption, complacency, get-quick-rich schemes, and weak leadership dominated management from the early 1980s through the 1990s in companies in all corners of the globe, not excluding Asia.
7. The tariffs were lowered for the most part, but were not totally dismantled.
8. Among the most common incentives included tax holidays on profits and subsidies for the cost of job training.

9. Singapore was an exception. Although it did not start its export-oriented industrialization until the mid-1960s, its exports since then consisted of higher valued-added goods such as electronic products. Singapore's education level, which was higher than other countries in the Pacific Rim region, played an important role in its shift towards EOI (Neher, 1991: p. 127). As will be explained in Chapter Three, the technological transfers and FDI from the U.S. and Japan were also instrumental in Singapore's rapid development in the electronics industry.
10. ASEAN, founded in 1967 in Bangkok, Thailand, is now comprised of Brunei, Cambodia, Laos, Indonesia, Malaysia, Myanmar, the Philippines, Thailand, Singapore, and Vietnam.
11. Short-term foreign portfolio investment is an indirect investment that lasts less than a year.
12. According to the 1997 report of the Asian Development Bank, the number of firms and their workers in the region represented 96 percent of the total number of electronic components firms globally. This also represented 97 percent of the total number of workers employed in such firms worldwide (Tan, 2000: p. 21).
13. The HPAEs consisted of Taiwan, Singapore, South Korea, Hong Kong, Malaysia, Thailand, Indonesia, and China. They were referred to by the World Bank as countries that developed a path to industrialization via exports of manufactured goods primarily to advanced nations. These countries did more than creating industrial bases only by substituting domestic manufactured goods for imports (Krugman and Obstfeld, 2000: p. 266). Their EOI strategies took it a step forward global economic integration as explained above.
14. The massive outflow of foreign investment capital reached up to 40 percent of its total since the late 1960s (Tran Van Hoa, 2000: p. 12).
15. The ringgit was at 4.88 per dollar in early January of 1998 (Tran Van Hoa, 2000: p. 12).
16. Korea was the exception to this trend. Because the country allowed some nominal exchange rate depreciation, its cumulative 12 percent real exchange rate appreciation over the 1990-1997 period was much less (Glick, 1999: p. 36).
17. The LTCM, based in Greenwich, Connecticut, was the "Mother of All Hedge Funds." Using computer models and borrowing heavily from various banks, LTCM put $120 billion at risk, hoping, implicitly, that the value of U.S. T-bonds would go down and that the value of junk bonds and emerging market bonds would go up in the Summer of 1998. The opposite actually occurred and the LTCM did not anticipate the extent of the global contagion (Friedman, 2000: p. xiv).
18. The overproduction in electronic industries caused a decrease of export growth particularly in Korea and Malaysia, the countries that exported significant amounts of electronic products (Glick, 1998: p. 37).
19. The result of which over-capacity in production in similar sectors across Asia became prevalent, especially in the first half of the 1990s (Jackson, 1999: p. 5).
20. In fact, clientelism played a long-term role in the economic decline of Japan after the early 1970s.
21. A prevalent aspect of moral hazard, which will be discussed throughout the book.
22. As stated before, the Asian-5 countries comprises of the Philippines, Korea, Malaysia, Indonesia, and Thailand.

23. The ratio of M2 (in dollar terms) to foreign reserves reflects the potential demand for foreign currency by holders of (broad) domestic money. The 400 percent ratio that plagued Asia also plagued Mexico prior to its 1994-1995 Peso Crisis. (Glick, 1999: p. 43).
24. Infrastructure includes transportation, water, electricity, communication, and health facilities.

Chapter Two
Taiwan's Economic Path after the Second World War

I.
Taiwan's Road Towards Development: The Essence of Land Reform

Since the late 1960s, the economic growth of Taiwan proves to be axiomatic. By 1995 Taiwan became the world's twelfth largest trading nation, even with an annual income of $12,300.00 and a population of 21.4 million (Fred Robins, 1998: p. 45). Among the chief reasons for the success of Taiwan's economy was the pragmatic nature of the government's industrial policies.

Taiwan was influenced by the economic ideology of Dr. Sun Yat-Sen who conveyed key emphasis such as: 1) equal sharing among the people of the fruits of the economy, 2) private ownership of business and property, 3) the preservation of the market functions, 4) the institution of checking measures to prevent corporate monopoly of the basic life-sustaining materials and services, and 5) the government's responsibility to build infrastructures to enable continuing economic growth. The government emphasized the importance of an economic environment capable of stimulating and nurturing the individual's ability to carry out his or her profit making activities (Hwang, 1991: pp. 59-61).

The land reform policy in the late 1940s through the early 1950s gave farmers the needed production incentives such as full ownership of their land and the sole benefits from their labor. In order to assist the farmers in shifting farming towards business enterprising, the government: 1) disseminated new agricultural technologies to farming communities, 2) made agricultural loans available, and 3) upgraded rural infrastructures. As the agricultural economy grew, the government helped the farmers find international markets for their products (Hwang, 1991: p. 61). As a result, tenants declined from 39 percent in 1949 to 9 percent in 1976, while agricultural owner-operators increased from 36 to 82 percent of the total population (Gwynne, Klak, and Shaw, 2003: p. 99).

The government's guidance in the agricultural economy made it a success. Such a success not only satisfied domestic demand for agricultural products, but it also generated enough capital to subsidize Taiwan's early industrial development. The Taiwanese government encouraged capital accumulation, and then channeled it away from real estate and short-term speculative ventures towards more highly productive activities. This type of local planning system was led by the government as well as by intense foreign development assistance-based economic aid (primarily by the United States) that has turned Taiwan around since 1951 (Fred Robins, 1998: p. 45).

II.
The Importance of the United States Post 1951

Prior to 1951, Taiwan's economy was primarily agricultural. Its high inflation, coupled with growing civil dislocation, prevented the provincial authorities of Taiwan from engaging in any large-scale reconstruction on their own (Robins, 1998: p. 47). By 1951, however, Taiwan began to experience a turnaround when the United States started its own development assistance-based economic aid. Between 1951 and 1953, the United States provided Taiwan with aid-financed imports of $150 million of basic food and consumer goods, which were instrumental in breaking the destabilizing high inflation rate (Robins, 1998: p. 47). Other than aid-financed imports, the United States also provided technical assistance. American personnel gave Taiwan the needed expertise to assist the government in agricultural extension services, further land reforms, civil aviation administration, public health, education, and other infrastructural projects. Furthermore, the United States bestowed upon Taiwan twenty-four percent of private investment (Robins, 1998: p. 49).

Thus, between 1951 and 1965, the United States gave Taiwan more than $4 billion in grants, loans, and military equipment. Of the $4 billion, $1.5 billion was given for non-militarily purposes, which were roughly 40 percent of total investments and imports during that period (Robins, 1998: p. 50). Furthermore, U.S. civilian aid constituted more than 10 percent of Taiwan's gross national product (GNP) by 1951. Between 1951 and 1964, aid provided by the United States had met 93 percent of Taiwan's foreign exchange deficit. The sale of U.S. aid commodities for local currency removed excess purchasing power from the economy and, thereby, stabilized prices. The investment funds provided by the United States were utilized for the development of transportation, communications, electric power, manufacturing, mining, and military projects (Robins, 1998: p. 50).

In summary, the role of the United States towards Taiwan's economic development was important, yet it must be asserted that the United States by itself was not the decisive factor in laying the foundation for Taiwan's future economic success. Of the current $1.3 billion account deficit between 1953 and 1962, aid financed approximately $1.1 billion (or 85 percent of that deficit). In addition, U.S. aid contributed roughly one-third of Taiwan's gross domestic investment (Fred Robins, 1998: p. 50). While eighty-six cases of FDI were received by Taiwan in the 1950s, fifty-eight cases of the FDI were provided by China. In addition, in the most dramatic expansion of manufacturing output from 1961-1970, domestic savings provided about eighty-five percent of gross domestic investment (Fred Robins, 1998: p. 50).

III.
Taiwan's Move from Import-Substitution Industrialization to Export-Oriented Industrialization: Post 1950s

A. The First Phase: Import Substitution, 1950 Through 1960

This first phase of Taiwan's modern economic development was underpinned by the 1949 currency reform, and the foreign assistance economic aid provided by the United States. The policies in the 1950s were designed to increase both local food production, and the saving of foreign exchange through import substitution. The share of non-durable consumer goods in total imports decreased from 20 percent to 6.6 percent between 1952 and 1957. Furthermore, multiple exchange rates were combined with a system of administered foreign exchange allocation and with tariff and non-tariff protection during this period. The average nominal tariff rate for all imports, for instance, increased from 20 percent to 45 percent between 1948 and 1955 (Fred Robins, 1998: p. 53).

The currency reform was essential because it was overvalued, which in turn penalized exports while discouraging the development of export industries. Larger government enterprises enjoyed the easiest access to foreign exchange, and were in competition in obtaining government licenses, rather than reducing costs and attracting customers. Controls upon foreign exchange and imports were strict in the midst of the inflation and the balance of payment crises (Fred Robins, 1998: pp. 53-54). Consequently, Taiwan's manufacturing sector saw rapid expansion, while import substitution proceeded in rubber, textiles, leather products, petroleum, coal, and metal products. In addition, new firms were able to establish strong domestic market presence free from both import and foreign-own competitions. By 1954, the small size of Taiwan's domestic market became a constraint and the decline of the high manufacturing growth rate of the previous years became axiomatic. However, import substitution in beverages, tobacco, textiles, clothing, paper, and cement were complete. Taiwan moved towards the outward-oriented development strategy of the early 1960s as its policy lost momentum (Fred Robins, 1998: pp. 53-54).

By 1953, Taiwan formed the Economic Stabilization Board (ESB). The ESB created Taiwan's first two Four-Year Plans as a condition for receiving U.S. aid. Although the ESB was disbanded by 1958, and the planning decentralized, Taiwan has continued to formulate Four-Year Plans until the present. The economic planning of the Taiwanese government since the 1950s, and again in the 1970s, has been broadly based and well-integrated. For instance, the government formulated concurrent plans for national construction, labor policy, and agriculture during those periods of the Four and Six-Year Plans (Fred Robins, 1998: p. 52).

In addition, Taiwan developed guidelines for the development of science and a National Council on Science Development by 1959. The integration of every element of government economic planning, with fiscal and monetary policy decisions at the macroeconomic level was aphoristic since the 1950s. However, with the exception of a few major industry and infrastructure projects, the "contents of these plans has not been imposed on the economy" (Fred Robins, 1998: p. 52). There was a major state-owned sector, mainly comprised of both: 1) the assets expropriated from Japan, and 2) the important Kuomintang (KMT) party-owned companies, which asserted their own influence, persuasion, and coercion at their disposals. However, the influence, persuasion, and coercion were not heavy-handed. Instead, as K.T. Li stated "....what we as policy makers did in Taiwan was to help various parts of the economy first to start, and then to walk; and then we let go" (Fred Robins, 1998: p. 52).[1]

It was only by the late 1950s did Taiwan begin to seriously promote manufacturing. Using Hong Kong as a model, Taiwan has relied more on smaller companies than on the interventionism of the government. After years of maintaining an overvalued exchange rate (to keep manufactured imports inexpensive), the government cut the value of the Taiwanese dollar by one-half (Gwynne, Klak, and Shaw, 2003: p. 99).

B. Export-Led Industrialization and the Initial Series of Economic Openness, 1960 Through 1973

Although industrial export growth, especially in textiles, actually began in the 1950s as a planned state priority, export-led industrialization was introduced by changes in trade and exchange rate priorities between 1958 and 1960 (Robins, 1998: p. 55). These changes included further devaluation of Taiwan's currency, removal of many import controls, and exchange rate unification. The Statute for the Encouragement of Investment of 1961 was applicable to both foreign and domestic investors. More specifically, the Statute included tax holidays, a ceiling on the corporate income tax rate, a tax regime favorable to enterprises, and accelerated depreciation. Furthermore, Taiwan also began to enjoy freedom of repatriating profit. The option of full ownership and managerial control had made Taiwan an attraction for FDI (Robins, 1998: p. 55).

Further liberalization continued throughout the 1960s through the establishment of export processing zones (EPZs), the creation of bonded factories, and the streamlining of some export incentives. The Third Four-Year Plan (1961-1964) under K.T. Li's coordinating committee incorporated a nineteen-point program of economic and financial reforms. The Fourth Plan (1965-1968) was recentralized under the Council of International Economic Cooperation and Development (CIECD) policy coordination. During in the Fifth Plan (1969-1972), the CIECD focused its attention on coordination rather than planning (Robins, 1998: pp. 51 and 55). Though the Taiwanese economy was still very much protected, exports alone could be manufactured under virtually free trade conditions. The complicated system of tax rebates was introduced, and it gave exporters the incentives to buy from domestic producers rather than from abroad without a financial loss. Furthermore, domestic producers remained protected despite selling finished goods to local buyers at prices established by the world market (Robins, 1998: pp. 56-57).

These reforms of the 1960s proved to be of immense benefits to Taiwan. It experienced an extraordinary non-inflationary boom, and enjoyed great increases of exports in clothing, electronic components, radio, television, light electrical machinery, textiles, and shoes. The value of exports increased from $136 million in 1963 to $379.4 million in 1973, a rate of roughly forty percent per annum. Furthermore, from 1963 through 1973, the gross national savings doubled to 33 percent of the GNP. Similarly, gross private savings rose to 22.6 percent per annum (Fred Robins, 1998: p. 57). During the 1960s, Taiwan's annual manufacturing growth rate fluctuated between 8 and 24 percent as textile and clothing exports boomed (Gwynne, Klak, and Shaw, 2003: p. 99).

Taiwan, however, continued to exercise industrial protectionism and did not engage in a full-scale liberalization until 1971, when it reduced many tariff barriers and eased quantitative import restrictions.[2] However, the protectionism exercised by Taiwan was carefully calculated, and not only did the protectionism yield near self-sufficiency in a large number of basic items, its levels were gradually reduced on selected industries by 1958 and onwards. The slow reduction of Taiwan's protection has been implemented often at an individual plant level (Robins, 1998: pp.57-58).

C. Secondary Import Substitution, 1973-1980

As a result of the First Oil Shock of 1973, Taiwan abandoned the Sixth Four-Year Plan of 1973-1976; which consisted of the partial decentralization under the new Economic Planning Council. The quadrupling of the oil prices in 1973 placed a burdensome toll upon Taiwan, especially since it imported 98 percent of its oil. Consequently, the inflation rose to over 40 percent per annum. The Taiwanese government counteracted the rising inflation by substantially raising many government-controlled prices and engaging in counter-actionary monetary policy. Furthermore, governmental expenditure decreased by 33 percent in real terms during the fiscal year of 1974: output growth was as low as 1.1 percent in real terms (Robins, 1998: p. 58). During the 1973-1976 period, Taiwan followed both Japan and South Korea in promoting heavy industries, although most of these industries were state controlled (Gwynne, Klak, and Shaw, 2003: p. 99). Taiwan enjoyed a period of stability and industrial expansion between the First Oil Shock and the Second Oil Shock (of 1978). The Seventh Six-Year Plan of 1976 through 1981, introduced in 1975, included ten major public and heavy industry development projects. Under this Plan, Taiwan renewed its drive for capital intensive endeavors and heavy industry mainly to meet domestic demand rather than for exports. As Robins further states:

> New state-owned enterprises were established to set up an integrated steel mill, the Kaohsing shipyard and petrochemical installations. As a result, the share of the public sector in Taiwan's manufacturing output expanded against the long-term trend to 15.4 percent in 1979. Developing these heavy industries also required new types of foreign investment and new public sector expertise; in addition to attracting inward investment, the knowledgeable evaluation of new production technologies was required (Robins, 1998: p. 61).

Taiwan next launched the "Twelve Major Development Projects" by 1978. In 1979, however, the government announced a plan for an export-oriented, large car plant to be developed by state enterprises. That plan, however, was not a success and although the Second Oil Shock brought lower growth over the period 1979 through 1982, the impact of the shock was not as profound as it was during the First Oil Shock. Therefore, drastic economic responses were not necessary, and the economy was able to adjust itself more gradually (Robins, 1998: p.60). In 1980, the Taiwanese government engaged in a systematic program for the development of science and technology to help raise industrial productivity. One way in dealing with such an engagement was to upgrade many public research organizations (Robins, 1998: p.60). The focus in further industrial improvements shifted from traditional capital-intensive industry to higher technology-intensive, non-polluting, energy efficient sectors (announced especially by the Eighth "New" Four Year Plan of 1982-1985) (Gwynne, Klak, and Shaw, 2003: p. 99). Some sectors were designated under a new Strategic Industry Development Program and supported by the Statute for the Encouragement of Investment (Robins, 1998: p. 60).

By the early 1980s, Taiwan emerged as the world's leader in its intermediate and consumer exports, such as machine tools, bicycles, and footwear. Manufactured exports made up one-third of the total manufactured production, with both textiles and electronics that accounted for half of the total. Although Taiwan became the leading exporter of equipment, its component exports were the smallest compared to Singapore and Korea (Yoshihara, 1978: p. 172). Despite the oil price crises, all sectors of industry prospered, new heavy industries were established, and telecommunications were improved immensely. Furthermore, small and medium-sized businesses (SMBs) of less than 300 employees accounted for 65 percent of the island's total exports (Robins, 1998: p.61).[3] Although these firms were resilient and highly flexible, they were, however, short-term in orientation with typically a three-year payback horizon.[4] Also, as Robins states, "as late as 1991, more than 40 percent of the finance raised by the SMBs still came from the private loan market rather than from the banks" (Robins, 1998: p.61).

D. A Leap Onwards towards Innovation, Higher-Technology, Higher Value Goods, and the Secondary Series of Economic Openness: 1980-Present

It is well-known that the role of the Taiwanese government, in the utilization of technology for industrial improvement, has been of profound importance during the 1970s, and close attention was paid particularly to science. The National Science Development Plan (1969-1980) was drafted in 1969, and the Industrial Technology Research Institution (ITRI) was created in 1973. In order to develop an integrated circuit production facility, and to nurture the semi-conductor industry, Taiwan established the Electronics Research and Service Organization (ERSO) in 1975 (Robins, 1998: p. 63).

These more focused planning developments were to lead to the establishment of the United Microelectronics (UMC) in 1978, and later the Taiwan Semiconductor (TSMC).[5] Furthermore, the Hsinchu science-based park was created in 1980 and was given the task of establishing the infrastructure needed: 1) to create and attract high value-added enterprises in Taiwan, and 2) to establish state of the art research and development capabilities. The high tech enterprises were recipients of generous assistance from the government: the assistance which included tax holidays, duty-free imports of key equipment and materials, exemption from commodity taxes on exports, low-interest loans, and matching funds for research (Robins, 1998: p. 63).

One example of the business-government collaboration was the entry of Taiwan's firms into the personal computer market, which began with a copy of Apple II in 1981 (over four years after the original product introduction). The ERSO joined the local industry and modeled an IBM PC based on Intel 8088. By 1983, Taiwan's industry introduced cloned computers, and when IBM introduced its PC/AT in 1984, Taiwan's clone computers were on the market by the following year. By 1990, Taiwan became the sixth largest producer of computer hardware in the world (Robins, 1998: pp. 63 and 69). Biotechnology and other higher-technology sectors became government priorities by the late 1980s (Gwynne, Klak, and Shaw, 2003: p. 99).

During the 1980s, Taiwan began a series of financial liberalization that has influenced the country's rapid development of its financial markets. The financial liberalization since the 1980s had essentially four characteristics: 1) the growth rate of both bank deposits and bank loans have declined, 2) the scale of direct financing has broadened, 3) both the bill market as well as the stock market has grown at a rapid pace, and 4) the transaction system has matured (Lee, 2001: p. 89). As a result, Taiwan's trade surplus reached 21 percent of its GNP, while the government approved outward investment jumped 80 percent by 1987. Within a year, the trade surplus not only precipitated a rapid appreciation of the New Taiwanese dollar, but it also precipitated the removal of the foreign exchange controls, the reduction of many tariffs, and the elimination of many non-tariff barriers.[6] In 1987, Taiwan established the International Economic Corporation Development Fund (IECDF) in order to encourage the use of the large foreign exchange reserves for investment in other regional countries (Robins, 1998: p. 65). Furthermore, securities companies were given permission to establish themselves in Taiwan (Lee, 2001: p. 89).

Another step Taiwan took was to lift its formal ban on the growing indirect trade and investment with China. Although Taiwan limited any single investment in China to $50 million, Taiwanese investors surpassed the limit by investing through Hong Kong and elsewhere. By 2001, Taiwan's investment in China was between $40 and $70 billion and became China's third largest trading partner after the United States and Japan (Gwynne, Klak, and Shaw, 2003: p. 99).

As a result of the series of initiatives, foreign investment doubled for the next two years. A year later, in 1989, Taiwan removed every ounce of control on deposit and lending rates and permitting foreign banks to play a bigger role (Robins, 1998: p. 65).[7] Private banks were given permission to establish in the country in 1991 while regulations governing bill-financing companies were relaxed three years later (Lee, 2001: p. 89). In addition, regulations on commercial banks engaged in bill businesses were relaxed in 1992 and again in 1995. Since March of 1996, overseas Chinese and foreigners who were not allowed to invest directly in the local stock market in the past found themselves able to do so (Lee, 2001: p. 89).

Thanks to Taiwan's moves for openness, between 1980 and 1993, it achieved an annual average growth in GDP of 7.7 percent, while its international trade expanded at over 11 percent per annum in U.S. dollar terms. As a result, Taiwan's per capita GDP was $10,852, which was two-thirds that of Hong Kong and Singapore, twenty time that of China, and 60 percent that of Australia (Robins, 1998: p. 67). As Saler points out:

> Taiwan's economy became among the most vibrant of any Asian nation, growing at an average rate of more than eight percent over the past decade. The Taiwanese currency has also been a boon to American investors over the past several years, adding a substantial foreign-exchange kicker to the relatively modest gains of the Taiwan bourse itself (Saler, 1996: p. 166).

Although Taiwan continued to use restrictions on foreign portfolio investments, it has shown its continuation in easing up on those restrictions which will carry on to adding depth and diversity; especially in the financial-services sector (Saler, 1996: p. 170). Taiwan's stock market is the third largest in Asia despite the restrictions over foreign investment. Although these restrictions were eased up, it was done so with some degree of inconsistency. Therefore, Taiwan enjoyed the lowest percentage of foreign participation of any Asian market. Taiwan's total foreign ownership of its securities was limited to merely 10 percent of the outstanding shares of any individual company, and a market aggregate of

$7.5 billion (Saler, 1996: p. 170).

From 1988 through 1994, Taiwanese equities returned 90 percent of its local currency, and 137 percent in U.S. dollars for a net out-performance of the Standard & Poor's 500 of three percent (Saler, 1996: p. 170).[8] Moreover, on fourteen separate occasions, the Taiwanese bourse fell by 10 percent or more in a single month, with the largest fall of 37 percent in August of 1990 (as a result of the Iraqi invasion upon Kuwait). Between 1988 and 1990, Taiwan's equity rose by more than 300 percent in U.S. dollars, before their slide of 60 percent by September of 1993 (Saler, 1996: p. 170). By 1993, the huge speculations that pushed the emerging market prices higher throughout that year reached Taiwan, as its valuations relative to the overheated bourses of Malaysia, Thailand, and Hong Kong, seemed more reasonable. Investors, therefore, began looking upon the Taiwanese government to further ease foreign investment restrictions. The Taiwan's Weighted Stock Index, which comprises nearly all publicly traded companies on the Taiwan bourse, had declined by 22 percent (Saler, 1996: p. 171).

IV.
Taiwan and the Asian Financial Crisis of 1997-1998

A. Taiwan's Sound Economic Performance

As mentioned before, Taiwan escaped from the Crisis relatively unscathed, but for five important reasons. *The first reason for the "shield" against the severity of this debacle was due to the strengths of Taiwan's private entrepreneur culture and resources from its educational and Research and Development sectors.* These sectors balanced the financial market practices often opaque and self-serving as was the case in the rest of the emerging Asian markets (Godement, 1999: p. 140). *The second reason why Taiwan was not severely affected by the Crisis was due to Taiwan's conventional economy.* Taiwan had the ability to structure itself to withstand the Crisis due to its heavy emphasis on strong savings over investment. As shown in Table 2.1, Taiwan had a higher rate of domestic savings per GDP than its rate of domestic investment per GDP since the mid-1980s.

Table 2.1 Taiwan's Savings and Investment

Saving and Investment Rates	1985	1990	1995
Domestic Savings/GDP (%)	32.5	28.1	26.3
Domestic Investment/GDP (%)	19.1	23.1	24.5

Source: Naughton, Tony. "Taiwan: An Island State with Economic Insulation?" *The Causes and Impact of the Asian Financial Crisis.* Tran Van Hoa and Charles Harvie, editors. London: MacMillan Press Ltd., 2000: p. 165.

The third reason for Taiwan's strong economic performance throughout the Crisis was due to its sound stabilization strategy in the financial market. The stock market remained subdued for most of the 1990s; and although the Crisis placed the market to a temporary halt, the return for stock investors for 1997 was positive (Naughton, 2000: pp. 163-165). Furthermore, the prime lending rate remained low while the interest rates remained modest and stable, as shown in Table 2.2 below.

Table 2.2 Taiwan's Financial Market Data

Financial Data (selected)	1993	1994	1995	1996	1997
Stock-market index (average)	4182	6252	5580	5975	9143
Prime lending rate (%)	8.22	7.91	7.91	7.69	7.65

Source: Naughton, Tony. "Taiwan: An Island State with Economic Insulation?" *The Causes and Impact of the Asian Financial Crisis.* Tran Van Hoa and Charles Harvie, editors. London: MacMillan Press Ltd., 2000: p. 165.

The fourth reason for Taiwan's "shield" against the severe effects of the Crisis was due to Taiwan's strong economic indicators of the 1990s. Taiwan maintained consistent current account surpluses and large foreign reserves. Furthermore, Taiwan's external debt remained *negligible*, and its short-term debt was only 22 percent of its foreign reserves (Tan, 2000: p. 86). The modest interest rates can be partly explained by the low inflation rates of the 1990s, as shown in Table 2.3.

Table 2.3 Taiwan's Economic Indicators (1991-1997)

The Indicators *(in percentage)*	**1991**	**1992**	**1993**	**1994**	**1995**	**1996**	**1997**
Real GDP growth (%)	7.55	6.76	6.32	6.54	6.03	5.70	6.20
Total Exports (U.S.$ billion)	76.18	81.47	85.09	93.05	110.66	118.88	124.82
Total Imports (U.S.$ billion)	62.86	72.01	77.06	85.35	103.55	106.86	117.55
Current account balance (U.S.$ billion)	12.02	8.15	6.71	6.15	4.82	10.48	8.11
Foreign exchange reserves (U.S.$ billion)	82.41	82.30	83.57	92.45	91.50	89.00	84.00
Total external debt (U.S.$ billion)	neg.	neg.	neg.	neg.	neg.	neg.	neg.
Debt Servicing (U.S.$ billion)	neg.	neg.	neg.	neg.	neg.	neg.	neg.
Exchange rate vs. U.S.$ (year-end)	25.75	25.42	26.67	26.30	27.26	27.50	31.50
Inflation (CPI %)	3.62	4.46	2.94	4.09	3.68	3.07	2.65

Source: Naughton, Tony. "Taiwan: An Island State with Economic Insulation?" *The Causes and Impact of the Asian Financial Crisis.* Tran Van Hoa and Charles Harvie, editors. London: MacMillan Press Ltd., 2000: p. 164. PERC, Ltd.

Table 2.3 further demonstrates Taiwan's strong export manufacturing sector. This sector was bestowed with FDI which was generally long-term.[9] Many SMBs remained immensely competitive in the global markets and had the capacity to respond and adapt to changes in their economic environment.[10] As Gerald Tan puts it rather pointedly, "Innovative entrepreneurship is a hallmark of Taiwanese management" (Tan, 2000: p. 86). Taiwan exercised technological upgradings periodically, flexibility in industrial structural adjustment, and its ability in maintaining financial risks for business corporations (Lee, 2001: pp. 91-92).

The final reason why Taiwan went through the Crisis relatively unscathed was due to its stable KMT party. Although the party exercised quasi-authoritarianism, it remained unusually well-organized and autonomous. Its strength and autonomy meant that Taiwan's economic policy was largely immuned from the "need to attract voters and campaign funds" (Noble and Ravenhill, 2000: p. 102). In other words, the Taiwanese government was successful in preventing the escalation of crony capitalism, which was among the hallmarks of the Asian Financial Crisis of 1997-1998. However, it must be said that Taiwan's small size and open economy rendered the party vulnerable to instability and manipulation by China. Furthermore, the KMT's diplomatic isolation meant that it could not expect aid from the IMF, Japan, or the United States. The KMT feared the probabilities of: 1) inflation and financial impropriety, and 2) capital flight and infiltration by investors acting on behalf of China (Noble and Ravenhill, 2000: p. 102).

B. Taiwan's Inability to Fully Escape from the Effects of the Crisis

Despite Taiwan's strong economic fundamentals, Taiwan was affected by the Crisis due to over-leveraging and heavy-cross shareholding in the stock market (Lee, 2001: p. 90). The New Taiwanese (NT) dollar encountered the severe speculative attack after the baht was devalued by mid-July of 1997. In response to the attack, the central bank spent $5 billion, and raised the interest rates up to 15 percent in order to defend the value of its currency (Tan, 2000: pp. 86-87). In the first week of October, the central bank spent $1.2 billion in order to prevent the NT dollar from depreciating below the NT$29 per U.S. dollar. On October 17th, however, the Central Bank allowed the NT dollar to float, and subsequently, the currency was depreciated by roughly 15 percent against the U.S. dollar. The currency has stabilized at this level since 1998 and this situation was a reflection of the currency that was not entirely convertible (Lee, 2001: p. 90).

Table 2.3 demonstrates that the 1997 figures indicate the impact of the broader Asian Financial Crisis on Taiwan: the depreciation of the currency, the rise in the cost of imports, and the deterioration in foreign exchange holdings (Naughton, 2000: p. 163). The growth rates of Taiwan's exports decreased from 17 percent per annum in 1995, to 4 percent per annum in 1996. Its heavy reliance on the export of electronics products made Taiwan vulnerable in the slowdown of the global electronics market in the mid-1990s. The Taiwanese stock market rose rapidly at the end of 1996 and by August 1997, the stock market index had broken through the 10,000 point barrier. However, the high interest rates used to defend the currency, the falling share prices in the regional stock markets, and the slowdown in the global electronics market, caused investors to sell their shares at rapid proportions. Therefore, the stock market slid after 1997, reaching 5,798 points by February of 1999 (Tan, 2000: pp. 87-88).

Taiwan made matters more precarious by allowing the establishment of sixteen new private banks and allowing nine more credit and trust institutions to operate as banks. These financial institutions, controlled by large business groups, had relatively little initial exposure to the property market. Several of the banks accrued up to millions of dollars of bad debts due to loans granted to their subsidiaries in the construction sector (Tan, 2000: p. 87). Due primarily to natural disasters, the construction sector was not entirely successful in their projects. Therefore, these subsidiaries could not service their loans and, consequently, the non-performing loans of the new banks were estimated at 8 percent. The percentage of the non-performing loans that were set to rise significantly at the exposure of the private banks to the property sector was anything but ideal (Tan, 2000: p. 87).

V.
Epilogue
Taiwan Then and Now: A Look at its Current Economic Well-being in the Post Asian Financial Crisis Era and its Outlook onto the Future

A. Taiwan's Road to Economic Growth and Sustainability-A Recapitulation

In using the economic ideology of Dr. Sun Yat Sen, the government's equal opportunity policy measures were designed to be pragmatic. These measures included: 1) making available to all people the resources required for entrepreneurial endeavors such as capital accumulation, marketing and product information, as well as technical and management assistance, 2) ensuring equal access to education, 3) providing low-cost, high-quality training in specialized, advanced business and technical fields, and 4) making venture capital available to farmers and SMBs (Hwang, 1991: p. 47).

The economic policies were applied only to facilitate the transition to new economic development orientations. The first ISI was short-lived because of Taiwan's desire to move to the EOI stage, and because of the United States' demand for Taiwan's economic openness. FDI and economic aid from the United States from the onset accelerated Taiwan's economic growth after 1951. After ISI, Taiwan moved towards export expansionism, the development of heavy and petrochemical industries, and the promotion of high-tech industries during the EOI stage.

While Taiwan shifted from ISI to EOI, it began its series of financial and industrial liberalizations such as tax holidays, a ceiling on a corporate income tax rate, and the freedom to repatriate profits. With these liberalization measures, Taiwan was bestowed with additional FDI and portfolio investments. These investments aided Taiwan in its heavy emphasis on science and technology. Therefore, Taiwan became a chief exporter in electronics goods by the mid-1960s onwards. Consequently, its GDP grew no less than 7 percent in the next three decades.

The success of Taiwan since the 1950s shows us: 1) that deliberate government involvement in the economy can bring long-term, material gain, and 2) that effective policy mechanisms reflect their time, purpose, and particular government and business environment. Flexibility and adaptability were the norms in engaging in economic policy coordination and developmental strategies that propelled Taiwan even through the Asian Financial Crisis.

Although Taiwan maintained strong economic fundamentals, its currency underwent severe speculative attack after the baht's devaluation of 1997. The rise in the interest rates by the Central Bank stabilized the currency through 1998. However, the establishment of new financial institutions, with little exposure to the property sector, made matters more precarious. These banks loaned money to their subsidiaries in construction projects that were largely unsuccessful. Consequently, the non-performing loans increased to 8 percent by 1999, and were expected to increase even more.

The lesson we draw from Taiwan is that stability, efficiency, and prudence were important for the sake of its economic development and sustainability. Even when efficiency was sacrificed for the sake of stability, Taiwan's decision making over the past three decades proved to be calculating and decisive. Although some may have questioned Taiwan's increase of the interest rates in response to the speculative attacks on its currency, the move proved to be not as damaging as anticipated, and its GDP growth is still at a respectable 5 percent minimum since 1998.

B. Taiwan in the Post-Asian Financial Crisis Era: Reforms, Recession, and Recovery

1. The Reforms

Since the Asian Financial Crisis of 1997-1998, Taiwan continues with its financial reforms in the banking sector and in the securities industries. In mid-February of 1999, Taiwan held the "Symposium on the Current Economic Problems and Resolution Schemes." The Symposium was held out of concerns that: 1) Taiwan's asset bubble burst in 1990 and the property market has stagnated since then and 2) the factors which led to Japan's past decade of stagnation and bank misery began to be felt in Taiwan (Lee, 2001: p. 95). The conclusions made by the Financial Reform Committee, formed in 1997, added to the urgency of the state of Taiwan's financial market and thus, necessitated this Symposium. The ten proposals reached during the aforementioned event were aimed at improving the operational efficiencies of banks as well as strengthening the banks' surveillance system (Lee, 2001: p. 95).

The proposals are as follow: 1) for banks to speed up bad-loan write-offs to cut the non-performing loan (NPL) ratio, 2) banks will be asked to increase bad loan provisions from 1 percent to 2 percent (with the revision of the Tax Law for this purpose), 3) commercial banks would be allowed to issue corporate bonds (otherwise known as financial bonds), 4) banks will be encouraged to issue preferred stocks to further increase their capital adequacy ratios without diluting earnings on common shares, 5) a creation of a new law on the supervision of state-owned financial institutions so as to prevent excessive interference in the operations of such institutions, 6) banks must engage in credit rating, with a new asset restructuring mechanism set up to buy poor quality assets from low-rated banks, 7) certain regulations must be instituted in order to control the use of common stocks as collateral for bank loans, 8) to encourage bank mergers, tax incentives will be provided, 9) chairpersons of banks should be full time and shall be held fully responsible in preventing corruption of their affiliates, and 10) bank guarantees or joint guarantees will be strictly regulated or even banned (Lee, 2001: pp. 95-96).

The Symposium also recommended the enactment of the Trust Business Law in order for more business to be created for banks. As mentioned before, this historically important event came a year later after the Financial Reform Committee reached a series of *conclusions* surrounding the state of Taiwan's financial sector (Lee, 2001: pp. 96-97). *First,* the state-owned banks must improve its operational efficiency. This is because after 1992, the market share of deposits in these banks fell from 55.96 percent to 46.92 percent in a four year period. The share of loans likewise dropped from 58.95 percent to 53.44 percent during the same period. Because the lack of an incentive system and the inflexibility in the budgeting processing were the major problems, the Committee has decided to privatize those state-owned banks to restore their competitive edge. *Second,* mortgage-backed securities (MBS) will be launched to create liquidity for bank loans. This is because securitization is an effective way of providing a secondary market for loans (Lee, 2001: p. 97).

Third, as the Committee suggested, the banks should be allowed to enter into investment banking areas in order to improve bank competitiveness. Banks should also be encouraged, for the sake of risk control purposes, to set up independent subsidiaries for securities-related business. In addition, banks should, as far as the Committee was concerned, be allowed to enter the bond market as underwriters, dealers, and brokers, with surveillance and risk control consolidated. This is, in effect, to make the dichotomy between banking and securities blurred (Lee, 2001: p. 97). Furthermore, the Central Bank has decided to engage in asset management by opening the business of money market fund management to banks under the Trust Law and Trust Business Law (Lee, 2001: p. 97).

Fourth and perhaps more importantly, banks should be required to self-regulate their own liquidity risk management according to the guidelines set forth by the Ministry of Finance. Limits on transactions, whether through lending, equity investments, or derivative contracts, should be strongly regulated. For the sake of limiting or eliminating moral hazards, penalties on illegal actions by banks will, according to the Committee, be increased and charged on a daily basis until those actions are dealt with and corrected (Lee, 2001: p. 97).

The financial reforms in the securities industries were initiated as a result of the semi-crash of Taiwan's stock market in the second half of 1998. The crash spelled out the need to eliminate highly risky operations and re-regulate the sector to restore orderly trading. Among the key reform initiatives is to strengthen the market mechanisms and enlarging market share (Lee, 2001: pp. 99-100). These were done by recommending that the Securities and Futures Exchange Commission (SFC) be given an independent budget while elevating its ranking in the governmental hierarchy. The SFC was also recommended to use its power to investigate, search, and make arrest for illegal activities. Other recommendations include: 1) increasing criminal penalties for inside traders and illegal churners, 2) discouraging short-term trading, 3) close investigation of funds raised through seasoned offerings, and 4) cross shareholdings and loans against stocks as collateral should be properly regulated (Lee, 2001: pp. 99-100).

As far as increasing market scale is concerned, greater transparency and market participation of companies top the list of financial and market reforms. For example, it's been recommended that listing standards on the exchange and OTC (over-the counter) markets should be reviewed and lowered if possible to encourage more companies to go public.[11] Also, it was recommended that consolidated financial statements should be prepared to improve the transparency of company information (Lee, 2001: p. 100).

2. The Brief Recession

Notwithstanding the series of reforms made after the Crisis of 1997-1998, Taiwan found itself in a series of economic predicaments by 2001. As you shall see in Table 2.4, while its GDP in 2000 was 5.9 percent, the GDP fell to -2.2 percent in 2001, with the precipitous fall in both merchandise export and import growths.

Table 2.4
Taiwan's Financial Indicators, 2000 through 2005

The Indicators *(in percentage)*	**2000**	**2001**	**2002**	**2003**	**2004**	**2005**
GDP Growth	5.9	-2.2	3.5	3.4	5.7	4.1
Gross domestic investment/GDP	22.6	17.4	16.8	17.3	20.7	20.8
Gross domestic savings/GDP	25.4	23.9	25.4	25.7	25.8	n/a.
Inflation rate (consumer price index)	1.3	0.0	-0.2	-0.3	1.6	2.3
Money supply (M2) growth	7.0	5.8	3.6	5.9	7.4	6.5
Fiscal balance/GDP	-1.3	-2.5	-3.0	-3.1	-3.4	-1.0
Merchandise export growth	21.8	-17.3	6.4	10.5	20.7	8.8
Merchandise import growth	25.9	-23.7	3.2	12.2	32.2	8.5
Current account balance/GDP	2.9	6.4	9.2	10.0	6.2	4.7
Unemployment Rate	3.0	4.5	5.2	5.0	4.5	4.1

Sources: Central Bank of China. ***Website***: *www.cbc.gov.tw*
The Asian Development Bank (Outlook 2003, 2005, 2006). ***Website:*** *www.adb.org*
The Gross Domestic Investment for 2005 and the Unemployment rate is provided by IndexMundi (for 2000 through 2004).
Website: *www.indexmundi.com*

Note: According to the Asian Development Outlook 2006, the GDP of 2004 was 6.1percent (its 2005 Outlook reported it as 5.7 percent)

By the Spring of 2001, Taiwan entered a recession, with unemployment that reached a record high of 4.5 percent in June. This was accompanied by the biggest monthly drop in industrial output since 1975 as well as the steepest drop in export orders since 1981).[12] By June of 1995, the following happened: 1) export orders slid by 19.9 percent, 2) orders for electronics fell by 33.8 percent, and 3) both industrial and manufacturing outputs fell by 11.2 percent and 11.8 percent respectively (BBC News, 07/23/2001: pp. 1-3).

3. The Continued Recovery from the Recession and the Crisis

However, the recession proved to be short-lived with the worst of it over by the beginning months of 2002. Taiwan's economy beat forecasts by growing close to 1 percent in the first three months of 2002. Moreover, a pickup in exports prompted the budget office to up it growth forecast from 2.29 percent to 2.55 percent. The exports not only featured electronics, but also included products such as steel, automobiles, petrochemicals, and, as Dong Tao, an economist with Credit Suisse First Boston, states "virtually all cyclical industries" (BBC News, 05/17/2002: pp. 1-3). The industry sector improved quite rapidly due to the aforementioned increased exports. Value added in industry improved by 5.4 percent over the 2001 level, thanks largely by a 6.6 percent broad-based expansion in manufacturing.[13] Exports grew by 6.4 percent as external demand conditions improved throughout the year 2002. Comparatively, the service sector growth was more modest at 2.7 percent (Asian Development Outlook 2003, 2003: p. 60).

While Taiwan continues its recovery from the brief recessionary period, private consumption rose by only 1.9 percent in 2002 while private investment remained moderate. This was because of the lingering levels of uncertainty in both the global and domestic economic recoveries. Moreover, unemployment increased to 5.2 percent in 2002, while the employed labor force rose by merely 0.8 percent (Asian Development Outlook 2003, 2003: p. 60). Private investment began to strengthen in the third quarter of 2002, ending seven straight quarters of contraction, while government consumption and investment contracted further by 0.9 percent and 10.9 percent respectively from last year's level. Therefore, gross fixed investment continued to decline by 2.0 percent in 2002. This means, as a result, that domestic demand improved only slightly by 1.3 percent (ADO 2003, 2003: p. 60).

The rise of unemployment occurred because to the closure or downsizing of enterprises due to Taiwan's sluggish economy and structural transition. Therefore, the monthly earnings for manufacturing workers fell by 1.2 percent over the year. The slow growth in domestic demand contributed to the deflationary effects of prices, with the CPI declining by 0.2 percent. Yet, the core CPI (not including fresh vegetables, fruits, aquatic products, and energy) rose by 0.7 percent due to surcharges on goods such as cigarettes, wines, and other products that were imposed in the aftermath of agreements between Taiwan and the World Trade Organization (WTO) since its entry into this global trade resolutive body (ADO 2003, 2003: p. 60).

Notwithstanding the continuation of weak household spending, imports improved by 3.2 percent, largely because of higher levels of imported intermediate goods and higher oil prices. However, both private and public investment remained weak, causing capital goods imported to decline by 31.6 percent and 3.5

percent for both 2001 and 2002 respectively. Therefore, trade surplus increased to $24.7 billion in 2002 (22.4 percent higher than the previous year) (Asian Development Outlook 2003, 2003: p. 61).

The continued uncertainty in the global and regional economic recoveries from the recession was reflected on the fluctuations of the stock prices. While both inflation rates and interest rates fell during 2002, the stock market remained volatile: it grew by 11 percent in the first quarter, declined in prices and volume terms in the next two quarters, and improved by November (Asian Development Outlook 2003, 2003: p. 61). By year's end, however, the overall value of the stock market fell by 11.2 percent. Much of the instability in Taiwan's stock market was influenced by turbulence of the U.S. stock market, particularly during the second half of the year (ADO 2003, 2003: p. 61).

4. The Role of the Central Bank of China & Monetary Policy Developments in Taiwan's Continuing Recovery Period

The Central Bank of China (CBC) continued its active role in stimulating the Taiwanese economy. Since December of 2000, the CBC cut the interest rates fourteen times and the rediscount rate twice (in June and November of 2002). In fact, the rediscount rate was cut from 2.125 percent in December of 2001, to 1.875 percent in the following June, and to 1.625 percent in November (Asian Development Outlook 2003, 2003: p. 61). The average lending rates, rates on commercial paper, as well as government bond offered by commercial banks, also decreased. However, because the banks showed reluctance in lowering their lending rates even further, the CBC responded by bringing forth a series of measures aiming at improving the transmission mechanism of monetary policy (thus improving liquidity in the market) (ADO 2003, 2003: p. 61).[14] The demand for liquidity remained moderate throughout 2002 due to the subdued nature of the economy. M2, which measures money stock and consists of M1 plus savings deposits, grew by only 3.6 percent in 2002, as opposed to 5.8 percent in 2001. Due to the continuous decline of the interest rates, bank deposits became less attractive to investors. Therefore, liquidity was transferred from bank deposits to the bond market. On a more promising note, however, was that despite the liquidity and lending concerns, the role of the CBC was decisive in its relatively loose monetary stance. Taiwan's economic revivalism began to emerge while the NPL ratio among domestic banks decreased from 8.04 percent in March to 6.12 percent in December, 2002 (ADO 2003, 2003: p. 61).

The NPL level remained high nevertheless and, along with elevated public debt level, this became among the pressing issues for policy makers (Asian Development Outlook 2003, 2003: p. 62). One measure taken to counter the problem was the establishment of the Financial Institution Merger Law and Financial Holding Company Law in 2001. Passed by the Legislative Yuan, the law-making body, this measure provides financial institutions greater flexibility in merging and providing a wider range of financial services. Another measure taken was the passing of the Financial Assets Securitization Statute in June of 2002. That statute was passed in order to re-invigorate the financial and real estate markets as well as to boost liquidity (ADO 2003, 2003: p. 61).

As stated above, the reduction of NPLs was a paramount concern, and in 2002, the Taiwanese government used the Financial Restructuring Fund of NT $140 billion to restructure forty-four problematic financial institutions and assisted in the establishment of sixteen asset management companies (AMCs) (Asian Development Outlook 2003, 2003: p. 62). The AMCs are designed to serve as a go-between for the government to deal with the NPLs. The goal is to develop a secondary market through which the NPLs can be traded. With the plan to use financial asset reduction securitization to expedite the reduction of the NPLs well under way, the AMCs started operations in 2002, buying up to NT $211 billion worth of NPLs. To further hasten the reduction of the NPLs, the Ministry of Finance proposed expanding the size and scope of the Financial Restructuring Fund (ADO 2003, 2003: p. 62).

Comparatively, efforts made to deal with the worsened public debt-to-GDP ratio proved to be not as effective and far-reaching as expected. The weak economy, coupled with accumulated tax incentives offered by the Taiwanese government, caused tax revenues to decline by 2.6 percent in 2002. While the president's promise to not cut taxes burdened the tax base even more, efforts were made not to engage in tax cuts, but to reform the tax system in broad strokes. The reforms included rationalizing the tax system, reducing some of the tax breaks that were given to high-tech companies, as well as improving the overall efficiency of the system (Asian Development Outlook 2003, 2003: p. 62).

External demands continued to lack certainty, especially due to a slow yet an uneven global economic recovery as well as various conflicts throughout the Middle East. To counter this predicament, the Legislative Yuan passed two laws in 2002 (Asian Development Outlook 2003, 2003: p. 63). One law allows the authorities to have a supplementary budget of NT $50 billion to increase infrastructure construction in 2003. Another law allows the government to create supplementary budget appropriations of NT $20 billion to produce short-term jobs for the unemployed in 2003. In addition, Challenge 2008 was created in 2002. This medium- to long-term program was formed to upgrade the structure of the Taiwanese economy. Challenge 2008 is the National Development Plan which involves mobilizing roughly U.S.$15 billion of government investment and is encouraging the private sector to invest U.S.$6 billion by 2008. Other goals were created for 2008, which include achieving economic growth for more that 5 percent per year, raising spending on research and development, making the economy the world leader in fifteen products or technologies, and connecting more that six million households to broadband communications (Asian Development Outlook 2003, 2003: p. 63).

C. Taiwan's Continuing Recovery in 2003 and Beyond

1. Taiwan's Rebound from SARS of 2003

Taiwan's GDP growth decreased from 3.5 percent in 2002 to 3.2 percent in 2003 primarily due to the SARS outbreak which affected the overall trading climate for the region and beyond.[15] However, with the improvement of both export and import performances, as well as with flexibility of Taiwan's monetary policy, Taiwan exceeded the forecast of economic growth and improvement for FY 2004. Despite the SARS debacle of 2003, the economy showed a robust growth of 5.7 percent in 2004, which was supported by the cyclical rebound in the global high-tech sector that boosted business investment. The 5.7 percent growth happened to be the fastest rate since 2000 and it reached a peak of 7.9 percent in the second quarter before losing some momentum in the second half of that year (Asian Development Outlook 2005, 2005: p. 86). The lost of momentum was because of the general slowdown of export growth due to higher global gas prices, an easing of global demand for high-tech products, and China's tightening macroeconomic policy.

It was domestic demand, especially private consumption and investment, which was the force for Taiwan's growth, not the external sector as was the case in previous years.[16] Private consumption, which rose by 3.1 percent in 2004, contributed 1.9 percentage points to the growth. Meanwhile, the recovery of the information and communications technology (ICT) industry, a significant part of the economy, boosted business investment. Therefore, private fixed investment grew sharply by 28.2 percent and gross fixed capital formation contributed 2.6 percentage points to GDP growth (Asian Development Outlook 2005, 2005: p. 86).[17]

Both industry and services contributed quite equally to the GDP growth at roughly 3 percentage points apiece. The industrial sector, which grew at an accelerated 8.3 percent, was helped by manufacturing, which grew by 9.4 percent and supported by the ICT subsector. The rebound in the service sector was due to Taiwan's emergence from the SARS outbreak, which notably improved tourism, travel, and retail trading. Unfortunately, agricultural production dropped by 7.1 percent due to a typhoon and floods (which consequently saw a rise in food prices). But because the agricultural sector only accounted for 1.7 percent of the overall economy, the GDP was hardly affected by the drop of its production. Outside the agricultural concerns, however, the overall economic picture continues to brighten as employment is showing improvement, as shown in Table 2.4 (Asian Development Outlook 2005, 2005: p. 86).

In 2005, however, the economic growth slowed to 4.1 percent GDP (from 5.7 percent in 2004). This was due mainly from a deceleration of growth in merchandise exports from 20.7 percent in 2004 to just 8.8 percent in 2005. The deceleration occurred despite the upturn in global electronics cycle, which by the way, lifted Taiwan's economic growth in late 2005 (Asian Development Outlook 2006, 2006: p. 137). But, the upturn in late 2005 appeared to not do enough to offset the effects of the first half of that year, which was soft and contractual in nature. Private investment fell by 1.3 percent during that period while inflation picked up (which resulted in the government's decision to raise the discount rate). Private consumption, however, continued to expand. This consumption, which accounted for 62 percent of GDP, grew by 3.0 percent in 2005 (the extent of growth that remained quite consistent in recent years) and contributed to 1.8 percentage points of GDP growth. The rise in private consumption corresponded to the overall improvement in both consumer confidence and the employment rate (Asian Development Outlook 2006, 2006: p. 137).[18]

Government consumption and investment grew only marginally by 0.7 percent and 0.3 percent respectively, reflecting the Taiwanese government's efforts to tighten expenditures. Fixed investment grew by 17.2 percent in 2005, but was noticeably offset by the slight drop in private investment, resulting in a 0.5 percent gain in total fixed investment (Asian Development Outlook 2006, 2006: p. 137). Furthermore, private investment is influenced by and contingent upon the export cycle, meaning, for instance, that investment increases when export performance picks up and improves. That was not the case in Taiwan in the latter half of 2005 when private investment fell as export increased (Asian Development Outlook 2006, 2006: p. 137). The possible cause of this unusual dichotomy was a sharp expansion of production capacity in 2004, which enabled manufacturers to meet higher export demand in the second half of 2005. In all, total investment (not excluding inventory investment) shaved 0.3 percentage points from GDP growth in 2005 (Asian Development Outlook 2006, 2006: p. 137).

The weather continues to play a decisive role in increases in food prices and in sectors' performances. Typhoons and floods caused the agricultural sector to contract from 7.1 percent in 2004 to 4.1 percent in 2005 (and the bad weather caused the sector to contract even in 2004). The manufacturing sector continued to improve, however, with its growth of 5.8 percent. The reason for the sector's good performance was electronics, the key driver of its expansion notwithstanding the fact that electronics did not perform so well in the first half of 2005 (Asian Development Outlook 2006, 2006: p. 137). While construction remained flat, the service sector grew by 3.8 percent, signaling the strength of consumption demand. With the rapid price increases in the sector, the nominal growth of services continued to outpace that of the industrial sector. Thus, the share of services in GDP on this basis has in twenty years improved from 50 percent to 74 percent while the share of industry has declined from 40 percent to 25 percent (Asian Development Outlook 2006, 2006: pp. 137-138). Part of the reason why the industrial sector has shown a decline has to do with the relocation of some traditional manufacturing production in recent years to low-costs economies such as China (Asian Development Outlook 2006, 2006: p. 138).

Price increases in food due to severe typhoons constitute a chief concern. Because of such increases, consumer inflation rose to an average of 2.3 percent in 2005 (although core inflation remained tame at 0.7 percent) (Asian Development Outlook 2006, 2006: p. 138). Furthermore, the appreciation of the New Taiwanese dollar (NT$) and price regulation of transport services and power had muted the direct effect of higher global oil prices. With further integration with the Chinese economy, which led to an inflow of lower-priced manufacturing imports, inflation remained damped. In addition, the employment picture continued to brighten. Employment rose by 1.6 percent in 2005, while the unemployment rate fell to 4.1 percent (which happened to be the lowest since 2000, when the rate was around 3.0 percent). On the debit side, however, the average earnings of non-agricultural workers rose by merely 1.4 percent, below the inflation rate (Asian Development Outlook 2006, 2006: p. 138).

2. The Macroeconomic Picture in 2004

The overall trading performance continued to show improvement in 2004, with merchandise exports that increased by 20.7 percent. And with exports to Asian nations that were up by roughly 25 percent and accounted for over half of total exports. In the meantime, imports of capital and consumption goods went up by 32.2 percent, which reflects strong domestic demand. The rise in imports had caused the trade surplus to shrink from $24.9 billion in 2003 to $16.5 billion in 2004 with the current account surplus narrowed from 10.2 percent to 6.2 percent during that time span (Asian Development Outlook 2005, 2005: p. 87). Furthermore, foreign reserves rose from $35.1 billion to $241.7 billion by the end of 2004. The rise in foreign reserves was made possible for two reasons. The first reason was the increased portfolio investment, which was driven by the opening of the capital market in October of 2003 that allowed foreign investors to trade on the stock market. The second reason for the rise of the foreign reserves was an appreciation against the U.S. dollar of the reserves denominated in euros and yen (Asian Development Outlook 2005, 2005: p. 87).

Fiscally speaking, the Taiwanese government fared less well in 2004. Despite the fact that the deficit decreased from 3.6 percent in 2003 to 2.9 percent in 2004, it still exceeded 3.0 percent of GDP since 2000. Weak revenue mobilization, along with various tax reductions and incentives as well as an increase in government borrowing, has become major causes of the deficit. Fiscal revenues eroded from 20.6 percent in 1990 to 13.5 percent in 2004 as public debt increased from 23 percent of GDP in 1998 to 38 percent in 2004 (Asian Development Outlook 2005, 2005: p. 86). Furthermore, inflation returned at 1.6 percent in 2004 after two years of deflation. The continual rise in food prices, wholesale price index (by 7.1 percent), commodity prices, and international oil were the principal causes of the inflation, although the rise in oil had a minimal impact since it made up of merely 2.3 percent of the CPI and because consumers were not required to bear the burden of its upsurge (Asian Development Outlook 2005, 2005: p. 87). However, the money supply (M2) improves to 7.4 in 2004, reflecting Taiwan's economic recovery. The New Taiwanese dollar appreciated by nearly 3 percent against the U.S. dollar to NT$33.4 on average for the year, although it depreciated against the yen to NT$0.309/yen1 from NT$0.297/yen1 in 2003 (ADO 2005, 2005: p. 86).

The government is becoming increasingly aware in the rise of both its spending and the fiscal deficit which resulted in part therefrom. The concessions and incentives distorted the tax system and seriously eroded the tax base (Asian Development Outlook 2005, 2005: p. 87). The policy makers predicted that the balancing of the budget could take five to ten years through the reduction of government employment, enlarging the tax base, raising the tax rates, and selling some state-owned enterprises (SOEs); although privatizing SOEs have met with some resistance with Parliament, from labor unions, and sometimes from companies themselves. In February of 2005, the government proposed a new minimum business income tax on local and foreign enterprises, although the timeframe for implementation was not yet given (ADO 2005, 2005: p. 87).

3. The Macroeconomic Picture in 2005

Even as trade improved markedly in 2004, its performances suffered a steep decline the following year, with merchandise exports falling from 20.7 percent to 8.8 percent and merchandise import dipping to 8.5 percent from 32.5 percent. As mentioned before, that alone played a main role in about 1.6 percent drop in GDP. The merchandise trade surplus increased to $18.0 billion during that year, although the current account surplus narrowed to $16.4 billion (primarily due to increased outward remittances of investment income) (Asian Development Outlook 2006, 2006: p. 138). In addition, although Taiwan benefited from a surge in net inflows of portfolio investment, much of that was offset by increased loans to foreign banks, which resulted in reduced financial account surpluses. Gross international reserves rose to $253.3 billion and the high volume of foreign funds into stocks as well as the speculation of revaluation of the Chinese yuan, led to the abundance of liquidity and strength in the Taiwanese currency. The improvement in global investor sentiment was the main reason for such a surge of foreign fund going into stocks. Consequently, the New Taiwanese dollar appreciated by 3.9 percent against the U.S. dollar in year average terms while its effective exchange rate appreciated by 0.2 percent (Asian Development Outlook 2006, 2006: p. 138).

The government and the banking sector continue with their heavy hands-on approach in dealing with financial and fiscal matters, especially when they concern low and negative interest rates with the rise of inflation. The monetary authorities gradually moved to a more neutral policy stance to help achieve price stability and ideal capital allocation. The Central Bank of China raised its benchmark discount rate by 12.5 basis points in each quarter of 2005, bringing the rate to 2.25 percent (from 1.75 percent in 2004) (Asian Development Outlook 2006, 2006: p. 138).[19] Although the growth rate in broad money (M_2) slowed from 7.4 percent in 2004 to 6.5 percent in 2005, the funds in the banking system remained abundant and thus, were able to absorb much of the effects of the rises of the discount rate. Besides, the growth rate in M_2 still remained within the Central Bank's 3.5 percent to 7.5 percent target range. In the context of the abundance of funds in the system, domestic credit expanded by 8.0 percent during that year to both private consumers and businesses. However, out of concern that such an expansion may yield to the rise in NPLs, the banks tightened lending policies.[20] Meanwhile, the government's hands-on approach in the overall economic well-being continued to pay dividends. Its efforts towards fiscal consolidation led to a lift in general government revenue by about 8.5 percent in 2005, with overall expenditure that declined by 1.0 percent. Therefore, the budget deficit continued to recoil to 1.0 percent of the GDP. Also, the ratio of outstanding government debt to GDP stood at 32.1 percent by year's end, marking "recent years' financing of budget deficits" (Asian Development Outlook 2006, 2006: pp. 138-139).

4. The Conclusion & Outlook

Although Taiwan was not as deeply affected by the Asian Financial Crisis of 1997-1998, as compared to Thailand and Indonesia, it went through some degree of turbulence especially in 2001 through the first quarter of 2002. However, despite the turbulence and the murkiness in the global and regional economic picture, the Taiwanese government continues to demonstrate its flexible, realistic, yet creative hands-on approach to the issues facing the nation's economy. Private investment and consumption are likely to improve even more in part due to the measures passed during the past three years.

However, the road ahead may not be so smooth. The GDP growth rate rests on an average of 2.7 percent in the past four years, a marked decline in economic performance from the 1990s which was 6.3 percent and from the 1980s which was 8.1 percent. Among the main causes included slow population growth as well as an outflow of FDI, the key engine of economic growth in the 1960s through much of the 1990s. The primary reason for the outflow was due to manufacturers relocating to lower-cost economies (Asian Development Outlook 2005, 2005: p. 88). Furthermore, the current war in Iraq, SARS and a sluggish yet uneven recovery from global economic recession, has created uncertainty regarding external demand. Structural and cyclical unemployment as well as income will likely remain pressing issues as economic recovery and demands for goods continue with their slow yet uneven pace. In addition, oil prices concerns, along with a sharp appreciation of the New Taiwanese dollar and the consequent reduction of the economy's export competitiveness, are matters to look at in 2005 and beyond. Indeed, the sometimes strained relations with China is not improving matters any and a risk that Taiwan could be left out of closer regional economic integration must not be taken lightly (Asian Development Outlook 2005, 2005: p. 89).

Furthermore, medium-term prospects for the economy depend on two principal structural factors. *The first factor* calls for more efforts to be made to nurture the larger firms and strengthen their capacity in branding, research and development, as well as distribution (Asian Development Outlook 2006, 2006: p. 139). In the past, the small and medium-sized firms were the ones that played crucial roles in Taiwan's economic development. They were the ones that supplied global electronics companies under original-equipment manufacturing arrangements. However, they never own the products brand, and as they pursued aggressive pricing strategies, the profit margins of these domestic suppliers were seriously squeezed, with a profit rate of 2 percent to 5 percent typical of original equipment manufacturers. Competition from low-cost economies likewise reduced Taiwan's advantage in this industry. Although a number of domestic firms have developed their own brands, more shall be done in that regard (Asian Development Outlook 2006, 2006: pp. 139-140). *The second factor* regards the services sector, which is now proven to be a larger piece of the Taiwanese economic pie. That sector must become a key factor in the country's long-term economic growth. Should the sector grow further in the coming years, Taiwan may be required to open more to foreign competition, engage further in regulatory reforms, and to put in gear consolidation of the fragmented banking industry (Asian Development Outlook 2006, 2006: p. 140).

Yet, some optimism remains. The Central Bank is continuing to exercise prudent monetary policy initiatives towards stability by raising the official discount rate by twenty-five basis points to 1.625 percent in September, 2004 (the first increase since mid-2000). The rate increased further to 1.75 percent in December and to 1.875 percent in March, 2005 (Asian Development Outlook 2005, 2005: p. 89). By the end of 2005, the rate increased further to 2.25 percent (Asian Development Outlook 2006, 2006: p. 139). In raising the discount rate, the Central Bank pointed to rising inflationary expectations, high utilization in manufacturing (80.3 percent in January, 2005), low real interest rates, and the overall improvement in the labor market. In this context, the goal of the Bank is to return the monetary policy to a neutral stance to help maintain price stability and prevent negative real interest rates from hampering fund allocation and long-term financial stability (Asian Development Outlook 2005, 2005: p. 89). Furthermore, in reversing the erosion of tax base due to exemptions, the government introduced earlier this year, the Alternative Minimum Tax program, which is likely to lift revenue in the near future. Under this legislation, the tax on income has a rate of 10 percent on business profits that exceeds NT$2 million and a rate of 20 percent on individuals who make over NT$6 million. It will broaden the tax base since it will reverse the exemptions firms and individuals enjoyed over the years (Asian Development Outlook 2006, 2006: p. 139).

Much work in Taiwan's economic recovery remains, however. Along with the aforementioned concerns, Taiwan must continue to be mindful of the depth and duration of the upturn (and downturn) in the electronics cycle, for its importance cannot be overlooked. Also, although the Minimum Tax Alternative legislation will broaden Taiwan's tax base, it is possible that it will discourage domestic investment and cause outsourcing to lower-cost economies (Asian Development Outlook 2006, 2006: p. 140). But, thanks to the dynamism of the Taiwanese government, the hands-on approach of China's Central Bank, the continuation of careful investment, and far-seeing programs and legislatures such as Challenge 2008, there's really no reason to fear for the worst, at least for now.

VI.
Notes

1. In fact, much of the economic planning engaged by the Taiwanese Government since the 1950s echoed that of Japan, especially in the form of capital investments and subsidies MITI (Ministry of International Trade & Industry) and the Ministry of Finance bestowed upon infant industries as head-starts. Like Taiwan, Japan also provided economic and financial guidelines towards development.
2. In addition, Taiwan did not make any significant move to cease control over foreign exchange and to ease access for imports to the domestic market until after 1985. Exchange control was lifted in 1987 while the maximum tariff was still at 58 percent (Robins, 1998: p. 57).
3. That percentage represents a highly decentralized production structure (Robins, 1998: p. 61).
4. The short term in orientation characterizing the SMBs procedures and strategies were due to the high cost of capital in the informal market (Robins, 1998: pp.57-58).
5. Both the UMC and the TSMC were joint state-private sector ventures, although the TSMC involved the participation of both Taiwanese and foreign capital (Robins, 1998: p. 63).
6. The move in opening up its domestic economy to foreign importers, though incomplete, was apparent in its application for membership of GATT/WTO in 1990. Also, Taiwan abandoned the monopoly systems for tobacco, and alcohol while public procurement was lifted (Robins, 1998: p. 65).
7. Without a doubt, Taiwan by 1989 began in its engagement towards financial deregulation.
8. In the meantime, Taiwanese stocks had more than five times the average downside volatility of their American counterparts (Saler, 1996: p. 170).
9. However, the short-term foreign portfolio investment was negligible (Tan, 2000: p. 86).
10. Moreover, the high-technology industry comprised more than 10 percent of Taiwan's GNP and almost 30 percent of its total exports (especially from the computer industry) (Tan, 2000: p. 86).

11. Over-the-Counter (OTC) is an option traded off-exchange, unlike a listed stock option. The OTC option has a direct link between buyer and seller, has no secondary market, and has no standardization of striking prices and expiration dates.
Source: www.bloomberg.com/analysis/glossary/bfgloso.html
12. Orders from the United States, Taiwan's biggest importer of its products, decreased by 20.3 percent, from Hong Kong by 16.4 percent, from Japan by 23.4 percent, and from Europe by 30.2 percent (BBC News: 07/23/2001: pp. 1-3).
13. In conjunction to Dong Tao's assertion, production in electronics and IT (information technology) increased by 11.4 percent, basic metals by 10.3 percent, machinery by 5.8 percent, and chemicals by 4.4 percent. Production related to food, however, contracted by 4.5 percent while construction declined by 2.9 percent (Asian Development Outlook 2003, 2003: p. 60).
14. Liquidity refers to a level of activity or rather, cash flow. It refers to an allowance of buying and selling with minimum price disturbance especially with relative ease. It's an antithesis of illiquidity.
15. The Severe acute respiratory syndrome (SARS) is a viral respiratory disease. Its symptoms include high fever up to and over 100.4 degrees Fahrenheit, chills, diarrhea, body aches, headaches, and a general feeling of discomfort. Its recognition came into being in November of 2002 when Chinese officials discovered the first victims of the illness.
Source: The Centers for Disease Control & Prevention. Website: www.cdc.gov
16. The external sector did not contribute to the growth, as strong export growth was offset by booming demand for imports (Asian Development Outlook 2005, 2005: p. 86).
17. Capital formation is an expansion of capital (money invested in a firm) or capital goods (goods used by firms to produce other goods like buildings, equipment, etc.) through savings which can sometimes lead to economic growth.
18. Rapid expansion of credit over several years also lifted consumer spending (Asian Development Outlook 2006, 2006: p. 137).
19. The basis point, in the bondmarket, is the smallest measure used for quoting. Each percentage point of yield in bonds equals 100 basis points. Basis points are also used for interest rates. For example, an interest rate of 5 percent is fifty basis points higher than an interest rate of 4.5 percent. A yield in turn is the percentage return paid on a stock in the form of dividends, or an effective rate of interest paid on a bond or a note.
Source: http://www.bloomberg.com
20. In fact, the NPL ratio for credit cards increased from 2.0 percent in 2004 to 2.4 percent a year later while banks wrote off the equivalent $2.2 billion of bad loans on credit cards in 2005 (Asian Development Outlook 2006, 2006: p. 139).

Chapter Three
Singapore's Vision for Economic Growth, Sustainability, and Re-Growth of Today and For Tomorrow

I.
Onto the Path of Economic Development: From Basic Industrialization towards Higher Valued-Added Economy (1960s to Present):

A. Introduction: Singapore's Strive for Industrialization and Development, 1960 - 1973

Singapore's industrialization was initiated to cope with the decline in entrepot trade as well as the unemployment rate, the latter that was expected to rise in the second half of the 1960s. The Economic Development Board (EDB) was established in 1961 to engage in Singapore's industrialization. The Jurong Industrial Estate became among EDB's important undertakings in the promotion of industrial investment (Kunio Yoshihara, 1978: p. 20).

The People's Action Party (PAP) initially pursued a policy of import-substituting industrialization, characterized by low tariffs on a narrow range of industries. However, Singapore's domestic market was too small for this policy to be viable, and consequently, Singapore campaigned to join the Malaysian Federation (Murray and Perera, 1996: p. 21).[1] Singapore joined the Federation of Malaysia in 1963 after both the prime ministers of Singapore and Malaysia supported the Federation. Although Singapore alone could not attract a large amount of import-substitution investments due to its small population, shipping goods freely from Singapore to Malaysia was possible, with Malaysia becoming part of Singapore's domestic market. The population of this market would increase from two million to ten million, with per capita income increasing several times higher than their neighboring countries (Kunio Yoshihara, 1978: pp. 20-21).

However, the formation of the common market between Singapore and Malaysia became problematic. Malaysian industrialization lagged behind the industrialization efforts of Singapore. Therefore, the government of Malaysia feared that their country will be flooded with goods coming from Singapore, and consequently felt reluctant to abolish the trade barriers between Malaysia and Singapore (Kunio Yoshihara, 1978: p. 21). In addition, there was a dispute over the insistence of its partners in Kuala Lumpur to create a Malay-dominated society. Malaysia was available as an export market, yet such availability meant that Singapore companies had to compete in Malaysian markets against producers in developed countries by lowering its production costs. Investors, who counted on special privileges in Malaysia, suffered a severe blow once the projected common market collapsed by 1965 (Kunio Yoshihara, 1978: p. 21).[2]

With the loss of the projected common market, the stagnation of entrepot trade, and the scheduled British withdrawal, the PAP turned to labor-intensive manufacturing for exports.[3] However, because the local private sector had no industrial experience, multinational corporations were invited in with generous investment incentives (such as tax breaks) (Murray and Perera, 1996: p. 21). The strategy worked, especially since most export-oriented investors came to grips with the reality that the Singapore market was not as small as initially determined. Singapore engaged in a large-scale building project after the separation from Malaysia, and enjoyed a rapid economic progression after 1967. Singapore's market was enlarged, and import-substitution investment began pouring in from Japanese firms (Kunio Yoshihara, 1978: pp. 21-22). By 1966, a Japanese electronics firm set up a joint venture to sell its products in Singapore's domestic market, while other companies began investing into that country. In 1968, the Japanese export-oriented investment started arriving in Singapore, first by firms producing umbrellas and watchcases, and then by toy and textile manufacturers. Mitsubishi Heavy Industries constructed a dockyard for shipbuilding in 1973, and Singapore became an export base for equipment assemblers. The number of textiles and electronics and the amount of shipbuilding and repairs dominated Japan's export-oriented investment in Singapore after 1970 (Kunio Yoshihara, 1978: pp. 21-22).

With world trade booming during the mid 1960s, the rush of offshore sourcing by MNCs occurred. Singapore, with its excellent geographical location, excellent infrastructure, free-trade policies, and a hardworking population, became an attraction of immigration and labor mobility. Furthermore, other than export manufacturing, in which the electronics industry was prominent, Singapore became the regional service and refining center for oil exploration and an extraction boom by the late 1960s. In addition, the government took over the naval facilities once occupied by the British forces and transformed them into major shipbuilding and repairing centers. Meanwhile, Singapore started new enterprises by itself or with foreign joint-venture partners (Murray and Perera, 1996: pp. 21-22).

B. The Rise of Predominance in the Electronics Industry, Post 1965

Singapore's economic success was largely due to the rapid development of the electronics industry; moving from the first television assembly plant established before 1965 to the world's largest exporter in disk drives by the mid-1980s. As mentioned before, the tax breaks offered by the Singapore government encouraged multinationals firms (MNFs) to establish regional operating headquarters. The qualifications for establishing regional operating headquarters included basing their regional Research and Development, distribution, service network, and financial system in Singapore (Murray and Perera, 1996: pp. 132-133 and 143). The industry was transformed in 1967 when an American electronics MNF, Texas Instruments, established an offshore sourcing semiconductor plant to perform labor-intensive assembly for export. Within a few years, every American manufacturer had a similar plant in Singapore, resulting in Singapore becoming the largest exporter of semiconductors in the world. In addition, the SGS-Thomson Microelectronics (a French-Italian joint venture) set up a plant in Singapore in 1969 and has further increased its industry-based presence since then. Concurrently, Germany's Siemens, the largest electronics company in Europe, has assembled 80 percent of its integrated circuits in a Singapore plant since 1970 (Murray and Perera, 1996: pp. 132-133 and 143).

Production costs rose and the labor market was tightened by the government due to its shift from low-wage to high-wage labor costs. This policy was part of the proclaimed "Second Industrial Revolution" in 1979, which was designed to restructure the economy toward high-tech industries (Neher, 1991: p. 127). Education levels, skill, and experience had risen to the point where Singapore could accommodate higher-skilled industries. Furthermore, the electronics firms had already initiated capital-substitution by the late 1970s as labor costs rose, and with the development of new products and technologies (Murray and Perera, 1996: p. 133).

The development of new products and technologies created, to a large extent, the replacement of semi-conductors with computers (and computer peripherals), and accessories as the dominant segment of Singapore's electronics industry.[4] The American disk drive companies were less labor-intensive and much higher value-added than semiconductors and other components and consumer products. By the mid-1980s, Singapore became the leading supplier of disk drives[5] (Murray and Perera, 1996: p. 113). However, the demand for world computers decreased by 1988, which resulted in the economic slump for the Singapore-based U.S. disk-drive industry. But, this slump was short-lived because Conner, among the chief disk-drive manufacturers in the world, expanded, and consequently, the industry largely recovered by April of 1989 (Murray and Perera, 1996: p. 113).

The rise of computer peripheral manufacturing, especially of computer-tape drives produced principally by Singapore, did not damper the semiconductors, components, consumer electronics, and telecommunication industries. By 1988, the semiconductor industry was comprised of nineteen manufacturers, with more than fifty others in the supporting industries. The output in semiconductors increased from \$2.3 billion in 1992 to \$4.2 billion in 1994. New investors of the automatic chip manufacturing included the NEC Corporation (from Japan) and Philips (Murray and Perera, 1996: p. 137). Furthermore, the semiconductor industry began to expand, diversify, and upgrade. By the late 1980s, eight multinational corporations such as AT&T, Microelectronics, SGS-Thomson, Chartered

Telmos, Hewlitt-Packard, National Semiconductor, Texas Instruments, Silicon Compilation Technology, and Silicon Systems, had commercially integrated circuit design centers in Singapore (Murray and Perera, 1996: pp. 137-138).

There was also an increased export-oriented investment in the manufacturing of telecommunications equipment (from AT&T and Ericsson), facsimile machines (Matsushita), and process control systems (Yogogawa). Furthermore, Sony, Sanyo, and Matsushita came into the picture more profoundly in the mid-1980s, employing more than 10,000 people to manufacture high-precision automatic inserting equipment for printed-circuit board development (Murray and Perera, 1996: pp. 137-138).[6]

By the 1980s, Singapore was experiencing greater rates of population growth and labor mobility into its markets, notwithstanding the limitations set by the government on the population of foreign workers. Singapore literally ran out of sea space and sea-front land, which placed constraints on land and labor (Murray and Perera, 1996: pp. 27 and 35). As a result, there were sharp increases in the cost of property and labor, which, with the appreciation of the Singapore dollar, virtually squeezed the profit margins. In order to continue to grow at relatively high rates, the government found it essential to reorganize the management of human and physical resources (Murray and Perera, 1996: pp. 27 and 35).

The Growth Triangle, an initiative introduced in the late 1980s, promoted the distribution of manufacturing operations between Singapore, the nearby Riau Islands of Indonesia, and Johor. In essence, the goal was to build a tri-national industrial park aimed at attracting activities ranging from agribusinesses and fisheries to electronics, petrochemicals, shipping, and tourism. Companies and MNCs were encouraged to undertake distribution processing into the Riau Islands and Johor (Murray and Perera, 1996: pp. 27 and 34-35).

The initiative worked, and over two-million jobs were created, especially for the Indonesian population. However, income distribution continues to plague Johor, and its infrastructure is not as advanced as Singapore's. Like Batam, the largest of the Riau Islands, geographical and economical isolation poses serious problems to Johor as well. Singapore, while promoting the Growth Triangle concept to this day, is searching further afield in the growing outward reaches of its economic strategy (Murray and Perera, 1996: pp. 55-67).

C. Onto the Path of Economic Development and Laissez Faire: A Movement towards a Status as a Regional Financial Center, 1960s to Present

A series of moves initiated by the government helped to give Singapore the reputation as a regional financial center. In the 1960s, Singapore passed both the Banking Act and the Finance Companies Act; which were passed for the protection of depositors, and for proper control of the activities of the commercial banks and finance companies. In addition, the government, by 1968, set up the

Development Bank of Singapore (DBS) in order to encourage long-term financing, as well as to abolish the withholding tax on interest payable to non-resident depositors: the beginning of the Asian Dollar Market (Murray and Perera, 1996: pp. 23 and 199). The government announced its policy to develop a higher level of expertise in the financial sector in order to increase capital inflow and investment. Two years later, Singapore admitted a foreign bank and in 1971, monetary and banking administration was centralized through the establishment of the Monetary Authority of Singapore (MAS). Furthermore, exchange control was liberalized on June 1, 1978 to remove restrictions on the movement of funds (Murray and Perera, 1996: pp. 23 and 199).

The financial instruments (such as the MAS, the Central Provident Fund (CPF), and the Post Office Savings Banks) were essentials in the assurance of prudence among financial institutions, as well as the protection of depositors. The importance of the MAS was the combination in the regulatory and supervisory role in nurturing the growth of size, and depth of money, capital, gold, securities, and foreign exchange markets (Murray and Perera, 1996: pp. 202-203). The MAS: 1) acts as a banker, fiscal agent, and financial advisor to the government, 2) has the duty to promote monetary stability, credit, and exchange policies conducive to the growth of the economy, 3) takes on the supervision and the regulation of the banking and financial sectors, 4) engage in developing the financial markets as well as introducing new instruments, and 5) is authorized to borrow, lend, buy or sell currencies, issue discount and rediscount securities treasury bills, commercial bills, and government securities (Murray and Perera, 1996: pp. 202-203).[7]

The Central Provident Fund (CPF) is a social insurance scheme because it mobilizes a large proportion of domestic savings for financing public sector developments. Domestic savings derived from contributions from employees, and employers, participating in the CPF.[8] The Post Office Savings Bank (POSBank) was established to encourage thrift and to mobilize savings primarily in the public sector. It provides facilities for savings and the transfer of funds (as well as loans) to government-owned enterprises and to statutory authorities. The POSBank also invests in government bonds, provides housing mortgages, and redeposites some funds with commercial banks (Murray and Perera, 1996: pp. 204-205).

By the early 1970s, Singapore became a regional financial center due to the influx of foreign banks. Although the need for increased employment from a growing population would be catered for through greater industrialization, the financial sector was of critical importance in Singapore's progress towards economic development. Singapore was already a regional trading center, and possessed the basic infrastructure on which to build and expand its role in international finance (Murray and Perera, 1996: p. 23). Although Singapore left the Malaysian Federation in 1965, it shared a common market until 1973 when it announced its intention to set up a separate stock market. The securities industry responded to the announcement quickly with the incorporation of the Stock Exchange of Singapore, a separate and an autonomous body.[9] In addition, the MAS formulated the concept of offshore banking, and gave approval for several internationally reputable banks to conduct offshore business from Singapore (Murray and Perera, 1996: p. 23).

The MAS also exempted the Asian Currency Unit (ACU) from an 18 percent liquidity ratio normally required for commercial banks, which was an important move for the development of offshore banking by the mid-1980s because: 1) it gave the Asian Dollar Market a boost, and 2) it was made possible through the creation of the Singapore-based Asian Dollar Market using the ACU to accept foreign currency, to call deposits, and to make loans to foreign currencies (Murray and Perera, 1996: pp. 199-200).[10] Furthermore, the government engaged in another series of market and financial reforms towards the ideal of laissez-faire. The government: 1) abolished stamp duties on Negotiable Certificates of Deposits (NCDs) and bills of exchange growth of an acceptance market and secondary market in NCDs, 2) engaged in tax reduction from 40 percent to 10 percent levied upon income derived from ACUs offshore transactions and dividends distributed out of such projects, and 3) abolished the stamp duty on ACU offshore loan documents and on Asian and Singapore dollar bonds (Murray and Perera, 1996: pp. 199-200). The abolishment of the stamp duties in NCDs was especially important for two reasons: 1) a number of banks have been given permission to issue NCDs denominated in Singapore dollars and various foreign currencies, and 2) local corporations could borrow from the Asian Dollar Market, even when there was no exchange control (Murray and Perera, 1996: pp. 199-200).

As mentioned before, there was one foreign commercial bank that was admitted by Singapore before 1971 and the licensing system of the MAS gave rise to more commercial banks in the country. *The MAS formulated three types of licenses for banks to open a branch or sub-branch in Singapore:*

A *full banking license* allows a bank to engage in all types of activities permitted under the Banking Act (essentially the same as those engaged upon by a commercial bank anywhere in the world). All thirteen locally incorporated and foreign banks admitted before 1971 qualified for the full banking license. A *restricted banking license* allows the same type of transactions similar to those of a full licensed bank. Banks may not, however, open any branches, operate savings accounts, or accept fixed deposits of less than $250,000 per deposit. Fourteen foreign banks received the restricted banking license by 1994 (Murray and Perera, 1996: p. 205).

Offshore banking remained the most dominate type of banking, with 83 banks having offshore banking licenses. An *offshore banking* license allows a bank: 1) to engage in wholesale banking with non-residents, 2) to extend credit and to provide facilities such as opening of letters of credit and issuing trust receipts, and 3) to give overdrafts up to the total limit of $100 million to non-residents without any prior governmental approval. A bank may not, however, accept fixed savings, or other interest-bearing deposits, from residents. Similarly, an offshore bank is not permitted to open branches, and merchant banks operating in offshore banking activities are subject to the same terms (Murray and Perera, 1996: pp. 205).

Even with the creation of the above-mentioned financial instruments and the licensing system, Singapore continued to focus on its development as an international finance center during the 1980s. The emphasis on Singapore's financial market shifted towards capital market instruments, and related activities such as the management of investments and risks. The domestic market was broadened, and offshore activities were generally promoted (Murray and Perera, 1996: pp. 211-212). Negotiable certificates of deposit, both in Singapore and U.S. dollars, were issued by several banks. Meanwhile, commercial paper and government securities (both of a wide range of maturities), as well as gold certificates, were made available. After the ACU was established, depositors have the opportunity to place funds in foreign currencies with these institutions. At the same time, the securities market was revitalized in 1987, and primary dealers, who underwrite auctions of treasury bills, notes, and bonds, ensure the liquidity in the market. However, registered dealers do not have the privilege and the obligation of bidding directly in the auctions of new issues (Murray and Perera, 1996: p. 212). Furthermore, banks have the ability to invest directly in government securities in the range of maturities and at a competitive market yield. Consequently, the attraction of placing funds with discount houses diminished significantly (Murray and Perera, 1996: p.212).

D. The Stock Exchange-A Brief Survey

As mentioned before, Singapore established its own stock market by 1973. By 1986, in the wake of the shock recession, Singapore engaged in a series of measures to strengthen the stockbroking industry. Among the measures were the passing of a new Securities Industry Act and the opening up of local stockbroking firms to ownership by local and foreign financial institutions. Brokerage rates were cut whereas brokerage houses adopted a graduated commission scale with a view of moving towards freely negotiable rates (Murray and Perera, 1996: p. 213). The measures worked, and the stockbroker industry became more capitalized, more competitive, and offered a better range, better quality of services, and better investor protection. Consequently, in terms of volume of transactions, the Stock Exchange of Singapore became the third largest in Asia after Tokyo and Hong Kong (Saler, 1996: p. 150).

II.
The Importance of Japan in the Economic Development of Singapore

A. The Essence and the Nature of Japanese Foreign Direct Investment, Post 1970

From 1975 to 1984, foreign-owned establishments, with more than fifty percent of foreign capital investment, comprised 23 percent of establishments. However, the establishments generated 55 percent employment, 73 percent of gross output, and 65 percent of capital expenditure (Lim Hua Sing, 1999: pp. 79-82). Japan, along with Europe and the United States, have been the predominate investors in Singapore. They were responsible for 90 percent of the investment in 1988, and 97 percent of the total FDI in Singapore's manufacturing sector in the first quarter of 1989. Although the United States had been the largest investor into Singapore from 1980 through 1985, Japan became its principal investor by 1986 through 1988. Whereas Japan's investments into Singapore's manufacturing sector was 27 percent of that of the United States in 1980, that percentage rose to 42 percent in 1986, leaving the United States behind with 37 percent and Europe with 18 percent. The primary reason for Japan's takeover in its overall investment in Singapore was due to the drastic Yen appreciation in 1985. Consequently, Japanese firms reduced imports of industrial parts and components from Japan, and the procurement of industrial parts and components in Singapore's local markets increased to coincide with Japanese firms shifting their production operations in Singapore (Lim Hua Sing, 1999: pp. 79-82).

Japan's viewpoint of Singapore's economical and industrial capabilities helped shaped its motivation towards investment into the country. More non-manufacturing Japanese firms than manufacturing Japanese firms looked upon Singapore as an important base for entrepot trade, especially for exporting their products to third-world countries, and for supplying industrial parts and components (Lim Hua Sing, 1999: pp. 80-81). Furthermore, the non-manufacturing Japanese firms looked upon Singapore as: 1) an important information center, due to its strategic location and its well-established transport and telecommunications systems, 2) an important consumption market, and 3) an important financial center.[11] Japanese manufacturing firms saw Singapore as a country having low labor cost, a center for the supply of industrial parts and components, and its usage of preferential tariffs. These viewpoints were reflected in the rapid increase of Japanese liaison and branch offices in Singapore from 1979 to 1984 (Lim Hua Sing, 1999: pp. 80-81).

There were other factors that made Singapore attractive to Japanese foreign direct investment. Although Singapore's small and medium-sized businesses (SMBs) played a limited supplementary or supporting role to Japanese firms, *its highly trained workforce and its educational levels were comparatively high among the ASEAN countries.* Furthermore, Singapore's well-developed economic infrastructure ensured that the country develop its high-tech, high-valued added, and knowledge-intensive industries (Lim Hua Sing, 1999: pp. 83-85).

As mentioned before, textiles and electronics manufacturing as well as shipbuilding and repairs, dominated Japan's export-oriented investment in Singapore after 1970. However, the manufacturing firms which produced ferrous and non-ferrous, chemical and petroleum products, also dominated Japan's export-oriented investment until 1985. The importance of Japanese FDI in the textile industry decreased greatly, especially by 1985, where it constituted 0.3 percent of the total Japanese FDI in Singapore. By 1980, the electronic firms under Japanese FDI increased from 3 percent in 1970, to 11.8 percent in 1980 (Lim Hua Sing, 1999: p. 88). Furthermore, the non-manufacturing sector gained the momentum in obtaining Japanese FDI, especially in foreign trade and commerce. As Lim Hua Sing states:

> Between 1970 and 1985, the number of Japanese firms increased six-fold in foreign trade and commerce, sevenfold in construction and engineering, and nine-fold in both finance and insurance and transportation and warehousing. If other "non-manufacturing" is included, the number of non-manufacturing firms has increased 7.4 times, from 63 firms in 1970 to 464 firms in 1985 (Lim Hua Sing, 1999: p. 88).

Table 3.1 on the following page illustrates the shift of Japanese FDI from textiles and lower value-added goods to higher value-added goods, commerce, and services. Japan's investment commitments in Singapore increased 3.3 times from $73.7 billion in 1982, to $244.1 billion in 1985. To be seen on this table, Japanese FDI in Singapore became more capital and technology intensive while labor-intensive industries (such as the SMBs) were not capable of automation or mechanization in time. Therefore, Japanese firms were compelled to either liquidate, or relocate to neighboring ASEAN countries. The survival of Japanese-affiliated firms with lower productivity, efficiency, and competitiveness were threatened due to the persistent global economic recession, and Singapore's sluggish economic performance during the 1985 through 1986 fiscal years (Lim Hua Sing, 1999: p. 90).[12] Singapore's local enterprises, mostly Chinese, have performed soundly in banking, finance, and other service sectors, but have been the least effective in the manufacturing sector (Lim Hua Sing, 1999: p. 113).

Table 3.1
Japanese foreign investment in Singapore by industry ($ million)
Singapore

Industries	**1989**	**1990**	**1991**[13]
Foodstuffs	438	3	8
Textiles	2	101	15
Lumber and pulp	4	23	0
Chemicals	42	53	45
Iron and steel/ non-ferrous metal	14	10	7
Machinery	30	410	14
Electric/electronic	91	54	54
Transport equipment	-	0	0
Others	58	14	34
MANUFACTURING TOTAL	678	269	177
Agricultural and Forestry	-	1	0
Fisheries	1	0	0
Mining	-	5	0
RESOURCES DEVELOPMENT TOTAL	1	6	0
Construction	91	2	2
Commerce	70	265	154
Finance and Insurance	339	87	97
Services	148	86	37
Transportation	228	46	58
Real Estate	345	52	83
Others	-	1	0
COMMERCE AND SERVICES TOTAL	1,221	539	431
BRANCHES	3	25	6
TOTAL	1,902	840	614

Source: Tejima, Shigeki. "Foreign Direct Investment by Japanese Firms in the Asia-Pacific Region." *Emerging Growth Pole: The Asia-Pacific Economy.* Dilip K. Das, editor. London: Prentice Hall, 1997: p. 130.

Japanese-owned subsidiaries and joint ventures have remained an important feature in Japanese FDI in Singapore. The combination of the number of Japanese-owned subsidiaries (271 firms), branch offices (101 firms), and liaison offices (127 firms) constituted 63.5 percent of the total number of Japanese firms in Singapore in 1982. Furthermore, joint ventures have been significant in transportation, warehousing, chemical, trade, and commerce industries (Lim Hua Sing, 1999: pp. 96-97).

Thus, the engagement in subsidiaries and joint ventures was one of the most important contributions arising from Japan's FDI in Singapore. Another important contribution pertained to the employment opportunities generated by Japanese firms. As Lim Hua Sing states,

> In 1980, 718 Japanese-affiliated firms in Singapore provided 70,323 employment opportunities for Singaporeans and guest employees, mainly from Malaysia, together with 2,909 Japanese and 171 other expatriates. Employees who worked for those Japanese firms constituted 6.7 percent of Singapore's total workforce (Lim Hua Sing, 1999: p. 102).

In 1982, the number of employment opportunities provided by 782 Japanese firms increased to 70,870. Japanese joint ventures employed 38,764 employees (which constituted 52.8 percent of the total workforce in Japanese firms). Japanese-owned subsidiaries, meanwhile, employed 29,397 workers (40.1 percent of the total work force in Japanese firms) (Lim Hua Sing, 1999: p. 102). The number of employees in the manufacturing sector was 54,692 (74.5 percent), which was comprised of 16.9 percent of Singapore's total manufacturing workforce. The bulk of the manufacturing employees that engaged in both the electric and electronic sectors comprised of 48.8 percent of the total workforce in the manufacturing sector (Lim Hua Sing, 1999: p. 102).

By 1988, however, the number of workers employed by Japanese firms in Singapore decreased to 69,179 (from 70,323 in 1982). As the Japanese FDI in Singapore continued to decrease, the total workforce employed by Japanese firms had diminished. Part of the reason for such a decline had to do with the Japanese manufacturing industries, especially in electronics, that sought cheaper labor (Lim Hua Sing, 1999: pp.105-107). The electronics industries required a huge number of guest workers mainly from the Malay Peninsula. They increasingly shifted these high-labor intensive operations to other ASEAN countries or to China where cheap labor was readily available. The trend is likely to continue as the Singapore government remains improbable to cease imposition of the higher employers' Central Provident Fund (CPF), and heavy foreign worker levies while aiming at expanding high-tech, high value-added, and knowledge-intensive activities (Lim Hua Sing, 1999: pp.105-107).

B. Japanese Style Management in Singapore

By the early 1980s, the Singapore government started to look into the possibility of introducing the Japanese-style managerial system into substantial enterprises in Singapore (especially those owned by Japan).[14] The Singapore government had three reasons to look towards Japan in regards to its managerial style. *First*, Japan's rapid economic development was seen by the Singapore government as a developmental model. *Secondly*, Japanese FDI in Singapore was perceived as crucial to Singapore's industrial reconstruction towards high-tech, high value-added, and knowledge-intensive activities. *Lastly,* the number of Japanese affiliated enterprises in Singapore has remained at a high level among foreign enterprises (Lim Hua Sing, 1999: p. 107).

The government of Singapore took steps in understanding the Japanese-style managerial system and Japanese experts on management and productivity were invited to serve as advisers or consultants to the National Productivity Board (NPB). The experts were also assisted by the NPB research staff, and published books on Japanese management under NPB's sponsorship. In addition, Japanese experts and academics were invited to give lectures initiated mainly by the Economic Development Board (EDB) along with both the Trade Development Board (TDB) and the NPB. Moreover, Singaporean government officials were sent to Japan where they gathered first-hand information from Japanese companies, factories, and governmental organizations (Lim Hua Sing, 1999: p. 107).

However, it was soon discovered that the Japanese managerial systems were not so harmonious to the enterprises of Singapore for the following reasons. *First,* Singapore is a society strongly influenced by Western culture (especially in regards to individualism and economic pragmatism). Lifetime employment system enjoyed in Japan is not applicable in Singapore where job-hopping for better remuneration and career advancement is common. *Second,* unlike Japan, Singapore is still a highly heterogeneous society, with the population comprised of 77.6 percent Chinese, 14.2 percent Malaysians, 7.1 percent Indians, and 1.1 percent Eurasians and others.[15] With the diversity very pronounced, and the fact that the Singaporean industries employed a huge number of foreign workers on a contractual basis, the implementation of the systems of lifetime employment and seniority wage was deemed impossible (Lim Hua Sing, 1999: pp. 107-110).

Lastly, Singapore has a very large number of MNCs of various nationalities. Not only has Singapore attracted the MNCs from both Europe and the United States, it has also attracted an increased percentage of investments from NIEs, such as Hong Kong, Taiwan, and Korea (Lim Hua Sing, 1999: pp. 107-110). Because Japanese FDI in Singapore continued to grow, a substantial number of employees, both managerial and rank and file, was severely needed by Japanese enterprises, especially since these enterprises were not as appealing to Singaporean graduate students as Western MNCs or public enterprises. This need will eventually provide Japanese firms with the incentives to modify their managerial systems to adapt to the Singapore's labor market (Lim Hua Sing, 1999: pp. 111-113).

C. Conclusion

Despite the lack of chemistry between Japanese managerial style and Singapore's labor market, Japanese FDI proved to be highly instrumental and essential for Singapore's rapid economic development. Indeed, FDI from Japan, Europe, and the United States, proved to be indispensable to Singapore's objectives in advancing its economy. Singapore became an important production base for Japanese manufacturing industries, especially during the shift towards higher valued-added goods. Japanese FDI since 1985 in Singapore's finance, insurance, commerce, service, and transportation sectors has attracted attention, and this trend seems to be further strengthened as Singapore's financial and commercial roles in the Asia-Pacific region gain momentum (Lim Hua Sing, 1999: p. 112).

III.
Singapore and the Asian Financial Crisis of 1997-1998: How did Singapore Manage to adapt to the Decreases in Trade and Investment in East Asia?

Like Hong Kong, Taiwan, and to some extent, Malaysia, Singapore had strong economic fundamentals. It managed to maintain a large current account surplus, which was 18 percent of its GDP in 1995. Although Singapore's trade balance was usually in a deficit, it was sufficiently compensated by its large net exports of invisibles.[16] Furthermore, the short-term foreign portfolio investment was a small fraction of the long-term FDI at 23 percent, and this investment accounted for 1 percent of Singapore's GDP in 1995. Singapore's external debt was 8 percent of its GDP, and its short-term foreign debt was merely 2 percent of its large foreign reserves of $69 billion in 1995 (Tan, 2000: p. 84).

The financial sector of Singapore was well-supervised and the capital-adequacy ratios of many of its banks have been consistently higher than the 12 percent ratio required by the MAS, or the 8 percent ratio recommended by the BIS. The Singapore dollar continued to be a strong currency, supported by its formidable reserves while fixed to the U.S. dollar in a managed float. The government's measures to curb speculation in the property market led to the decrease in property prices (Tan, 2000: p. 84).

However, Singapore could not insulate itself completely from the indirect contagion effects of the currency crisis. Many of its banks and industrial firms had considerable exposure to Malaysia, Indonesia, and Thailand. Since the 1980s, many firms set up their subsidiaries in these countries for lower production costs and land prices. As these countries began to be affected by a series of currency devaluations, the contagion effects reached Singapore unavoidably. Furthermore, the decline in the global demands for electronics decreased Singapore's exports from 18 percent per annum in 1995 to 5 percent per annum in 1996. Part of the reason was that Malaysia, Thailand, and the Philippines accounted for 25 percent of Singapore's exports and 22 percent of its imports in 1996 (Tan, 2000: pp. 84-85 and 134). The depreciation of the baht by July of 1997, resulted in the depreciation of the Singapore dollar by roughly 17 percent in December. The stock market, affected by expectations of a severe slowdown in Singapore's economic growth, fell from 2,215 points in January of 1997 to 1,561 points in December (Tan, 2000: p. 86). Although Singapore's GDP still grew by 5.6 percent in the first quarter of 1998, it fell into a recession in the second quarter (Godement, 1999: p. 179). The productivity growth rate slackened, and unemployment almost doubled to 4.5 percent of the workforce (Tan, 2000: p. 137).

In face of a rapidly deteriorating regional financial crisis, the government's strategy included cutting governmental costs, improving efficiency, and intensifying market liberalization. Singapore's effort to launch an international mechanism for export financing was achieved in large part to relieve Indonesia's industrial and primary material firms. The plan involved backing Indonesia's central bank together with its well established foreign banks (Godement, 1999: pp. 183-189).

The Singaporean government also moved towards greater transparency and availability of information in the financial sector. In January 1998, the MAS instructed banks to publicly expose their non-performing loans and hidden reserves. In shifting from regulation towards supervision, the MAS focused on the evaluation of risk management and internal control processes of Singapore's financial institutions. While the MAS moved to improve standards of banking disclosure and to strengthen market discipline, financial institutions were given more freedom in their operations (Tan, 2000: pp. 200-202). By 1999, the MAS announced further financial liberalization such as: 1) the lifting of foreign ownership restrictions, 2) the granting of six full banking licenses, 3) the abolishment of the 1 percent fixed commissions for share transactions, and 4) the introduction of an additional 40 percent tax rebate for commercial and industrial properties. Furthermore, the government intensified its investments towards education, training, and labor skills. Investments in infrastructure were made in order to boost aggregate demand (Tan, 2000: pp. 200-202).

These measures were designed to prepare the economy should Singapore recover from the Crisis. By March 1999, there were signs that Singapore's economic recovery was on the horizon when the value of the Singapore dollar stabilized to roughly S$1.7 to the U.S. dollar. Furthermore, when the stock market seemed to have bottomed out, yet by March 1999, the Straits Times index rose steadily to reach 88 percent of its January 1997 level. However, Singapore continued to be plagued by falling wages, increasing levels of unemployment, declining domestic export levels of non-oil goods, and the depressing property market (Tan, 2000: pp. 202-203). Nonetheless, Singapore, along with Hong Kong, will be looked upon as a buffer and intermediary in every kind of transactions, shielding more rudimentary economies and societies, while fulfilling the needs of many large foreign firms still operating in the region (Godement, 1999: p. 209).

IV.
Epilogue
Singapore Then and Now: A Look at its Current Economic Well-being in the Post Asian Financial Crisis Era and its Outlook onto the Future

A. Singapore's Economic Growth and Sustainability – A Recapitulation

Singapore continues to remain in an enviable financial position. Massive capital inflows of direct investment, a strong fiscal policy, and a high savings rate made Singapore's balance sheet the model for emerging and developing economies. Since the 1960s, Singaporean investment has averaged 59 cents for every dollar consumed, more than doubling the world average. By the 1990s, that figure increased to 75 cents for every dollar consumed (Saler, 1996: p. 150). Furthermore, the strong overall balance of payment positions has led to a steady appreciation in the Singapore dollar against the U.S. dollar. The Singapore dollar has been a consistent ally of American investors, appreciating by approximately 90 percent against the U.S. dollar since the 1960s (Saler, 1996: p. 151).

The phenomenal economic success of Singapore was due to the following factors. *The first factor* was undoubtedly the brilliant work of Lee Kuan Yew, who led Singapore from its 1957 independence from British rule to his resignation as prime minister in November of 1990. He was highly instrumental in placing highly educated and technically proficient officials in charge of development programs. His officials, in turn, established effective policies free from corruption (Neher, 1991; p. 123). Although he leaned towards authoritarianism even more by the end of his tenure (Singapore has been run by a one-party system), he won popular support thanks chiefly to Singapore's remarkable economic growth (Neher, 1991; p. 21).

Second, Singapore's strong fiscal policy allowed the government to run budgetary surpluses in every fiscal year except one since 1971, with recent surpluses averaging nearly ten percent of GDP (Khan, 1997: p. 93). *Third,* Singapore placed a heavy emphasis on savings and investments more than consumption, resulting in the saving rate that increased from 17.2 percent in the 1965-1970 period to 47.5 percent in 1993 (Khan, 1997: p. 93). Furthermore, as of 1993, the net Singaporean public and private investments reached more than 43 percent of its GDP, compared with 16.5 percent in the United States, and slightly over 20 percent for the world as a whole (Saler, 1996: pp. 150-151). *Fourth,* the rates of inflation remained low in every decade except in the 1970s (Khan, 1997: p. 93). *Finally,* Singapore's economic growth was accompanied by fundamental structural transformation and a shift from entrepot, labor-intensive economy into high valued-added, capital intensive economy (Khan, 1997: p. 93).

The Asian Financial Crisis had indirect effects on Singapore for the most part. Although Singapore maintained sound economic fundamentals, it could not avoid the contagion effects of the Crisis. This was because as the demands especially for electronics decreased to unprecedented levels on the eve of the Crisis, exports in the Pacific-rim region slowed precipitously. Therefore, bank shares on the Singapore stock exchange fell by 27 percent during a two week period in January 1998. Singapore's financial sector, which accounted for 13 percent of its GDP, was also affected by the Crisis. Projects that required financing became fewer in number, and, there were not enough finance companies that could issue new bonds or float new equity issues (Tan, 2000: pp. 135-136).

The measures designed to turn the economy around were not without some success. As mentioned before, the Singapore dollar stabilized after 1999 and the stock market showed signs of promise. However, the unemployment concerns, lower wages, property depression, and the general decreases in trade of non-oil products are hindering Singapore's efforts for a more fuller economic recovery.

B. Singapore's Brief Recessionary Period after the 1997-1998 Crisis Era:

As you will see in Table 3.2, Singapore's economic performance was sound in the year 2000, despite the rise in unemployment, lower wages, property depression, and general decreases in trade of non-oil products. However, these factors did influence Singapore's sharp economic downturn in the following year, with GDP dropping to -2.3 percent from 9.4 percent in 2000. Singapore's economy shrank by 10.1 percent from April through June of 2001, its second successive quarterly contraction (BBC News, 07/10/2001: p. 1). Technically, Singapore entered into a recession. Its second-quarter contraction had turned annual GDP growth to a -0.9 percent year on year. The reason for the drop was a more than expected plunge of global demand for high-tech equipment, the industry that has continued to be a mainstay of Singapore's economic growth and sustainability since the 1960s. Moreover, manufacturing, half of which was high-tech, accounted for one-quarter of Singapore's GDP (BBC News, 07/10/2001: p. 1). Furthermore, with Singapore being vulnerable to the ebbs and flows of the global economy, its domestic demand, even during its recovery in 2002, remained subdued as fixed capital investments and private consumption decreased

(Asian Development Outlook 2003, 2003: p. 89). Therefore, the Singapore dollar dropped a series of eleven-year lows, to roughly 1.835 against the U.S. dollar (BBC News, 07/10/2001: p. 1).

Table 3.2
Singapore's Major Economic Indicators, 2000-2005

The Indicators *(in percentage)*	**2000**	**2001**	**2002**	**2003**	**2004**	**2005**
GDP Growth	9.4	-2.3	4.0	2.9	8.7	6.4
Gross domestic investment/GDP	32.3	24.2	20.6	13.4	28.2	23.0
Gross Domestic savings/GDP	47.9	43.6	44.2	47.1	47.3	n/a.
Inflation rate (consumer price index)	1.3	1.0	-0.4	0.5	1.7	0.4
Money Supply (M2) Growth	-2.0	5.9	-0.3	6.9	6.2	n/a.
Fiscal balance/GDP	2.5	-1.8	-0.1	6.4	2.5	7.9
Merchandise export growth	20.0	-11.0	3.2	15.0	24.2	14.0
Merchandise import growth	24.1	-15.1	0.1	9.4	27.1	13.6
Current account balance/GDP	14.5	19.0	21.5	30.9	26.1	28.5
The Unemployment Rate	3.1	3.3	4.4	4.7	3.4	3.2

Sources: IndexMundi (on the unemployment rate, 2003 and 2004 as well as gross domestic investment for 2005). *Website:* www.indexmundi.com
The Asian Development Bank (Outlook 2003, 2004, 2005, and 2006).
Website: www.adb.org
Note: The latest GDP growth figures (2001-2005) are from the Asian Development Outlook 2006

The nature of the slowdown in Singapore's economic performance surprised the Singaporean government, and the trade and industry ministry was prompted to drop its economic growth forecast for 2001 from 3.5 percent-5.5 percent to 0.5 percent-1.5 percent (BBC News, 07/10/2001: p. 2). However, the government's response to the predicament was not without resiliency. Whereas the government exercised the least levels of liberalization during the Crisis of 1997-1998 when it increased trade barriers and regulation, it decided to reverse its policy course during the brief recessionary period. In July, the MAS unveiled its first economic stimulus package worth S$2.2 billion, which was the second phase of the financial deregulation plan announced in 1999. This meant that more foreign banks would be allowed to open branches in Singapore. Furthermore, all five of Singapore's banks, which were traditionally under the government's protection, were now allowed in engage in takeover bids. By reviving the financial sector, the government hoped that it would, in some ways, compensate for the weaker than expected performance of export-oriented manufacturing (BBC News, 07/10/2001: p. 2).

On 12th October of 2001, the government had brought to light its second economic stimulus package. Announced by Deputy Prime Minister Lee Hsien Loong, the package focused on heavy tax cuts, including rebates on personal and corporate taxes as well as a range of incentives for business, all with the goal of stimulating domestic demand and encouraging business activity (BBC News, 10/12/2001: pp. 1-2). Furthermore, the package included curbs on speculation in property, effectively banning the sale of residential and commercial land sites for the whole of 2002. Due to the global slowdown, which was made worse by the terrorist attacks of September 11th, the government predicted the economy to shrink by 3 percent, its worst performance since 1964. However, notwithstanding a rather broad welcome to the package, not everyone was convinced that this latest economic programme would be instrumental in reversing the sluggishness of the Singaporean economy. This was because, as they saw it, Singapore, being among the most trade-dependent in the world, has continue to remain heavily exposed to external forces beyond its government's control (BBC News, 10/12/2001: pp. 1-2).

Given that Singapore's annual exports were worth three times its annual GDP, the opponents' concerns were well taken. However, the package was pushed forward nevertheless, which included S$11.3 billion (a S$9.1 billion increased from the first package announced in July). As Mr. Lee Hsien Loong put it, this latest programme was worth 7 percent of its GDP. Moreover, the "New Singapore Share" scheme was expanded so as to urge the citizens to purchase quasi-government bonds as means to encourage savings and investments (BBC News, 10/12/2001: pp. 1-2).[17]

C. Singapore's Recovery from the Recessionary Period, 2002

1. Sector and Trade Improvements

Like Taiwan, Singapore beat the recession by the spring of 2002, thanks largely to its government's quick, decisive, and creative responses. The recovery was more modest than expected, with GDP expanded by only 4.0 percent. As mentioned before, the slower than expected recovery was due to a more subdued domestic demand, which was accompanied by decreases in both fixed capital investment and private consumption (Asian Development Outlook 2003, 2003:

p. 89).

However, the manufacturing sector showed some promising improvements: it grew by 8.3 percent in 2002. Much of it had to do with the recoveries in electronics, rubber, instrumentation equipment, and plastic products (Asian Development Outlook 2003, 2003: p. 89). Electronics in particular performed well in 2002, growing at 4.1 percent after its precipitous drop of 21.3 percent a year ago. The sharp improvement, boosted by a modest recovery in the global electronics market, was due to increased production of semiconductors, data storage, and office automation equipment, despite the lower output the personal computers and communications segments (ADO 2003, 2003: p. 89). The construction subsector remained weak, however, as Singapore saw no improvements in both private and public construction activities. It declined by 10.8 percent in 2002 and the shrinkage in private construction was largely due to low levels of commercial, industrial and civil engineering works (Asian Development Outlook 2003, 2003: p. 89).

Finance, likewise, did less well in 2002. After its modest growth of 3.7 percent in 2001, it fell by 4.8 percent in the following year. The less-than-ideal well being of the financial sector was a result from lopsided performances of the various segments of this industry (Asian Development Outlook 2003, 2003: p. 89). Commercial banking, as well as investment advisory services, and foreign exchange trading showed some modest growth. However, such a growth was overshadowed by a sharp decline in both insurance and stockbroking (ADO 2003, 2003: p. 89).

Trade performance improved overall in 2002, with merchandise export that expanded by 3.2 percent (after a drop of 11 percent a year before). Much of the improvement was due to better sales in both electronic and non-electronic products (such as pharmaceuticals and petrochemicals) (Asian Development Outlook 2003, 2003: p. 90). The improvement of import was much more modest, however, with an increase of merely 0.1 percent during the year. While non-oil imports contracted by 0.3 percent, key electronic merchandises, pharmaceuticals, measuring instruments, and petrochemicals rose more significantly (ADO 2003, 2003: p. 90). Furthermore, both wholesale and retail trade sectors grew by 2.7 percent in 2002, after its 3.3 percent decline a year before. Its ricochet was duly credited largely to better performance of entrepot trade, with a solid increase in non-oil exports. All of the improvements occurred despite an overall drop in domestic demand, which fell by 2.3 percent due to a persistent downfall in gross fixed capital formation, increased inventory cutbacks, and unfavorable private consumption. However, the trading scenario was sound enough that the current account surplus improved from 19.0 percent of GDP in 2001 to 21.5 percent in 2002 (ADO 2003, 2003: p. 90).

2. Singapore's Economic Initiatives

During Singapore's recessionary period, *maintaining current stability remained its first priority as far as monetary policy was concerned.* Consequently, the MAS remained, as a policy, neutral since July of 2001, with a stable, trade-weighted Singapore dollar nominal effective exchange rate. However, by October, that policy broadened in order to allow more flexibility in exchange rate management, only to become narrowed once again in January of 2002 as market and economic conditions reached greater stability (Asian Development Outlook 2003, 2003: p. 90).

Among the key initiatives in the budget for the 2002 fiscal year included: 1) enhancing the tax incentives for the financial sector, 2) introducing employee stock option incentive schemes, and 3) reducing corporate as well as personal income tax rates. Furthermore, part of the budget plans called for the increase in both the goods and tax rates from 3.0 percent to 4.0 percent effective January, 2003 in order to offset the loss of revenues from the reduction in income taxes. As a result of the initiatives, the budget deficit narrowed from S$94 billion in 2001 to S$94 million in 2002 (Asian Development Outlook 2003, 2003: p. 90).

The Singaporean government's plans to revamp the economy remained its top priority also, and in October 2001, in order to assess its development strategy and formulate a blueprint in how to restructure the economy, the Economic Review Committee (ERC) was formed for that purpose (Asian Development Outlook 2003, 2003: p. 90). The ERC, in early 2003, purpose two fairly broad measures: 1) a more immediate measures to deal with current uncertainties and 2) longer-term strategies to restructure the economy. The ERC recognized and enunciated the key yet immediate issues to address, namely to lower costs while staying competitive. Moreover, the Committee suggested long-term national goals, such as expanding external ties, maintaining competitiveness yet flexibility, developing human resources, encouraging entrepreneurship, and promoting growth in both manufacturing and services (Asian Development Outlook 2003, 2003: p. 90).

Other than issuing recommendation in how to improve productivity in the service sector, the ERC's service subcommittee (one of several committees the ERC has), also recommended ways in which overregulation, corporatization, and privatization to public suppliers should be addressed in order to introduce competition, institutional support, and training of human resources (Asian Development Outlook 2003, 2003: p. 91).

The third and final top priority of Singapore is to continue to enhance its financial system, its institutional and regulatory framework, and its market structure. Within that framework, two key issues were raised. *One issue* dealt with the creation of a more conducive regulatory environment to foster market dynamism and ensuring financial sector stability and soundness. Therefore, the MAS has shifted it policy focus from regulation to risk-preventive measures, such as supervision, disclosure, higher standards of corporate governance, as well as market discipline (Asian Development Outlook 2003, 2003: p. 91). *The other issue* brought to light the need to accelerate financial liberalization in order to promote competition and discipline. Steps were already taken in that regard. For instance, local banks have upgraded risk management systems and introduced new products and services. In addition, more government securities were made available to improve market liquidity and to create a benchmark yield curve (Asian Development Outlook 2003, 2003: p. 91).[18]

D. The Singaporean Continual Economic Improvement, 2003-2004

1. The Better Overall Economic Picture with Lingering External and Internal Concerns

In 2003, as Singapore's economy continued to improve, there were ample reasons to assume that the government would remain on course in maintaining the current monetary policy through managing the exchange rate. Stability in the Singapore dollar continues to be deemed as critical for the country's continuing economic recovery through supporting financial activities and entrepot trade and steps will more likely be made to maintain the abundance of market liquidity.

However, as in the case with Taiwan, external forces will continue to be the key factor in the extent of Singapore's economy growth and recovery. As global trade is showing signs of improvement since 2003, Singapore, as well as other countries in the East Asian region will continue to reap the benefits from the expansion in trade. According to the WTO, global trade improved by 4.5 percent in 2003 (BBC News, 04/05/2004: pp. 1-3). According to Supachai Panitchpakdi, then WTO's general director, "clearly the improved economic situation in the United States and Asia has given an important boost to world trade" (BBC News, 04/05/2004: pp. 1-3). But global market conditions remain uncertain due to the SARS outbreak, the conflicts throughout the Middle East and Iraq, and the sluggish economic recovery of the United States and much of Europe (particularly Germany).

Whereas Singapore's GDP remained at 2.9 percent in 2003, it grew to 8.7 percent in 2004 notwithstanding the aforementioned concerns such as SARS and the overall global economic picture, which, while showing some improvements, remains chancy at best. The rather phenomenal recovery of 2004 was a reflection of a broad recovery in both domestic and external demand, as well as the SARS-induced low base of the previous year. This induced the government to shift from its accommodative macroeconomic policy stance to such which is moderately more tightening in nature (Asian Development Outlook 2005, 2005: p. 114).

As far as domestic demand is concerned, private fixed investment improved to 13.9 percent in 2004 from a 4.2 percent contraction in 2003. The upsurge in the global electronic cycle boosted business confidence in Singapore's manufacturing subsector, which resulted in higher spending on machinery and equipment (Asian Development Outlook 2005, 2005: p. 114). In fact, The Ministry of Trade reported that the 10 percent growth in manufacturing in the third quarter of 2005 was driven by the biomedical, transport engineering, and chemical sectors (BBC News, 10/10/2005: pp. 1-2).[19] Indeed, electronics, petrochemicals, as well as pharmaceuticals played a huge role in increasing merchandise exports to 24.2 percent (from 12.1 percent in 2003). Booming regional demand especially for intermediate inputs for electronic products, machinery, and equipment, likewise contributed to the surge not only in exports, but imports as well, which grew from 8.5 percent in 2003 to 27.1 percent in 2004 (Asian Development Outlook 2005, 2005: p. 114).

Although public investment continued to fall, by 10.6 percent in 2004, private consumption saw a revival, which rose by 8.6 percent (Asian Development Outlook 2005, 2005: p. 114). Moreover, governmental operating expenditures increased by 3.6 percent, primarily due to rise in spending on education, security, and social welfare. Likewise, development spending rose by 6.7 percent due to increased expenditure on transport infrastructure as well as research and development. Paradoxically, the primary operating deficit decreased from S$2.5 billion (1.6 percent of GDP) in 2003 to S$2.1 billion (1.1 percent of GDP) in 2004 (ADO 2005, 2005: p. 114).

Although inflation edge up a bit in 2004, thanks to prices on oil-related items such as electricity and gasoline as well as increased costs of some services such as education and health care, the overall economic picture continues to improve. For one thing, the banking system was persistent in showing considerable liquidity while maintaining the prime lending rate of 5.3 percent (Asian Development Outlook 2005, 2005: p. 114). The stock markets in the Asia-Pacific region continued to generate renewed interests, reflecting on the 15 percent gain of the Straits Times Index in 2004. Secondly, the labor market conditions continue to be more favorable as the economy gathers momentum. In fact, 66,200 jobs were encouraged in 2004 while the unemployment rate improved to 3.4 percent (from 4.7 percent a year ago) (ADO 2005, 2005: p. 114). Lastly, the overall trading picture continued to improve also. Trade surplus rose to $31.1 billion in 2004 and the current account surplus improved to $27.8 billion, which was the equivalence to 26.1 percent of GDP. Due to increased borrowings by the non-bank sector, the net outflow on the capital and financial account declined from $20.1 billion in 2003 to $13.0 billion in 2004 (ADO 2005, 2005: p. 114). However, both direct investment inflows and outflows elevated significantly thanks to the government's efforts to attract FDI and by its domestic companies' overseas merger and acquisition activities. In fact, Singapore, being the largest recipient of FDI among ASEAN countries, received $16.1 billion of such investment in 2004 (Malaysian Industrial Development Authority (MIDA), 2006: p. 18). Meanwhile, gross international reserves increased to $112.8 billion by the end of 2004 (Asian Development Outlook 2005, 2005: p. 114).

2. Singapore's Macroeconomic Policy Developments, 2002-2004

The initial economic policy response after the brief recession in 2001-2002 was accommodative and flexible in nature as there was a need for policy stimulus to help jump-start the economy. However, as the economy continues to grow and become even more self-sustaining, Singapore switched from its flexible accommodative macroeconomic policy to a moderate tightening approach to economic monitoring (Asian Development Outlook 2005, 2005: p. 115). With the goal at reducing the risk of imported inflation in mind, the MAS changed its stance from zero appreciation of the trade-weighted nominal effective exchange rate to a modest and gradual appreciation in April, 2004. The Singapore dollar appreciated by 4.1 percent against the U.S. currency thanks to stronger capital inflows and the overall improvement in the region's economic outlook. However, the dollar weakened against the euro, sterling, and regional currencies such as Korean won and the Taiwanese NT dollar, resulting in a slight appreciation of the trade-weighted nominal effective exchange rate throughout 2004 (Asian Development Outlook 2005, 2005: pp. 115-116).

The 2004 budget continued to squeeze tax policy in an effort to improve competitiveness and attract FDI. Such an effort included a reduction of corporate income tax rate from 22 percent to 20 percent as well as tax exemptions for newly incorporated companies and foreign-sourced income and Singapore-sourced investment income (Asian Development Outlook 2005, 2005: p. 116). Furthermore, with an aim to attract internationally mobile talent, Singapore had planned to reduce the upper end of the personal income tax from 22 percent to 20 percent as well as revamping the tax system with measures to support financial services, logistics, and tourism such as: 1) a waiver of stamp duty on transfers of Singapore properties into real estate investment trusts for a five-year period, 2) a removal of stamp duties for Islamic real estate transactions, and 3) a concessional corporate tax rate of 10 percent for companies that deals with tourism events in the next five years (Asian Development Outlook 2005, 2005: p. 116).

E. The Economic Picture in 2005

1. The Overall Cooling down in GDP

The economy cooled down somewhat in 2005, with the GDP growth contracted to 6.4 percent from 8.7 percent a year before. Part of the reason for Singapore's cooler economic performance was due to the cyclical downturn in the global electronics industry as well as a decline in output from the pharmaceuticals industry (Asian Development Outlook 2006, 2006: p. 220). These developments, which occurred in the first-half of 2005, influenced the overall GDP growth rate for that year, even though both manufacturing and pharmaceuticals expanded rather sharply in the second-half. In fact, manufacturing improved by 9.3 percent, led by transport, engineering, biomedical manufacturing, and electronics subsectors. High global shipping freight rates and increased oil exploration, due to high oil prices and the damages to oil rigs in the Gulf of Mexico by Hurricane Katrina, boosted orders for Singapore's offshore and marine engineering industry, which in turn played a major role in ship conversion and oil-rig building. Furthermore, as the result of the global electronics inventory correction completed by mid-2005, electronics improved consequently thereafter (Asian Development Outlook 2006, 2006: p. 220).

Whereas construction continued to decline for the seventh straight year, the service industry picked up by 5.8 percent in 2005, thanks to the strong performances in wholesale and retail trade as well as by financial services (Asian Development Outlook 2006, 2006: p. 220). Domestic wholesale and retail trade was helped by both buoyant regional trade and the recovery of domestic consumption while the financial services benefited from expansion of asset management and capital market activities. The expansion of these activities was fueled by increased international investment in Asian equities, higher turnover in the domestic stock market, and greater volatility in the foreign exchange market (Asian Development Outlook 2006, 2006: p. 220).

Singapore's GDP growth remained fairly sluggish in the first quarter of 2006, where the growth was posted at a 1.2 percent rate. But expansion was still strong and analysts argued that this low rate of growth was not unusual after such a strong expansion, where GDP growth was 12.5 percent in the final quarter of 2005. The manufacturing sector grew by 16 percent while services, which accounted for about two-thirds of Singapore's $118 billion economy, rose by 7.6 percent also in the first quarter. Construction, however, continued to contract, posting a minus 0.6 percent growth rate for that period (BBC News, 04/10/2006: p. 1). While export growth appeared to remain strong, this seemingly sluggish GDP growth of the first quarter may likely yield to the targeted 6 percent to 8 percent growth rate for the year.

2. Singapore's Macroeconomic Considerations, 2005

After a surge in both merchandise export and merchandise import in 2004, both cooled down significantly in 2005 (see Table 3.2). On the demand side, Singapore's economic growth was driven primarily by external demand, but as mentioned before, cyclical downturn in global electronics industry affected not only its GDP growth, but also the overall trading performance itself. Much of what constituted merchandise export growth in 2005 came from exports of information technology and telecommunication products, which were spurred by the overall improvement in global growth during the latter half of that year. Merchandise imports, driven largely by exports, expanded by 13.6 percent in 2005, which could've been higher had it not been due to weak domestic investment in machinery and equipment (Asian Development Outlook 2006, 2006: pp. 220-221). However, the net exports in national accounts rose by 16.5 percent and contributed 4.6 percentage points of Singapore's 2005 GDP growth (Asian Development Outlook 2006, 2006: p. 221).

Although private consumption continued to recover, fixed investment contracted by 1.9 percent (after its rise to over 10 percent a year earlier). However, a 15 percent year-on-year rebound in gross fixed asset formation in the last quarter of 2005 suggested greater business confidence in the continuing improvement of external economic environment. Furthermore, the employment picture remained promising, with its expansion of 110,800 jobs and its generation being broad based (Asian Development Outlook 2006, 2006: p. 221). The government had much to do with the more favorable employment conditions by enhancing labor market flexibility in recent years, aided by job redesign and retraining. With the job market tightening, wages rose by 3.5 percent in 2005, quite similarly in pace in 2004. In addition, with higher wages, inflation slowed to 0.4 percent, mainly because car prices fell as a result from a decline in the premium paid in Singapore for vehicle permits. Also, the direct effect of high global oil prices has been considerably muted thus far due to "relatively small share of energy in total costs and contracting gross margins in downstream oil sector" (Asian Development Outlook 2006, 2006: p. 221).

Monetarily and fiscally speaking, the government remains vigilant in strengthening domestic recovery and fiscal position. The MAS maintained its monetary policy target of a modest and gradual appreciation of the trade-weighted nominal effective exchange rate in 2005. The Singapore dollar did weaken against the U.S. dollar although it strengthened against other major currencies. With domestic monetary conditions continued to tighten, the three-month interbank interest rate rose to 3.25 percent in December of 2005, up 181 basis points from a year earlier possibly due to the strengthening of the U.S. dollar (Asian Development Outlook 2006, 2006: p. 221). However, the average prime lending rate remained at 5.3 percent, reflecting weak demand for bank loans (ADO 2006, 2006: p. 221).

Meanwhile, fiscal conditions continued to improve. Despite the rise in operating revenue by 6.5 percent, the government's fiscal position has strengthened, while total expenditure increased to just 1.3 percent in 2005. This was due to the fall in development spending and as a result, the primary operating deficit fell to S$0.7 billion from S$2.1 billion in 2004 (Asian Development Outlook 2006, 2006: pp. 221-222). The overall fiscal balance remained strong and the trade surplus improved to $38.0 billion. In addition, Singapore's current account surplus increased to $38.0 billion, an equivalence to 28.5 percent of its GDP. Much of that surplus was offset by active investment abroad by Singapore companies, which were responsible for driving up capital outflow from the country (Asian Development Outlook 2006, 2006: p. 222).

F. In Conclusion

Singapore recently reported that the average annual rate of return over the past thirty years was 18 percent, although the return posted an average of merely 3 percent over the past ten years mainly due to the Asian Financial Crisis of 1997-1998. Even though the disclosure was far from complete, it was nevertheless important for it shows Singapore on its mission towards greater transparency in the management of government surpluses (and of government accounts overall) (Asian Development Outlook 2006, 2006: p. 220).

Another step Singapore has taken was its strengthening of external economic linkages through bilateral and multilateral trade arrangements. In 2004, it signed a free trade agreement with Korea, which means, among other things, that almost 75 percent of domestic exports to Korea (which amounts to about S$3 billion) will benefit from the immediate elimination of tariffs (Asian Development Outlook 2005, 2005: p. 116). India and China are also being pursued by Singapore's in its push for more bilateral trade agreements which could potentially play a role as a bridge between the two dynamically emerging economies of the regions (Asian Development Outlook 2005, 2005: pp. 116-117).

Singapore is undergoing significant structural adjustments in the midst of accelerating globalization and increased competition from other regional economies. In response to these challenges, the government became engaged in a series of structural reforms to diversify the economy and to enhance its competitiveness. Singapore is now moving up the manufacturing value chain into selected knowledge-intensive activities like pharmaceuticals. Traditional manufacturing industries, the backbones of Singapore's economic emergence since the 1960s, had relocated elsewhere while other traditional companies are staying put and upgrading their products. Niche industries such as, for instance, interactive media and water technology are likewise developing. Furthermore, with its efforts to make wages and other business costs more flexible, Singapore continues to attract MNCs and their FDIs (Asian Development Outlook 2006, 2006: p. 223). The endeavor worked, for according to the bi-annual KPMG study, which covers 128 cities in nine countries, Singapore ranks first in cost-competitive league, meaning that it's cheapest to do business in the country (BBC News, 03/21/2006: pp. 1-3). The study itself is based on the costs of setting up and running businesses across different industries over a ten-year cycle and its takes into account key factor such as wages, business taxes, rent, and energy costs. Singapore's lower labor cost, with average wages well below other countries in the study, was the main reason for its top ranking in cost-competitiveness, notwithstanding the fact that the country now boasts GDP per capita equivalent to some European countries. Labor costs happen to be most deciding factor for companies when determining where to do their business, followed by other factors such as cost of finding and securing premises and taxes (BBC News, 03/21/2006: pp. 1-3).

However, Singapore still has areas of concerns. *One concern* is an aging population that is becoming more of a pervasive issue throughout the world. Singapore is meeting such a challenge by improving the fertility rate and broadening the immigration criteria (Asian Development Outlook 2005, 2005: p. 116). *The second concern* is that Singapore is still vulnerable to external shocks, for it is still highly exposed to world market conditions. The government is responding to this by targeting some exported-oriented services like tourism, entertainment, education, and health care as new sources of growth. Furthermore, Singapore has figured that a larger population would help build domestic demand to better balance the fluctuations in global demand, which explains its strategy to relax immigration and improve the fertility rate. *The third concern* is that although the unemployment rate is improving (even though structural unemployment still lingers), the nominal wage issue is still an important one. Wage is on an increase, but it can still fluctuate and even decrease due to the dependency on global trade and the effects it has on the labor market (especially when international transactions with Singapore concerns oil). Wage itself is a kind of issue that requires close monitoring for consumption growth remains a critical aspect in Singapore's economic well-being. *Lastly,* income disparities and persistent skill mismatches remain lingering concerns as well. However, as in the case with Taiwan, Singapore's government will remain prudent and decisive in its quest for a more robust and an endurable economic recovery from the deleterious effects of the Asian Financial Crisis of 1997-1998 (Asian Development Outlook 2005, 2005: p. 116).

And much of that prudency and decisiveness continue to pay off. Singapore's economic recovery remains endurable, and in fact, according to the BBC News, Singapore's GDP recorded a robust growth of 7.7 percent in 2006 (and 5.9% for the fourth quarter alone). That growth was attributed to construction, biomedical manufacturing, and transport engineering (the latter two that grew in double figures). However, weaker electronics and chemicals output slowed the manufacturing sector in the fourth and final quarter of 2006. Furthermore, growth in services fell from 6.6 percent in the first three quarters to 6.0 percent in the last quarter due to slower growth in the wholesale and retail trade sector. The news was nevertheless encouraging, and the stock market continues its "recent strong run" (BBC News, 01/03/2007: pp. 1-2). The overall economic picture in the Asia-Pacific region is brightening as we speak, despite persistent concerns with today's matters and with fully reversing the lingering effects of the Crisis. Singapore remains among the recovering countries that is paving the way in that regard.

V.
Notes

1. Singapore, a compact urban society, has no agricultural base to build on and with no natural resources it could tap to generate wealth (Neher, 1991: p. 127).
2. Malaysia left the Malaysian Federation in 1965 (Kunio Yoshihara, 1978: pp. 21-22).
3. Entrepot trade surrounds goods that are received in warehouses for distribution, repackaging, and trans-shipment.
4. The shift from semiconductors to computers and computer peripherals was due to the shift from labor-intensive to higher value-added goods after 1980.
5. By 1987, Singapore accounted for 77 percent of global output of Winchester (hard) disk drives and 60 percent of the U.S. market (Murray and Perera, 1996: p. 133).
6. In the case of Sony, its Singapore headquarters covered the multinational's entire operations in the Asia-Pacific region outside Japan.
7. The MAS also provided to commercial banks three types of licenses to open a branch or sub-branch: full, restricted, or off-shore. The reason for the licensing? The future lay in offshore banking (Murray and Perrera, 1996: p. 23).
8. The membership and participation of employees and employers in the CPF is mandatory (Murray and Perrera, 1996: p. 23).
9. The Stock Exchange of Singapore began operations in June of 1973 (Murray and Perrera, 1996: p. 23).
10. The ACU is a separate book-keeper procedure (Murray and Perera, 1996: p. 199).
11. The non-manufacturing firms include engineering, construction, foreign trade, commerce, transportation, warehousing, and other services.
12. The general decreases of Japanese FDI onto Singapore and the rest of Southeast and East Asia were also reflections of Japan's stagnating economic crisis after 1989. Table 3.1 on page 66 reflects that in its 1991 column.
13. These firms included textiles, ferrous and non-ferrous products, transportation machinery, electric and electronics (all in the manufacturing sector), construction, engineering, foreign trade, commerce, transportation, and warehousing (all in the non-manufacturing firms) (Lim Hua Sing, 1999: p. 90).
14. The Japanese-style managerial system consisted of: 1) lifetime employment system, 2) a seniority wage system, and 3) an in-house union.
15. According to the 1992 census.
16. Invisibles refer to products not ordinarily found in financial statements or reflected in statistics or listings.
17. The *"New Singapore Shares" scheme*, initiated in the Summer of 2001, is a plan of the government to give all its citizens "shares" in the country as a mean to distribute part of any budget surplus back to the population. The scheme will pay a dividend each year for a fixed term, with an additional bonus payment (provided that the economy is doing well in the first place). The shares were to be redeemable in small lots for cash, though cashing in an entire allotment at once remains illegal. *The scheme relies on the continuation of Singapore's budget surplus* (BBC News, 08/20/2001: pp. 1-3).

18. The benchmark yield curve is a graphic depiction of the relationship between the yield on bonds of the same credit quality but different maturities. The yield curve can accurately forecast the turning points of the business cycle. It is a benchmark because it involves an investment strategy as well as the performance of a predetermined set of securities, which are used for comparison purposes.
Source: Investopia.com.
website: http://www.investopedia.com/university/advancedbond/advancedbond4.asp
19. With the exception of construction (which contracted for six straight years), all manufacturing and services subsectors registered the overall growth of 13.9 percent in 2004. Biomedical manufacturing grew by 25.7 percent whereas transport engineering rose by 24 percent. Electronics grew by 14.9 percent, underpinned by the rapid expansion of semiconductors and information technology as well as of consumer electronic products. This trend, although volatile in character, continued until and throughout 2005 (Asian Development Outlook 2005, 2005: p. 114).

Chapter Four
The Dynamics Behind Malaysia's Economic Growth: An Uneasy Road for Prosperity still Followed

I.
The State of the Malaysian Economy since 1957: From Import Substitution to Capital Intensive Industries

A. Malaysia, 1957 through 1960

At the time of its independence from British rule on August 31, 1957, Malaysia enjoyed one of the highest standards of living in Asia. In that year, the primary sector in agriculture, forestry, and mining accounted for 45 percent of the GDP. Meanwhile, the secondary sector in manufacturing and construction and the third sector in services accounted for 11 percent and 44 percent of Malaysia's GDP respectively (Gomez & Jomo, 1999: pp. 15-16).

The First Five Year Plan (1956-1960) accorded agriculture its top priority. However, the Plan placed strong emphasis on the more advanced urban sectors such as industry, machinery, and manufacturing.[1] This emphasis was based on the belief that backward linkages would operate to convey development into the rural economy (Cho, 1990: p. 53). To provide the mechanism to the linkages, the Plan gave prominence to the building of physical infrastructure facilities so that transport, utilities, and communications would consume slightly more than half of the planned expenditures over the five year period (Cho, 1990: pp. 53-54).

Furthermore, there was a planned development of economic infrastructures such as marketing mechanisms. Concurrently, Malaysia made provisions for rural credit and loan facilities, tariff protection to mainly foreign manufacturing companies seeking to secure or increase their market, and the setting up of farm co-operatives. These measures went hand-in-hand with Malaysia's continuing efforts in encouraging import-substituting industrialization, while preserving its open, export-oriented economy. However, rural producers were expected to remain vigilant in agricultural development, particularly in the newly developing rubber industry (Cho, 1990: p. 54).

The First Five Year Plan announced no policy on industrialization. Investment requirements were first determined for meeting targets for the growth of national income. Thereafter, the investment budget was allocated among sectors (Cho, 1990: p. 60). The industrialization was confined with passive measures such as site development, provisions of infrastructure, and a favorable climate for private investment. Import restrictions were condemned because they were deemed detrimental to the standard of living of the population. Moreover, tax concessions were discouraged since they would create tax differentials in favor of new firms (Cho, 1990: p. 54).

Concurrent with the publication of the Report of the Working Party on the Encouragement of Industrial Development in the Federation of Malaysia in 1957, the government engaged in the series of measures towards an industrialization policy. The Pioneer Industries Ordinance was passed in 1958, which offered tax relief allowances on profits for pioneer firms, with the length of relief depending upon the size of the company's investment.[2] The Ordinance was the source for lucrative opportunities with foreign capital investment in Malaysia. The tax incentives as well as the tariff protection tended to favor large, capital-intensive, usually foreign companies (Gomez & Jomo, 1999: pp. 16-17).

However, Malaysia's industrialization remained problematic for the following reasons: *First,* the development of domestic industry remained limited due to Malaysia's continued commitment towards economic openness. In addition, Malaysia had more limited incentives and support bestowed upon manufacturing and technological bases developed by Malaysians. The bases, therefore, continued to remain small and often dependent on foreign technology, especially of Japan, as we will see later. *Secondly,* although Singapore continued to promote large, capital intensive industries, most foreign companies participating in ISI merely established subsidiaries for the assembling, finishing, and packaging of goods produced with imported materials from profitable sale within the protected domestic market. In addition, materials and technologies were generally imported from parent companies abroad, and did not fit well with domestic goals geared towards economic development. Although wage rates increased in the capital-intensive industries, little employment opportunities were offered. *Third,* the size of the local market was limited in scope by level and distribution. *Finally,* the enforcement of these policy initiatives lacked coherence and consistency (Gomez & Jomo, 1999: pp. 16-17).

B. Malaysia, 1960 through 1971

The Second Five-Year Plan (1961-1965) called for: 1) the continuing provision of infrastructural facilities with up to 46 percent of the total planned expenditure, 2) the expansion of social services such as health, education, housing, and welfare, 3) providing employment opportunities, 4) raising the productivity of the economy while protecting per-capita standards against the anticipated decline in rubber prices, and 5) diversification of the economy. The Plan met its objectives, although economic diversification did not occur (Cho, 1990: pp. 55-56).

However, the targets of the first two Five-Year Plans were vague and some objectives were not met in full and in a timely manner. The First Malaysian Plan (1966-1970) sought to reverse these weaknesses. It called for: 1) the integration of the peoples and the states of Malaysia by promoting welfare to all, 2) a steady increase in the level of income and consumption per head, 3) an improvement of the standard of living (especially in the rural areas), 4) the provision of employment opportunities, 5) a diversification program in agriculture and industry so as to reduce the dependency upon rubber and tin, 6) an educational program for all Malaysians, 7) a program for effective family planning to reduce the demographic pressure, 8) a land settlement scheme to provide the land-less with economic-sized farms, and 9) an efficient and sufficient infrastructure (Cho, 1990: p. 57).

The First Malaysian Plan differed from the previous plans due to its more profound focus on the socio-economic and welfare concerns, as well as on developmental strategies. From 1966 to 1970, the total merchandise exports from Malaysia increased by less than one percent per year due to the expected decrease in the prices of natural rubber and palm oil, along with the diminishing exports in the volume of tin and iron ore. The planners at the Economic Planning Unit (EPU) of the Prime Minister's Department argued that import-substitution was an essential part of the growth strategy, and the best prospects were to be found in the industrial sector (Cho, 1990: pp. 58-59).

The planners had a point, for the total merchandise exports during the First Malaysian Plan experienced an average annual growth rate of 4.8 percent. The export performance of new activities was particularly significant in contributing to this growth rate (Cho, 1990: pp. 58-59). However, problems of import-substituting industrialization continued to persist, and the Malaysian Industrial Development Authority (MIDA) was set up to encourage industrial investment. Many MNCs were beginning to relocate their more labor-intensive production process abroad in order to reduce production costs. Therefore, the government encouraged MNCs, foreign experts, and international consultants to switch from ISI to EOI (Gomez & Jomo, 1999: p. 17).[3]

In 1968, the Investment Incentives Act was introduced, which provided tax holidays to approved firms for a maximum of eight years, company income tax exemptions to encourage employment, exception from an import duty for capital equipment and raw materials for export-oriented production, investment tax credits, and other export incentives and accelerated depreciation allowances (Gomez & Jomo, 1999: pp. 17-18). Three years later, the Free Trade Zone Act was introduced. This Act established free-trade zones in order to encourage investments; especially by companies manufacturing for export. It also provided exemptions from customs regulations for free-trade zone companies importing and exporting equipment, inputs, and outputs for export-oriented industries. In addition, the licensed manufacturing warehouses were introduced to allow greater flexibility in the location of these export-oriented industries (Gomez & Jomo, 1999: p. 18).

These moves were the symbolism of the Malaysian government's movement towards EOI, with its greater reliance upon foreign capital to promote it.[4] Foreign firms in the free-trade zones mainly used imported equipment and materials for production and were immuned from governmental pressures to set up joint ventures with domestic firms unless they produced for the domestic market. In short, foreign firms continued to dominate industries in technology and marketing (Gomez & Jomo, 1999: p. 18).

C. Malaysia: 1970 to the Present: The New Economic Policy and the Malaysian Plans

Malaysia continues to enjoy unrelenting yet robust economic growth and low inflation since 1957 (which a huge exception in 2001 to be seen later). However, income inequality increased, and poverty continued to be pervasive throughout the country. The primary objective of the New Economic Policy (NEP), announced in 1970, was "to reduce and eventually eradicate poverty, by raising income levels and increasing employment opportunities for all Malaysians, irrespective of race; [and] ...accelerating the process of restructuring Malaysian society to correct the economic imbalances, so as to reduce and eventually eliminate the identification of race with economic function" (Cho, 1990: p. 68).

While the passing of the NEP met with little opposition, many observers argued that its emphasis on wealth restructuring, and its actual implementation, hindered economic growth. Such a hindrance against growth was due to the emergence of cronyism, the distribution of rentier opportunities to companies controlled by politicians, retired bureaucrats, parties of the ruling coalition, and politically well-connected entrepreneurs. Transparency, critics argued, in government policymaking and implementation became a concern. Indeed, a patronage network grew under the NEP. Through the Policy, rents have been created, captured, and disbursed ostensibly as part of the government's policy of restructuring to attain greater inter-ethnic wealth parity and to develop Bumiputera entrepreneurs (Gomez & Jomo, 1999: pp. 25-26). This would give rise to political clientelism resulting in the deployment of economic resources and corruption. Yet the NEP responded to the problems of poverty, unemployment, and inter-ethnic imbalances. Consequently, the official poverty rate decreased from 49 percent in 1970 to 16 percent in 1990. Also, the government-owned enterprises that participated in activities in all public and private sectors of the economy increased considerably during the 1970s (Gomez & Jomo, 1999: p. 29).

The Economic Plans coincided well with the NEP in decreasing the level of poverty while restructuring the Malaysian society. The Second Malaysian Plan (1971-1975), and the Third Malaysian Plan (1976-1980), sought to reverse the ill-effects of poverty through direct engagement in the restructuring of society.[5] The Fourth Malaysian Plan (1981-1985) called for the continuation of the agricultural sector as a source of export earnings and raw materials for the manufacturing sector. The Plan expected an expansion of agricultural production and the growth of both the manufacturing and mining sectors. However, the employment growth fell short than expected while the Malaysian economy was dualistic in structure. To make matters more precarious, the economy depended heavily on commodity export trade and was therefore vulnerable to the swings in the world economy (Cho, 1990: pp. 77-78).

The Fifth Malaysian Plan (1986-1990), was premised on the completion of the objectives of the NEP with a drive towards privatization, regional development, and perhaps, a new National Economic Policy. Among other things, the Plan called for an increased role of the private sector to import dynamism into the economy, efficient management of the economy, domestic resource mobilization, stimulating industrial development, revitalization of the agricultural sector, and a greater emphasis on research and development (Cho, 1990: pp. 79-80). Unfortunately, the performance of the private sector had been dismal, achieving merely 1.8 percent growth out of the targeted 10.7 percent under the Fourth Malaysian Plan. The participation of the public sector in the domestic economy was likewise reduced significantly, due to the increase of foreign debt (especially to Japan) as well as huge budget deficits (Cho, 1990: p. 81).

In June of 1991, the government announced the New Development Policy (NDP) to succeed the NEP. The NDP replaced the racially based economic and social policy with national unity. The NDP emphasis on human resource development was reflected in the Sixth Malaysian Plan (1991-1995). The Seventh Malaysian Plan (1996-2000) continued to place strong emphasis on technical and vocational skills training and investment in research and development capabilities in order to reduce Malaysia's dependence on foreign investment and technology (Chowdhury, 1997: p. 60).

Prime Minister, Datuk Seri Dr. Mahathir Mohamed, who served as Malaysia's leader from July 16th, 1981 to October 31st, 2003, continued to emphasize growth, modernization, and industrialization as national economic priorities. On July 10th, 1991, Dr. Mahathir announced his series of objectives of the post-1990 economic development policy known as "Vision 2020" (which happened to be the Sixth Malaysian Plan incidentally). Vision 2020's nine main objectives (or challenges) were to establish: 1) a united, peaceful, integrated and harmonious Malaysian nation, 2) a secured, confident, respected, and robust society committed to excellence, 3) a mature, consensual and exemplary democracy, 4) a fully moral society with citizens strongly imbued with spiritual values and the highest ethical standards, 5) a culturally, ethnically, and religiously diverse, liberal, tolerant, and unified society, 6) a scientific, progressive, innovative, and forward-looking society, 7) a caring society with a family-based welfare system, 8) an economically just society with inter-ethnic economic parity, and 9) a fully competitive, dynamic, robust, resilient, and prosperous economy (Gomez & Jomo, 1999: pp. 168-169).

II.
Japan's Foreign Direct Investment and Style of Management in Malaysia

A. Introduction: Malaysian's "Look East" Policy and Japan's Managerial Style

Dr. Mahathir publicly announced the "Look East" policies in December of 1981. This policy, which stemmed from his long-term interests in studying Japanese management, aimed at introducing Japanese work ethics and managerial systems in order to improve the economic performance and productivity of Malaysia. This policy had gained momentum and became an important part of Malaysia's national policy. The "Look East" Policy proposed to combine Malaysia's resource-based industrialization with Japanese technology and capital. Most praised the Policy because it could potentially become an important part of Malaysia's New Economic Policy. Others questioned the Policy because it overlooked the critical differences between the societies: Japan's population has been homogeneous in nature while Malaysia's population continues to be more diverse and heterogeneous (Lim Hua Sing, 1999: p. 1).

However, the "Look East" policy *proved to be an important stepping-stone for Malaysia's recipience of Japanese FDI.* Although the Policy was widely regarded as a reflection of Prime Minister Mahathir's personal national development philosophy aimed at introducing Japanese values for the purpose of economic development, it, nevertheless, gained support by the Japanese government and the Japanese business community. Japan undoubtedly appreciated the gestures through the introduction of the Policy. As long as Malaysia maintained this policy, the Japanese government would, according to Lim Hua Sing, "continue to cooperate with the implementation of the Malaysia's 'Look East' policy" (Lim Hua Sing, 1999: p. 22). Furthermore, the policy has created a better understanding and has enhanced more opportunities for economic cooperation between Malaysia and Japan. As Lim Hua Sing further elaborates:

> Presently, it appears that economic cooperation in trade and investment has received the most attention in Malaysia-Japan relations while cultural exchange seems to have been of lesser significance or given inadequate attention. Generally, although cultural exchange does not directly contribute to economic cooperation; it forms a necessary basis for the deeper understanding of Malaysia's overall developmental achievements (Lim Hua Sing, 1999: p. 23).

Nevertheless, as in the case of Singapore, the issue of loyalty continues to surface in Malaysia. Workers in Malaysia continue to engage in job-hopping to other companies with higher remuneration, better promotion, better career prospects, and/or more flexible working hours. Furthermore, Malaysian workers tend to value family higher than their companies, and are willing to refuse overtime or extended work assignments in order to stay close to their families (Thong, 1991: pp. 143-144). This issue has proven to be even more difficult by the fact that a number of Japanese subsidiaries continue to engage in aspects associating with Japanese managerial style in human resources (especially in the practices of hiring, training, promotion, layoff, consensus decision making and consultation, conflict and grievance handling, and in quality control circles) (Thong, 1991: pp. 140-142).[6]

B. Malaysia's Trade with Japan

Malaysia in the 1970s, which had been more successful in export-oriented industrialization than Indonesia, Thailand, and the Philippines, began to receive export-oriented investments from Japan. Unlike Japan, Malaysia has been a resource-rich country, and therefore, it did not need the imports of industrial and agricultural resources from abroad (Yoshihara, 1978: p. 16). Therefore, Malaysia's exports of tin, petroleum (both crude and refined), timber, natural rubber, latex, and fixed vegetable oils (crude, refined, and purified) to Japan has been promising (Lim Hua Sing, 1999: p. 27).

While Malaysia had a trade surplus with Japan from 1976 through 1980, it ran into a trade deficit with Japan in 1981 through 1983. The trade deficit occurred because the commodity prices dropped suddenly, which seriously affected Malaysia's exports to Japan. At the same time, the demand for Japanese imports, especially for heavy industrial and chemical products, began to increase (Lim Hua Sing, 1999: p. 28). Although Malaysia experienced a trade surplus with Japan in 1984 through 1989, it went back to a trade deficit in 1990 through 1993, largely due to the substantial rise of the its imports of heavy chemical and industrial products from Japan. Among heavy chemical and industrial products, exports of machinery and equipment had been significant, especially since they maintained 67 to 74 percent of Japan's total exports to Malaysia during the 1985-1993 span. Meanwhile, exports in heavy chemical and industrial products maintained an 88 to 91 percent of Japan's total exports to Malaysia during that same period (Lim Hua Sing, 1999: p. 28).[7]

Essentially, the Japan-Malaysia trade relations have been vertical for the most part: Malaysia imports manufactures such as heavy chemical and industrial products from Japan, while Japan imports raw materials from Malaysia. Malaysia's export of manufactured goods constituted 28 and 32 percent of its total exports from Japan in 1992 and 1993 respectively (Lim Hua Sing, 1999: p. 30). As Malaysia continues to restructure its economy towards capital and technological oriented, it will continue to require the influx of capital and technology intensive industries, as well as substantial imports of capital and intermediate goods and products from Japan (Lim Hua Sing, 1999: p. 30). In the meanwhile, Japan will expect an increase of manufactured goods (particularly electrical machinery and equipment) imported from Malaysia. On the debit side, however, such an increase is not likely to be significant, since the NIEs are becoming more advanced in producing these products also. In addition, the NIEs are better than Malaysia in social and industrial infrastructure, managerial know-how, capital, technology, and human resources (Lim Hua Sing, 1999: p. 30). Therefore, the degree of success with Malaysia's industrialization policies in years to come will have some influence on Malaysia-Japan trade relations, which in turn will determine the volume of Japan's FDI coming into the country.

C. Japan's Foreign Direct Investments: Its Nature and its Importance

As mentioned before, Japan's investment in Malaysia was particularly prompted in the early 1980s by the introduction of both the "Look East" policy in 1981, and The Fourth Malaysian Plan.[8] The "Look East" policy and the Plan have attracted pursuit by Japanese investors looking for business expansions in Malaysia (Lim Hua Sing, 1999: p. 30).

As a result, Japanese investment in Malaysia, based on paid-up capital, increased from $32.6 million in 1980 to $69.1 million in 1981, and then to $139.9 million in 1982 (which by then constituted 26.5 percent of total foreign direct investment in Malaysia). In addition, Japanese investment cases rose from 35 to 45 percent, and then to 36 percent during those three years. Therefore, Japanese investment in Malaysia's heavy industrial projects has continued its upward momentum (Lim Hua Sing, 1999: p. 31).

The trend of Japanese FDI continued its upward momentum from 1985 through 1992. Whereas Japanese investment in 1985 was $79.3 million, it rose to $879.8 million in 1991 (similarly in its tenor into Singapore and other ASEAN and NIEs countries). Furthermore, Japanese FDI in Malaysia's manufacturing sector had been predominating compared to such in the non-manufactured sector during that period. However, it shall be noted that the non-manufacturing sector gained momentum, absorbing Japanese FDI in the amount of $44.9 million in 1985 to $93 million in 1986 and to $202.5 million in 1989.[9] Japanese investors took greater interests in Malaysia's finance and insurance sectors after the 1985 Yen appreciation. Meanwhile, the Japanese FDI into Malaysia's manufacturing sector increased 18.7 times from $32.8 million in 1985 to $612.7 million in 1991. Japanese FDI in Malaysia's manufacturing sector has been concentrated in electronics and electrical products, and to a lesser extent chemicals, machinery, and metal and non-metal products (which altogether constituted 73 percent of Japanese FDI in 1991, but dropped to 51 percent in 1992) (Lim Hua Sing, 1999: pp. 31-36).

While Japanese FDI in the manufacturing sector will continue to be larger than that in the non-manufacturing sector, this trend will likely decrease as the non-manufacturing sector (especially commerce, finance and insurance, as well as services) is likely to gain momentum. This is the result, as Lim Hua Sing states, "of the immense increase of the Japanese FDI in the manufacturing sector which required strong back-up from investments in the non-manufacturing sector" (Lim Hua Sing, 1999: p. 37).

Part of the increase in both the manufacturing and non-manufacturing sectors in Malaysia was due to both the Yen appreciation of 1985 and a set of governmental economic and financial policies after 1987. By March of 1987, foreign companies were allowed to have 100 percent of their equity shares for five years, on the condition that 20 percent of their manufacturers were for export. Also, the Malaysian government announced that from January 1, 1989, corporate tax would be reduced from 40 to 35 percent, with the development tax reduced from 5 to 4 percent from 1990 (Lim Hua Sing, 1999: p. 31). Furthermore, the Malaysian government had taken steps in: 1) improving its social and industrial infrastructure, 2) expanding its domestic markets due to higher consumption power, 3) further improving and developing its labor resources, and 4) keeping its industrial and agricultural raw materials abundant. Japan was given further incentives to invest in Malaysia by the higher, more expensive operation costs in the NIEs, trade and economical frictions with the West, and increased competition from those NIEs (Lim Hua Sing, 1999: p. 36).

D. Japan's Development Aid

Japan was among the countries that provided economic assistance to Malaysia by financing Malaysia's industrial project and development of its human resources. According to the Official Development Assistance (ODA) from the Organization for Economic Cooperation and Development (OECD), Japan provided Malaysia $372.6 million in aid. Between 1966 and 1992, Japan extended fourteen loan aids to Malaysia, amounting to a total of 473.19 billion in yen (Lim Hua Sing, 1999: pp. 37-42).

The ODA disbursements were divided into grants and loan aid. Loan aid was generally larger than the total amount in grants, and by 1991, loan aid constituted 66 percent of Japan's total ODA disbursements to Malaysia (Lim Hua Sing, 1999: pp. 38-39). This aid was given for two purposes: 1) to improve infrastructure such as the Port Kelang power station project, the highway toll system project, the Perlis Port construction project, and the development of industrial projects such as the Sabah gas grid, ASEAN urea project in Malaysia, and the polished rice plant construction, and 2) to provide advanced equipment such as broadcasting equipment, LL equipment, audio-visual equipment, and setting up institutions for research and training. Additionally, Japan endowed Malaysia with trainers, experts, developing surveyors, Japan Overseas Co-operation volunteers, and project-type technical cooperation and development survey. However, Malaysia is now facing serious problems repaying the loan aid (made even more difficult by its sustained currency depreciation and the Yen appreciation in 1985). Malaysia's request to have loan repayment reduced was rejected by the Japanese Premier Takeshita Noboru during his last visit to Malaysia (Lim Hua Sing, 1999: p. 42).

E. Conclusion

The future relations between Japan and Malaysia depend on Malaysia's industrialization and economic policies. As stated before, the NIEs are better than Malaysia in social and industrial infrastructure, managerial know-how, capital, technology, and human resources. The loan repayment issue will also have an influence in the relations between these countries. However, Japanese FDI into Malaysia is decreasing due to the economic slowdown in Japan and Malaysia's recovery from the Asian Contagion of 1997. The Japanese investment, however, is not likely to end partly because of the recovery efforts of the Malaysian government after 1999.

III. Malaysia and the Asian Financial Crisis: How did the Government rid itself from the Initial Political Indecisiveness?

A. Recapitulation: Malaysia's Success Story

Until the onset of the currency crisis, Malaysia was deemed as the best development success story among the second tier newly industrializing economies (NIEs) in East Asia.[10] Malaysia's achievements performance was remarkable from the 1980s when there was a decisive shift towards greater outward-orientation of its' economic policy. Thanks largely to privatization after the mid-1980s, Malaysia, from 1987 through 1996, enjoyed economic growth at an annual rate of 8.8 percent, with the increase of per capita income from $1,850 to $4,425. Malaysia's rapid economic growth was accompanied by rising living standards, improvement in the distribution of income, and ameliorating the twin problems of poverty and racial imbalances. As far as political stability and policy continuity were concerned, "the stage was well set for advance through an outward-oriented development strategy....Malaysia's aim of entering the league of developed industrial nations by 2020 (as envisaged in Prime Minister Dr. Mahathir's Vision 2020 Speech) was generally considered feasible" (Athukorala, 1999: p. 28). To be seen in Table 4.1, the economy enjoyed full employment from 1990 through 1996, with the inflation rate a modest 4.5 percent.

Table 4.1
Malaysia's Macroeconomic Indicators, 1991-1997

The Indicators *(in percentage)*	1991	1992	1993	1994	1995	1996	1997
Real GDP	8.7	7.8	8.3	9.2	9.5	8.6	7.7
Inflation rate	4.4	4.7	3.6	3.7	3.4	3.5	2.7
Unemployment Rate	4.03	3.7	3.0	2.9	2.8	2.6	2.6
Fiscal Balances (% of GDP)	-2.0	-0.8	0.2	2.3	0.9	0.7	2.4
Current Account (% of GDP)	-9.2	-3.8	-4.8	-6.3	-8.5	-4.9	-5.1

Source: Chin, Kok Fay and K.S. Jomo. "Financial Reform and Crisis in Malaysia." *Financial Big Bang in Asia.* Masayoshi Tsurumi, editor. Singapore: Ashgate, 2001: pp. 225-250.

Before the Crisis, the banking sector was both robust and sound. Non-performing loans decreased from 5.5 percent in 1995 to 3.9 percent in 1996, thus falling well below the critical level of 15 to 16 percent used by the Bank of International Settlement (BIS) to identify troubled banking systems. Furthermore, the average capital adequacy ratio for commercial banks, merchant banks, and finance companies were 11.8 percent, 13.3 percent, and 10.6 percent respectively. Foreign currency exposure of the banking system remained low due to the central bank, Bank Negara Malaysia (BNM) policy of specifying stringent net open positions (NOPs) on foreign borrowing. By mid-1997, the aggregate net open position of the banking system was less than five percent to total bank liabilities (Athukorala, 1999: p. 32).

B. The Coming of Malaysia's Financial Crisis and Economic Collapse

Malaysia was not hard hit by the Asian Financial Crisis of 1997-1998 as compared to, say, Thailand and Indonesia. This was due to the strength of foreign industrial investment and its foreign debt that was largely publicly held. Furthermore, Malaysia's communitarian policies had virtually preserved its social and religious stability, without smothering economic initiatives (Godement, 1999: p. 13). Because Malaysia succumbed to the Crisis with only a little foreign debt exposure of its banking system, it was successful in surviving the economic crisis, though without an IMF sponsored rescue package (Athukorala, 1999: pp. 28-29).

However, by late 1997, Malaysia experienced the devaluation of its currency of more than 30 percent.[11] Part of the reason was an over-reliance on short-term capital. During the 1980s through the early 1990s, Malaysia had been dominated by FDI rather than by short-term private sector borrowing and portfolio investment. In 1996, net inflow of private short-term capital increased significantly, primarily driven by the boom in the Malaysian share market. As a result, capital inflow accounted for 43.3 percent of the total annual capital inflow by the end of 1996. The increased reliance on short-term capital increased the vulnerability of the ringgit to speculative attacks, because investments can leave the country quickly, thus exerting devaluation pressures (Athukorala, 1999: p. 31).

To fight a speculative run on its currency, a key determinant in doing so is a country's volume of foreign exchange reserves. Of a variety of measures, M2 is regarded as a compromise measure of liquidity assets for this purpose. M2 means currency plus demand and savings deposits in a commercial bank. The higher the M2/reserve ratio means that a country's inability to defend the currency increases proportionately, thus subject to speculative attacks more profoundly. Malaysia's M2/reserve ratio was at 4.7 by June of 1997 and was increasing (Athukorala, 1999: p. 31).

C. From Financial Crisis to Economic Collapse: The Nature of the Predicament

By the first quarter of 1997, the real exchange rate appreciated by roughly 15 percent. This real appreciation was deemed to have been a major factor in the formation of the Crisis (Athukorala, 1999: p. 31). Malaysia, to the surprise of most, began to denounce foreign hedge funds for economic sabotage in September of 1997 (Perkins and Woo, 2000: p. 227). The exchange rate of the ringgit varied in a narrow range of 2.36 to 2.51 RG per U.S. dollar. After the baht came under heavy speculative attack by mid-May of 1997, the ringgit also experienced heavy selling pressure and Bank Negara Malaysia (BNM) responded by selling close to $1.5 billion to prop up the currency, only for it to float by July 14th due to market pressures (Athukorala, 1999: p. 29).

Although the exchange rate showed some signs of stability during February and March of 1998, it continued to slip heavily in the succeeding months until it was fixed at a rate of M$3.80 = $1.00 (Perkins and Woo, 2000: p. 237).[12] The collapse of the stock market caused even greater concerns, and between July 1997 and mid-January 1998, the all ordinaries index of the Kuala Lumpur Stock Exchange (KLSE) declined by over 65 percent, erasing roughly $225 billion of share values. This decline was the biggest stock market plunge among the five Southeast Asian countries under the Crisis. Even before the Crisis, the KLSE was the third largest in the Asia-Pacific region after Tokyo and Hong Kong, thanks to a market capitalization of roughly $200 billion by the mid-1990s (Perkins and Woo, 2000: p. 237).

In relation to GDP, the stock market capitalization in Malaysia (over 300 percent of that GDP) was substantially higher than any other significant economy. The KLSE composite index went from 506 in 1990 to 1238 in 1996. This rise in share prices allowed Malaysians to borrow more from the banks to acquire more assets (Perkins and Woo, 2000: p. 237). At the onset of the Crisis, however, foreign investors accounted for only 30 to 40 percent of the activities in the market (Athukorala, 1999: pp. 29-32). It was a sign of the reversal of foreign capital flows by mid-1997: capital flight became a reality, to the severe disadvantage of the economy.

The reversal of foreign capital flows accelerated at the end of 1997 and exacerbated the decline of the Malaysian stock market. Moreover, as the stock market began to crash, capital outflow depreciated the ringgit even further against the dollar. Thus, the value of the ringgit per dollar increased from 2.5 in 1997 (second quarter), to 4.2 in 1998 (second quarter) (Athukorala, 1999: pp. 29-32). Deputy Prime Minister and Finance Minister, Anwar Ibrahim, reacted to the acceleration in capital flight by implementing an IMF-style high interest rate policy to stabilize the exchange rate and to restore market confidence (Perkins and Woo, 2000: p. 237). In this reform package announced on December 5th, 1997, the key measures included: 1) cutting government spending by 18 percent, 2) postponing all public sector investment projects indefinitely, 3) ceasing new overseas investment by Malaysian firms, 4) freezing new share issues, 5) company restructuring, and 6) cutting salaries of government ministers by 10 percent. With these measures, the previous budget forecast for economic growth was reduced from 7 percent to 4-5 percent. (Athukorala, 1999: p. 34) As a result, the annualized growth rate of reserve money went from over 25 percent in 1997 to 15 percent in 1998 (second quarter). As credit became tightened in early 1998, the lending rate increased from 10 percent in 1997 (fourth quarter) to 12.2 percent in 1998 (second quarter) (Perkins, and Woo, 2000: pp. 237-238).

However, the ringgit continued to decline notwithstanding Ibrahim's high interest rate policy. Investment spending was reduced significantly and contributed to the downslide of the stock market: The KLSE composite index fell from 1238 in 1996 to 455 in 1998 (second quarter). It must be argued, however, that Dr. Mahathir's occasional excoriation of conspiratorial speculation by foreigners helped undermined Ibrahim's policy. Each outbursts made by the Prime Minister caused the ringgit to fall even further, as investors deemed them to be a prelude to the imposition of capital controls (Perkins and Woo, 2000: p. 238).

The confrontations between Ibrahim and Dr. Mahathir were not new. Whereas Dr. Mahathir pursued his attacks on currency speculators, Ibrahim focused on soothing the "nerves of currency traders and foreign investors by taking a more moderate stance" (Tan, 2000: pp. 126-127). Before the December 5th reform package, Dr. Mahathir created a "contending center of economic policymaking authority in the National Economic Action Council (NEAC)" (Haggard,

2000: p. 61). The NEAC was led by its chairperson Diam Zainuddin, who, as a former finance minister, was arguably the architect of the high-growth strategy of the late 1980s and the early 1990s. However, the NEAC generated substantial uncertainty over economic policymaking authority. Ibrahim was made deputy chairperson of the NEAC, but this appointment undermined his authority as finance minister. Principles and ideologies between Ibrahim and the NEAC under Zainuddin became different. Whereas the council argued that a fiscal stimulus and lower interest rates were necessary for recovery, Ibrahim argued for higher interest rates (Haggard, 2000: pp. 61-62).

Zainuddin's argument for a fiscal stimulus and a low interest rate won, as he himself was elevated to cabinet status on June 24th, 1998. On July, monetary policy was eased to deal with the severe crisis of the financial sector. Ibrahim meanwhile launched a number of important new institutions for: 1) recapitalizing the banks (Danamodal), 2) acquiring, rehabilitating, and disposing of assets (Danaharta), and 3) restructuring corporate debt. In seeking support from Japan, Singapore, Taiwan, and the World Bank, the government accelerated its efforts to raise foreign funds to finance these efforts (Haggard, 2000: pp. 61-62). However, the plan to float $2 billion of bonds for Danaharta was placed on hold after international agencies cut Malaysia's credit ratings. For example, Standard and Poor determined that non-performing loans had reached 30 percent of total loans. What made matters worse was that the GDP shrank by 6.8 percent by the second quarter of 1998 (Haggard, 2000: pp. 61-62).

The political climate ran contrary to the efforts towards economic recovery and reform, however. Deemed morally unfit to be a political leader, Ibrahim was dismissed by Dr. Mahathir on September 2nd, 1998. This action fueled numerous demonstrations, some of which became violent especially in Kuala Lumpur. While a movement demanding political reform, *reformasi,* was launched, Ibrahim's wife, Dr. Wan Azizah Ismail, launched a movement for social justice, *Adil,* in December of 1998. In the following April, she established a new multiracial political party called the National Justice Party to contest the next general elections to be held on April 1st, 2000. Although the political confrontations were admittedly not as severe as in Indonesia or as not as unstable as it was in Thailand, it nevertheless posed serious challenges to the efforts towards economic recovery (Tan, 2000: pp. 127-128).

The collapses in both the domestic stock market and the foreign exchange market were accompanied with a large decline in aggregate demand. The abrupt withdrawal of foreign funds, high interest rates, and doubtfulness of economic recovery in East Asia, caused severe downturns in private consumption and private investment. Although the depreciation of the ringgit yielded some positive effects, the depressed demand conditions in the Pacific-rim region offset them, making export value of $35 billion in the first half of 1998 lower than the export value of $39 billion in the first half of 1997. This predicament spelled loses in profits, and many large bumiputra conglomerates became financially illiquid or insolvent. These conglomerates began to suffer a decline in their share prices, which reduced the value of the collateral pledged against their bank loans. The end result was that the loss of profits due to Malaysia's economic collapse made the conglomerates incapable of servicing their bank loans (Perkins and Woo, 2000: p. 238). Malaysia's highly leveraged corporate sector accrued up to 400 billion ringgit in debts. With the rising interest rates up to 12 percent in 1998, many firms were struggling to repay their loans. Downsizing became a principal alternative for the firms to not only service the loans, but to also stay alive in the business world (Tan, 2000: p. 125). Consequently, the number of non-performing loans began to plague the banking sector (to be discussed further below).

The banking sector experienced a massive accumulation of outstanding domestic credit as well as a heavy exposure of the banking system to the property sector.[13] The annual growth rate of bank credit to the private sector increased continuously from 18 percent in 1990 to 33.5 percent in 1997. Moreover, the ratio of GDP of outstanding credit increased from an average level of 85 percent during 1985-1989, to 120 percent in 1994, and then to over 160 percent in mid-1997, when the financial crisis began to take hold of the country. Malaysia's credit building was the highest among countries in East Asia. Although some may find this a blessing in disguise, a symbol of almost unlimited opportunities for investors, it was nevertheless a cause for concern. Speculators in particular regarded a massive credit build-up of this nature as: 1) a sign of a government's reluctance to use the interest rate as a policy tool should a speculative attack on the currency occur and 2) an implication of a growing share of lending to less creditworthy borrowers. Rapid credit expansion was accompanied by a sharp increase in the share of total credit going to the property sector: by the end of 1996, this sector accounted for over 45 percent of outstanding bank credit (Athukorala, 1999: p. 32).

The concerns regarding massive credit build-up were not without legitimacy. Due to both the property market crash and massive capital outflows, the Malaysian banks began to experience an increase of non-performing loans. According to BNM, the proportion of non-performing assets increased from 2 percent in July of 1997, to 3.6 percent in December, and finally to 11.8 percent in July of 1998. However, as many companies began to roll-over their debt for the purpose of avoiding insolvency, the proportion of non-performing assets was deemed by market analysts to be much higher and severe than what was reported by the official figures. Independent estimates of the non-performing loan ratio ranged from 25 percent to 30 percent by the mid-1998. The result of the increase in non-performing loans was far-reaching beyond expectation: it was reflected in a sharp downturn in borrowing and financing, which contributed to the liquidity squeeze (Athukorala, 1999: p. 30). Bank Negara Malaysia ordered ailing banks and finance companies to either merge or face closure, probably due to a large number of branch closures and job losses (Tan, 2000: p. 125). Meanwhile, both traditional export industries and export-oriented manufacturing expanded significantly, reflecting the substantial gain in competitiveness through the real exchange rate appreciation. Unfortunately, the expansions were not sufficient to compensate for the "growth retarding effect of domestic deflation" (Athukorala, 1999: p. 30).

What made matters worse was that crony capitalism was no stranger to Malaysia. In fact, much of the recent expansion of bank lending to the activities of the property sector had taken the form of connected (state-directed) lending. In other words, a long standing relationship between the government and business provided an impetus for much of the bank lending activities. Rapid expansion in the stock market was also affected by crony capitalism. As Athukorala states,

> Rapid expansion of the share market was not, however, due to initiatives to redress underlying weaknesses of corporate governance. Most of the listed companies in Malaysia are tightly controlled by a handful of powerful families. These families often retain majority stakes even in public companies. Moreover, in many cases the interests of company bosses and politicians are closely interwoven. Manipulation of inter-company share transactions in order to augment profit in privately owned companies at the expense of listed companies has been a common occurrence in the Malaysian corporate world (Athukorala, 1999: p. 33).

As with the banking sector, crony capitalism in the stock market, in many respects, woefully undermined the soundness of Malaysia's economic and financial performances. This malpractice made stock trading vulnerable to financial panic because a minority of shareholders not connected to the politicians wondered how they would be treated in event of a market downturn. Consequently, foreign participants began pulling out in order to avoid currency risk A series of murky stock market dealings in the immediate aftermath on the onset of the financial crisis compounded this suspicion and thus aggravated the stock index slide discussed above (Athukorala, 1999: p. 33).

In October of 1997, the Malaysian government announced expectation of a growth rate of 7 percent for 1998. By December of that year, the government adjusted the expected growth rate to 4 if not 5 percent, and again in March of 1999, with the expected growth rate of 2 if not 3 percent. For the first and second quarters of 1998, the national accounts recorded 2.6 percent and 6.8 percent contration rate of the economy (Athukorala, 1999: p. 30). The unemployment rate increased from 2.5 percent in 1997 to 6.5 percent in 1998, primarily due to a sharp decrease of output in the manufacturing sector: over 560,000 people became unemployed by the end of that year (Tan, 2000: p. 126).

D. The Initial Weaknesses in Crisis Management

Once the financial and economic crises took hold on Malaysia's economy, the government exacerbated them by not attacking the sources of vulnerability decisively, while it did not restore investors' confidence. At first, the government denied that the Crisis even existed. Prime Minister Mahathir blamed currency speculators, and argued that a Jewish conspiracy was in hand to jeopardize the Malaysian miracle (George Soros, an American financier of Jewish heritage, was implicated during that attack). The attacks made by Mohathir precipitated a further slide of the ringgit, despite Ibrahim's efforts to soothe the nerves of currency traders and foreign investors by taking a more moderate stance (Athukorala, 1999: p. 34).

On August 27, 1997, Mahathir announced the ban on short selling in one-hundred designated stocks in an effort to eliminate speculative activity in the stock market. However, as a result of this policy move, the stock market lost 4.2 percent of its value, and the currency depreciated from roughly 2.5 to 2.9 ringgit to the dollar the next day (Tan, 2000: p. 181). During the government's denunciation of foreign hedge funds on grounds of economic sabotage in September 1997, the prime minister announced a 60 billion ringgit fund to buy shares from locals at a premium, though from foreigners at market prices on September 3, 1997. On September 4th, however, the stock market declined by 2.6 percent and the currency depreciated from 2.9 to 3.0 ringgit to the dollar (Tan, 2000: p. 181).

In response to this development, Dr. Mahathir reversed some of his policy announcements on September 4th, not excluding the ban of short selling of one-hundred designated stocks. Needless to say, the reversal of the announcements sparked a rally on the stock market and an appreciation of the ringgit. However, after Mahathir denounced currency trading during his visit to Hong Kong on September 20, he later announced that Malaysia would seek to limit currency trading, allowing it only for activities related to trade. On September 22, the stock market fell to 3.5 percent, and the currency depreciated from 3.0 to 3.09 ringgit to the dollar (Tan, 2000: pp. 181-182). After Mahathir's further denunciation on currency trading during his visit to Chile on September 30th, the stock slipped further and the currency depreciated to from roughly 3.10 to 3.35 ringgit to the dollar. Therefore, Mahathir chose not to make any further public statements regarding currency trading (Tan, 2000: pp. 181-182).

The government's imposition of comprehensive controls on capital outflows in 1998 did not help matters initially. On the eve of Ibrahim's dismissal, Malaysia was placed on capital controls on September 1, 1998. The exchange rate was fixed to 3.8 ringgit per dollar. As the interest rates were substantially reduced, an expansionary government budget was announced on October 23, 1998. Those policies added fuel to the already collapsing economy: GDP was contracted by 7.5 percent in 1998, a clear departure from the average annual growth rate of 8.7 percent from 1990 through 1997 (Perkins and Woo, 2000: p. 227 and 240).

In essence, Malaysia was plagued by an absence of a clear policy guideline necessary for its recovery. By mid-1998, while the economy was in a recession, there were no signs of achieving currency and share price stability. For instance, by mid-1998, GDP growth registered a -1.8 percent growth, while the money supply was growing at less than ten percent (Tan, 2000: p. 185). The stage was set for a dramatic policy turnaround in favor of an unorthodox and risky policy posture whose "key elements were capital controls and expansionary macroeconomic policy" (Athukorala, 1999: p. 29).

E. Malaysia's Move towards Growth Stimulation and Quasi-Economic Recovery

Malaysia increased its infrastructure spending in order to raise the general governmental budget deficit to 4.2 percent of GDP in 1999. This increase in infrastructure spending represented a major reversal of the budget surplus tradition, which had produced surpluses of 4 percent in 1997, and 0.7 percent in 1998. The non-financial public enterprises became an essential vehicle in the reflation efforts (Perkins and Woo, 2000: pp. 240-241). Petronas, the state oil company, kept financially precarious firms operating by its acquisition of them. The deficit spending of the non-financial public enterprises caused the budget surplus of the consolidated public sector to "go from 4 percent in 1996 and 6.3 percent in 1997 to -1.0 percent in 1998, -5.4 percent in 1999, and (expected) -4.5 percent in 2000" (Perkins and Woo, 2000: pp. 240-241).

In early 1999, Dr. Mahathir and Diam Zainuddin announced that bailouts of troubled firms would increase, and banks were urged to boost their lending. As part of Malaysia's recapitalization of the banking system, Danaharta and Danamodal were created as two new state agencies to restore the financial sector to financial solvency, so that bank lending could resume. Danaharta was responsible for taking over bad loans, whereas Danamodal's role was to recapitalize the banks (Perkins and Woo, 2000: p. 241). Danaharta had purchased non-performing loans worth 22 billion ringgit (which was roughly one-third of the total non-performing loans in Malaysia's banking sector). Danamodal deployed 11 billion ringgit to recapitalize several banks (Tan, 2000: p. 189). Meanwhile, the central bank imposed a mandatory target of 8 percent growth for bank loans in 1998. In February 2000, the bank introduced a 300 million ringgit subsidized loan program targeted at small and medium-sized businesses owned by bumiputras (Perkins and Woo, 2000: p. 241). Furthermore, foreign companies had purchased assets worth 7 billion ringgit in eight indebted private companies (Tan, 2000: p. 189). However, the use of bailouts in the reflation efforts raised a very important issue. As Perkins and Woo point out,

> If the bailouts were mostly for bumiputra firms that were rendered illiquid by the financial panic (e.g., companies that were unable to roll-over their short-

> term debt), then the underlying growth of the economy will be unaffected. But if the bailouts covered mostly bumiputra firms that had their insolvency hastened by the high interest rates and lower aggregate demand, then the survival of these low-growth potential firms will lower the trend growth rate. Furthermore, these inefficient firms are likely to weaken the future fiscal situation by requiring more subsidies, and to raise the costs for downstream firms by obtaining increased import protection in the future (Perkins and Woo, 2000: p. 242).

The implementation of liquidity, with leakage minimized by capital controls, lowered the short-term interest rate steadily from 11.1 percent on July 1, 1998 to 6.6 percent on December 9, 1998, and then to 3.17 percent in December 21, 1999. Meanwhile, the stock market index rose steadily from 471 on July 1, 1998 to 791.2 on December 21, 1999 (Perkins and Woo, 2000: p. 241).

The pegging of the ringgit at 3.8 per dollar since September 1998 has rendered it undervalued vis-à-vis the other major currencies in the region. As a result, Malaysia's exports saw a dramatic increase from $72 billion in 1998 to $82 billion in 1999. Furthermore, the exemption of new foreign-owned firms from bumiputra ownership requirements, regardless of the export orientation of the new foreign-owned firms, helped Malaysia to resume its recipience of FDI from abroad (Perkins and Woo, 2000: p. 242).

There is no question that the reflation measures, together with a reversal of the regional financial panic, gave Malaysia a growth rate of 4.7 percent by 1999 (Perkins and Woo, 2000: p. 242). The question is whether the government can avoid confrontations surrounding policies in order to rid the effects of the financial crisis completely. Meanwhile, the dismissal of Ibrahim is still in the minds of many.

IV.
Epilogue
Malaysia Then and Now: A Look at its Contemporary Economic Well-being in the Post Asian Financial Crisis Era and its Vision onto the Future

A. Malaysia: Its Visionary Growth and Sustainability - A Revisit

The government's directive industrial policy was instrumental towards Malaysia's economic growth after 1957. Where the level of poverty was at 49 percent by 1970, it decreased to 16 percent by 1990, and decreased further to a 7.2 percentile by the year 2000 (with increased employment outside agriculture). Because of import-substituting industrialization in the early 1960s and the mid-1980s, with the booming of export-oriented industrialization, manufacturing has become the single largest sector in Malaysia and the services grew correspondingly (Gomez & Jomo, 1999: p. 171). Japan and the United States were decisive in Malaysia's phenomenal economic growth through FDI and technological transfers, and Malaysia has reached a critical juncture in its march towards becoming a fully developed country (Chowdhury, 1997: p. 62).

However, Malaysia continues to rely too heavily on non-renewable natural resources. Currently, Malaysia's natural resources are a steadily declining share of GDP, or exports, and of government revenue (Perkins and Woo, 2000: p. 251). Furthermore, Malaysia's industrialization continues to be handicapped by: 1) a narrow manufacturing base, 2) weak industrial links, 3) insufficient local supply of intermediate products, 4) inadequate development of indigenous technology, 5) too little value-added manufacturings , 6) relatively high production costs, 7) infrastructural bottlenecks and labor shortages of skilled personnel, 8) lack of sufficient diversification of products as well as markets, 9) problems due to protectionism, trade blocs, and managed trade, and 10) the need for agrarian reform as well as resource and environmental protection (Gomez & Jomo, 1999: pp. 172-173).[14] However, the government recognizes these problems and Prime Minister Mahathir's "Vision 2020" should do much in erasing many if not most of the above-mentioned weaknesses.

The Asian Financial Crisis placed a temporary hold on "Vision 2020." Plagued by government indecisiveness and political fragmentation, Malaysia's economic recovery was in doubt. However, Malaysia's move towards capital controls and expansionary macroeconomic policy were highly instrumental in its economic recovery after 1999. Consequently, the latest figures suggest that Malaysia's economic growth rate can be sustained. By the year 2000 (fourth quarter), the growth rates at over five percent were higher than generally expected (BBC World Service, 2000: p. 3). A few domestically owned and controlled firms became successful exporters of manufactures and a few services (Perkins and Woo, 2000: p. 250). But, the above-mentioned weaknesses and concerns over political stability will continue to be challenges for Malaysia to overcome.

B. Malaysia's Economic Recovery, 2000-Present

Malaysia's recovery from the Asian Financial Crisis proves to be aphoristic. As you shall see in table 4.2, Malaysia's economic growth rate and recovery are quite sustained. By the year 2000 (fourth quarter), the growth rate at over five percent were higher than generally expected (BBC World Service, 2000: p. 3). *However, despite a sharp drop in GDP performance in 2001, Malaysia's full economy recovery was still on the horizon.* The 4.2 percent GDP growth of 2002 is worth noting given the lack of certainties and confidence that plagued much of the global community (which in turn dampened international trade). The aforementioned growth had much to do with strong consumption demand and recovery in exports, despite the performance of the latter below capacity (Asian Development Outlook 2003, 2003: p. 78).

Table 4.2
Malaysia's Macroeconomic Indicators, 2000-2005

The Indicators *(in percentage)*	**2000**	**2001**	**2002**	**2003**	**2004**	**2005**
GDP growth	8.3	0.4	4.2	5.4	7.1	5.3
Gross domestic investment/GDP	27.1	23.8	24.4	21.8	22.5	20.3
Gross domestic savings/GDP	47.1	42.2	41.8	42.1	43.0	n/a.
Inflation rate (consumer price index)	1.6	1.4	1.8	1.2	1.4	3.0
Money supply (M2 growth)	5.2	2.2	5.8	11.1	25.4	n/a.
Fiscal balance/GDP	-5.8	-5.5	-5.6	-5.3	-4.1	-3.8
Merchandise export growth	17.0	-10.6	6.1	12.4	20.5	11.0
Merchandise import growth	26.3	-10.3	8.1	5.4	25.8	8.5
Current account balance/GDP	9.4	8.3	7.6	13.0	12.5	15.7
Debt service ratio[15]	5.4	6.1	6.0	6.2	4.3	n/a.
Unemployment Rate	2.8	3.7	3.8	3.6	3.0	3.5

Sources:

1) The Asian Development Bank (Outlook 2003, 2005, and 2006). *Website* www.adb.org
2) IndexMundi (on the unemployment rate for 2004 as well as gross domestic investment for 2005). *Website:* www.indexmundi.com
3) Bank Negara Malaysia (debt service ratio for 2003 and 2004) in its 2004 Annual Report. *Website:* www.mida.gov.my/beta/pdf/BNMAnnual2004/pdf

Note:

The latest and revised GDP growth figures for 2003 through 2005 are from The Asian Development Outlook 2006.

The GDP growth continued to a 7.1 percent growth in 2004, the fastest expansion since 2000. The economy benefited from both stronger external and domestic demand and despite some moderation in global growth in the second half of 2004, the Malaysian economy remained resilient. It was the private sector (in consumption spending) that primarily gave Malaysia its economic resiliency and expansion (Bank Negara Malaysia Annual Report 2004, 2005: p. 1). The robust external and domestic demand outweighed a reduction of fiscal stimulus and consumption alone accounted for 5.7 percentage points to GDP growth (Asian Development Outlook 2005, 2005: p. 103). In 2005, however, the GDP growth moderated due to weakened external demand for electronics. This industry recovered later that year and was projected to improve further in 2006 (Asian Development Outlook 2006, 2006: p. 208).

1. The Economic Performances by Sectors

Manufacturing and services both played decisive roles in strengthening output growth in 2002. After its decline by 6.2 percent in 2001, manufacturing output improved by 4.1 percent the following year. The sharp improvement was due to the resiliency of consumption demand as well as a turnaround in manufacturing exports. Therefore, the growth of export-oriented industrial production gained strength throughout the year, although domestic-oriented industrial production slowed in comparison. Taken as a whole, the overall industrial production improved in 2002, with electronics which outperformed other subsectors and recorded the highest growth, followed by chemicals and vehicles (Asian Development Outlook 2003, 2003: pp. 78-79). Exports, therefore, grew by 6.1 percent in 2002 while imports improved by 8.1 percent. In addition, the services and construction sectors are likewise performing well, with their growths of 4.5 percent and 2.3 percent respectively. Only agriculture, which accounted for 8 percent of GDP, remained the most modest, with its growth of 0.3 percent in 2002 (ADO 2003, 2003: pp. 78-79).

In 2004, manufacturing improved further to 9.8 percent from 8.2 percent in 2003 while agriculture continued to perform well, despite a slight decrease from a 5.5 percent growth in 2003 to 5.0 percent in 2004 (Asian Development Outlook 2005, 2005: p. 103). In the manufacturing sector, both export and domestic oriented industries expanded strongly with "high capacity utilization, in line with the upturn in the global electronics cycle as well as stronger domestic demand" (Bank Negara Malaysia Annual Report 2004, 2005: p. 2). The services sector likewise improved (from 4.4 percent in 2003 to 6.6 percent in 2004), mainly due to higher consumer spending amidst the rise of disposable incomes as well as higher tourism and increased in trade-related activities (Bank Negara Malaysia Annual Report 2004, 2005: p. 2). The softening of the SARS outbreak since 2003 contributed to the rise especially of tourism as well as hotel and catering services.

In fact, nearly every sectors of the economy were growing, and in some cases, more so than anticipated. Mining and quarrying output increased by 4.1 percent, which were shored up by higher production of crude oil supported by strong external demand and high prices (Asian Development Outlook 2005, 2005: p. 103). In the agricultural sector, crude palm oil and rubber continued to perform well whereas forestry production showed improvement in response to higher demand from wood-based industries. The enhancement of the financial sector derived from a better stock market performance as well as from increased demand for bank loans and insurance. However, construction was the only sector that showed a contraction (of minus 1.9 percent) due to cuts in public investment (ADO 2005, 2005: p. 103). With the improvement in productivity growth, new capacity expansion in sectors that continued to experience strong growth and a more competitive environment, were factors that contributed to price stability, thus making inflationary pressures containable (Bank Negara Malaysia Annual Report 2004, 2005: pp. 3-4). Both CPI and core inflation stood at 1.4 percent and 1 percent respectively for 2004 and labor conditions continue to improve as the unemployment rate continues to decline (Bank Negara Malaysia Annual Report 2004, 2005: pp. 3-4).

On the supply side, the services sector continued to grow effervescently in 2005. This was due to both spending of households and foreign tourists as well as to new areas of growth, such as outsourcing of business services. Services contributed 3.3 percentage points to growth whereas the industry sector, harmed by weaker demand for electronic goods, contributed to 1.8 percentage point. Although inflation rose to 3.0 percent, the unemployment picture remained at an ideal low, despite its slight edging to 3.5 percent in 2005 (Asian Development Outlook 2006, 2006: p. 208).

2. The Trading and Investment Picture

Notwithstanding the struggles Malaysia had to endure to maintain the level of both exports and imports growths since 2000, when they recorded 17.0 percent and 26.3 percent expansions respectively, the country saw another surge in 2004. Exports grew remarkably well from 12.4 percent in 2003 to 20.5 percent in 2004 while imports grew from 5.4 percent to 25.8 percent during the same time span. The export growth was fueled by the overall improvement of the global economy as well as the recovery of the electronics cycle. Given the high import content of manufactured exports, import growth outpaced that of exports, which resulted in a trade surplus of $26.8 billion in 2004 (Asian Development Outlook 2005, 2005: p. 103). However, in 2005, both merchandise exports and merchandise imports cooled somewhat to 11 percent and 8.5 percent respectively (Malaysian Industrial Development Authority (MIDA), 2006: p. 10). The slowing down, partly due to weakened demand especially for electronics, generated a bigger trade surplus to roughly $35 billion (Asian Development Outlook 2006, 2006: p. 209).

Reflecting on the above-mentioned developments, the trade account of 2002 recorded a surplus of $18.1 billion, which was less than in 2001. With the growth in services deficit and income outflows, along with lower trade account surplus, the current account surplus decreased from $7.3 billion in 2001 to $7.2 billion in 2002 (Asian Development Outlook 2003, 2003: p. 79). However, the FDI applications for manufacturing projects were up by 13.7 percent in comparison to the previous year, suggestive of a gradually improving investor confidence.[16] The continual inflows of FDI as with a sustained current account surpluses gave Malaysia a favorable reserve position, with its net international reserves that increased from $30.8 billion in 2001 to $34.6 billion in 2002 (ADO 2003, 2003: p. 79).

With the trade surplus of $26.8 billion in 2004, the current account surplus remained a sizable 12.5 percent of GDP, underpinning a healthy balance-of-payment position. FDI continued to increase from $2.5 billion in 2003 to $4.7 billion in 2004 and with the continuation of capital inflows along with a favorable current account surplus, international reserves soared to $66.7 billion from $21.9 billion in 2003, a near doubling over the two years (Asian Development Outlook 2005, 2005: p. 103).[17] This in part reflects Malaysia's strong economic fundamentals as of late but also a reflection of the depreciation of the U.S. dollar against major currencies in 2004 (Bank Negara Malaysia Annual Report 2004, 2005: p. 5). Furthermore, the inflows of portfolio funds were also following stronger economic growth and improved corporate earning. In fact, portfolio investment inflows were significant in both equities and debt securities markets, reflections of positive investor sentiment despite sovereign ratings upgrades and speculations that some local currencies including the ringgit had the possibility for an upward revaluation (Bank Negara Malaysia Annual Report 2004, 2005: p. 4).

It was an excess of savings over investment that gave Malaysia a surge of current account surplus of $20.5 billion (or 15.7 percent of GDP) in 2005. While the surplus per se was good news, the lack of enthusiasm among companies to increase investment remained a source of concern for the government. In actuality, the investment rate has suffered a decline for five years, reaching 20.7 percent of gross national product during that year. This dented investment potential was due to two factors: 1) Malaysia's displacement as a low-cost manufacturing center and 2) domestic firms protracted progress in climbing the value-added ladder. However, gross FDI inflows rose by 6.4 percent in 2005 (Asian Development Outlook 2006, 2006: p. 209). Among ASEAN countries, Malaysia remained the second largest recipient of FDI inflows behind Singapore, garnering $4.6 billion of FDI in 2004 (Malaysian Industrial Development Authority (MIDA), 2006: p. 18).

3. Malaysia's Fiscal Policies and Monetary Considerations

Going back to the consistent GDP growth, which cumulated to 7.1 percent in 2004, it must be mentioned that part of the growth was driven by not only strong consumption demand and recovery in exports, but also by a series of fiscal measures. The stimulation packages and infrastructural spending were well documented in the previous section and the same fiscal pump-priming policy were maintained by the Malaysian government to boost domestic demand aimed at preventing recession and high unemployment. Also, the government, in 2001 and 2002, continued its expansionary fiscal policies to stimulate investment and production. Its monetary policy remained accommodative, liquidity remained in abundance, and interest rates were kept low (Asian Development Outlook 2003, 2003: p. 78). The government also aimed at improving fiscal consolidation by targeting a lower deficit at 4.7 percent of GDP (from a 5.5 percent out-turn in 2001). The aforementioned goal went along with the government's continued stimulation programs, this time for private sector activities. This budget included numerous important tax measures, such as a reduction of personal income tax rates, lower import duties on selected intermediate goods, adjustments in investment allowances and depreciation, and changes in tax holiday coverage for enterprises. The formula worked, for public consumption grew by 17.6 percent and 13.8 percent in 2001 and 2002 respectively, even though private consumption remained more modest, at 2.8 percent and 4.2 percent over the same period (Asian Development Outlook 2003, 2003: p. 78).

As mentioned above, Malaysia sought to boost domestic demand in the short term. However, it is not losing sight on its long-term goal, namely to enhance industrial competitiveness and labor productivity through spending on infrastructure development, education, and human-resources development (the similar endeavors that brought Malaysia to its economic predominance after the 1950s) (Asian Development Outlook 2003, 2003: p. 80). Furthermore, Malaysia's 2003 budget aspired towards fiscal consolidation in line with its goal of achieving a balance budget by the end of the Eighth Malaysia Plan (2001-2005). Based on projections of an improved economy, Malaysia targeted its budget deficit for 2003 at 3.9 percent of its GDP. In recognizing the private sector as the engine of economic growth, the budget increased expenditures for education and training, labor productivity improvement, Research and Development as well as technology, SMEs, and services in the areas of finance, agriculture, as well as computer software (Asian Development Outlook 2003, 2003: p. 80).

By 2004, however, the Malaysian government determined that there was no longer a need to further pump priming. The officials therefore tightened the fiscal policy and the budget deficit as a share of GDP narrowed to a five-year low of 4.1 percent (which was below the official target of 4.5 percent) (Asian Development Outlook 2005, 2005: pp. 103-104). Furthermore, for the sake of reducing the exposure of Malaysia's external debt, the government's funding requirement was sourced domestically, which did not crowd out private investment for liquidity remained ample (Asian Development Outlook 2005, 2005: pp. 103-104). Besides, Malaysia's external debt increased only moderately to $51.9 billion, which was attributed to higher short-term borrowing by the banking sector. This was due, in large part, to hedging activities for trade-related transactions and treasury activities. The share of short-term debt to total, overall debt remained low at 21.8 percent and given the prudent debt management policy, Malaysia's share of external debt improved from 50.2 percent in

2003 to 46.6 percent in 2004 (Bank Negara Malaysia Annual Report 2004, 2005: p. 5). In 2005, total outstanding government debt went down further to 46.2 percent (Asian Development Outlook 2006, 2006: p. 209). Meanwhile, as Table 4.2 shows, the debt servicing ratio improved from 6.2 percent in 2003 to 4.3 percent a year later.

Going back to the inflation rate, briefly, it must be pointed out that the rate in 2004, which was an average of 1.4 percent over the year, was the lowest in Southeast Asia. Price controls and fuel subsidies constrained the inflation rate despite costs pressures reflected in higher food prices and transport charges (Asian Development Outlook 2005, 2005: p. 104). The ringgit remained pegged to the U.S. dollar with the historically low interest rates. Moreover, due to the aggressive sterilization operations by Bank Negara Malaysia (to deal with the upsurge in reserves especially foreign ones due to investment inflows), the rise of monetary aggregates, M3, grew by 12.4 percent in December, 2004, which was sustained at a level consistent with the pace of real economic activity (Asian Development Outlook 2005, 2005: p. 104). The interest rate edged-up to 3.0 percent in 2005, largely due to a series of fiscal policy decisions such as reductions in fuel subsidies, higher duties on cigarettes and liquor, and increased highway toll charges (Asian Development Outlook 2006, 2006: p. 208).

In 2002, bank lending to the business sector as well as to consumers improved, thanks to the government's flexible fiscal policies. Major recipients of loans were manufacturing, SMEs, wholesale and retail trade, insurance, and construction. This, at least in part, led to the improvement of the banking sector as a whole. The NPL ratio, which remains on a 6-month classification basis, fell to about 7 percent (Asian Development Outlook 2003, 2003: p. 79). In addition, given the lower-than-expected economic performance, coupled by excess capacity, the CPI rose by merely 1.8 percent, irrespective of Malaysia's accommodative monetary stance. Two years later, with monetary conditions remaining accommodative for the seventh straight year in 2004, the asset quality of the banking system continued to improve, with the slowdown of new NPLs as well as better loan recovery and bad debt write-offs (Asian Development Outlook 2005, 2005: p. 104). In addition, the widening loan base brought down the net NPL ratio of the banking system, based on 6-month arrears, to 5.9 percent, which happened to be the lowest level since the 1997-1998 Asian Financial Crisis. This was influenced in part by the banking institutions' risk-weighted capital ratio at roughly 13.7 percent, which was considerably higher than the Basle minimal requirement of 8 percent (Asian Development Outlook 2003, 2003: p. 79).[18]

4. Macroeconomic Policy Developments

The foci of the Malaysian government are essentially twofold. The first focus is to maintain stability and improving the risk-bearing capacity of the economy in the midst of Malaysia's shift to a more market-driven approach to interest rate determination. The stable macroeconomic conditions allowed the Bank Negara Malaysia to introduce the New Interest Rate Framework on April 26th, 2004, which represented a change in implementing its mechanism for monetary policy. That change was instituted for the sake of strengthening the monetary policy transmission mechanism and promoting more efficient pricing by the financial system. The Overnight Policy Rate (OPR) is designed as both a signaling device to indicate monetary policy stance and a target rate for the central bank's daily liquidity operations (Bank Negara Malaysia Annual Report 2004, 2005: p. 6). To reflect the stable monetary stance, the OPR was set at the prevailing overnight rate of 2.7 percent but with enough flexibility to move within a corridor of +/- 25 basis points supported by a standing facility. Changes in the OPR would be announced through the monetary policy statements which are issued at least four times a year alongside the quarterly GDP announcements (Bank Negara Malaysia Annual Report 2004, 2005: p. 6). What the Bank also did was to develop the Institutional Securities Custodian Programme (or ISCAP). The effort was done as soon as the Bank began to use repo endeavors as part of its monetary policy instruments to manage liquidity in the banking system, for preventing an excessive buildup in liquidity remains a key challenge for the Bank. ISCAP was implemented to enable lending of securities as well as to improve the supply of instruments to undertake repo operations. The importance of repos rests in the fact that they enhance the overall functioning of the bond market (Bank Negara Malaysia Annual Report 2004, 2005: p. 6).

The second focus, not so unrelated to the first one, is to continue to provide infrastructure and an enabling environment for businesses to compete globally (Asian Development Outlook 2005, 2005: p. 104). This focus involves formulating a reform agenda to deal with corruption, improving the delivery of government services, improving overall efficiency while reducing red tape, as well as lowering the cost of doing business (such as, for example, simplifying reporting requirement for exporters to reduce administrative costs). In addition, efforts are being made to limit broader fiscal risks by reforming the government-linked corporations (GLCs). Although the government was involved in huge, prestige projects in the past, the new administration is turning its attention, and increasingly so, to smaller projects that have a greater multiplier effect. The administration is likewise putting greater emphasis on diversifying sources of growth into sectors such as services and agriculture (Asian Development Outlook 2005, 2005: p. 104).

In regards to the exchange rate, there is little pressure on the ringgit peg, suggesting that Malaysia continues to enjoy strong economic fundamentals, marginal misalignment against regional currencies, and the narrowing of the interest-rate differentials between interest rates of the United States and Malaysia (Asian Development Outlook 2005, 2005: pp. 104-105). This condition remains favorable especially since the global foreign exchange markets continue to be volatile and cut-throat. However, there's a growing consensus that a basket peg may be a better option for Malaysia and other countries in Southeast Asia and beyond. As the authors of the Asian Development Outlook argue, a basket peg offers greater flexibility should serious exchange rate corrections occur. John Williamson, Senior Fellow of the Institute for International Economics (based in Washington, DC) took the argument further in his paper "The Case for a Common Basket Peg for East Asian Currencies" in asserting that by shifting to a basket (or common) peg, the exchange rate will not be affected and the exchange rate corrections will not have any serious impact on a country's balance of payments performance, inflation, or even output should major variations in the exchange rates among industrialized countries occur. The destabilizing impacts will be at the very least, minimum, while a country like Malaysia could manage excess liquidity with greater ease (Williamson, 1996: pp. 1-13). In 2005, two key changes in monetary policy were made. The first change entailed the adoption of a managed currency float against a basket of currencies in July, which ended the peg of the ringgit against the U.S. dollar. The second change involved the government's decision to raise the interest rate, the first of such a move in seven years (Asian Development Outlook 2006, 2006: pp. 208-209).

With the banking sector that has recovered from the Asian Financial Crisis of 1997-1998, Danamodal, the agency established with the sole purpose of recapitalizing the financial institutions during the Crisis, was closed in early 2004. The closure came two years after the adjournment of the Corporate Debt Restructuring Committee, which was created to help corporate debt resolution (Asian Development Outlook 2005, 2005: p. 105). Furthermore, Danaharta, Malaysia's national asset management agency, closed in 2005. Its final report was prepared on September 30th of that year.

Malaysia is taking steps in opening up its financial services to foreign participation, such as, for instance, the acquisition by Temasek Holdings, Singapore's state-owned investment company, of a substantial stake in Alliance Bank. Going further in establishing greater bi-lateral trade and economic cooperation, the Malaysia and Singapore securities exchanges agreed to jointly develop a cross-trading link, which will increase both liquidity as well as access to capital (Asian Development Outlook 2005, 2005: p. 105). Furthermore, legislation was amended to allow mergers of commercial banks and finance companies within the same banking group in order to improve operational efficiencies, such as enhancing the safety of regulatory delivery and payment systems. With the introduction of the Financial Process Exchange (an internet-based payment system), the ultimate goal is to combat fraud and raise consumer confidence (Bank Negara Malaysia Annual Report 2004, 2005: p. 8).

With the goal of improving efficiency and profitability in mind, the Malaysian government placed GLCs under the oversight of Khazanah, the government's investment corporation. Khazanah will in turn revamp the GLC's operations in order to make them into market-driven entities through changes in board and management as well as introducing key performing indicators such as fixed-term contracts and performance-related compensation for management. Even though privatization have slowed, the reforms of the GLCs are likely good enough indicators as to where Malaysia is going as a force in the global market (Bank Negara Malaysia Annual Report 2004, 2005: p. 8).

C. Malaysia: An Exigent Look Towards a Challenging Tomorrow

1. An Historic Change in Leadership

An historic change in leadership occurred on October 31st, 2003. Dr. Mahathir Mohammed, who was Asia's longest-serving leader of twenty-two years, stepped down on that historic day and peacefully handed power to his hand-picked successor, Abdullah Badawi (Perlez, 2003: pp. 1-3). Better known on the international stage for his crude outburst, especially against the Jews, Dr. Mahathir is hugely credited for transforming his country into a major economic force in the world. Malaysia, once a disparate ethnic mix of a Malay majority and a Chinese and Indian minorities as well as a nation economically dependent on tin, rubber, and palm oil, became an unified major trading nation in Southeast Asia and the exporter of most of the world's Dell laptop computers and Intel high-end processors under Dr. Mahathir's leadership. It has been, as Joseph Stiglitz states, "a remarkable transformation" (Perlez, 2003: pp. 1-3).

2. The Challenges Facing Abdullah Badawi's Current Leadership

Among the new challenges facing Malaysia per se are: 1) the issues of protectionism, 2) its fiscal balancing, 3) continued handling of fiscal consolidation without slowing the economy down too abruptly, 4) economic growths of both China and India, which continue to effect East Asia and which influence the levels of FDI and portfolio inflows not only to Malaysia, but to the Southeast Asian region as a whole, and 5) the employment picture. Most manufacturers and services are oriented toward the domestic market, which means that many of them still require protection from international competition. Furthermore, a few domestically owned and controlled became successful exporters of manufactures and a few services (Perkins and Woo, 2000: p. 250). Since the Malaysian domestic market is not particularly large, firms, whose growth is based solely on that market, will not be able to take advantage of many economies of scale. On the other hand, should Malaysia continue to enjoy GDP growth, many of these import-substituting firms will have to become exporters of goods and services (Perkins and Woo, 2000: pp. 250-251).

In addition, *lack of business opportunities*, caused in part by the dominance of state enterprises in several sectors (like telecommunications), and, for some firms, limited access to capital due to rough collateral requirements and frail balance sheets, are main concerns for the officials as well. These are the factors that are curtailing investment. Also, although foreign participation is increasingly being allowed in parts of the services sector, significant barriers are still in place and the level of market access is subject to conditions. For instance, to practice law or accounting in Malaysia, one must either be a Malaysian citizen or its permanent resident and must pass a Malay-language exam (unless exempted) (Asian Development Outlook 2006, 2006: pp. 209 and 211). Opening up to foreign competition even further will encourage innovation, investment in new technology, and enhanced protection of intellectual property rights (Asian Development Outlook 2006, 2006: p. 212).

Another challenge involves its' natural resource base and ownership restructuring as well as income distribution. As of the year 2000, Malaysia's natural resources were a steadily declining share of GDP, or exports, and of government revenue. As far as ownership restructuring and income distribution are concern, Malaysia's internationally competitive manufacturing sectors are exempt from ownership requirements and are being dominated by direct foreign investors. Meanwhile local firms have started by concentrating on the domestic market. While some have grown and prospered under the requirements of laws such as the Industrial Coordination Act (ICA), fewer firm managed to grow beyond domestic borders.[19] Furthermore, Malaysia should cease its reliance on state ownership to further implement social objectives (Perkins and Woo, 2000: p. 251).

Malaysia, according to Perkins and Woo, should also relax the ownership restrictions of the ICA to enable the needed recapitalization of the banks and large firms. The United Malay National Organization (UMNO), the bumiputra led by Dr. Mahathir and the one which has traditionally dominated the ruling coalition and Parliament, should commit itself to the permanence of the ICA reforms should the troubled firms succeed in issuing new shares. The ICA reforms will yield an additional benefit: small and medium businesses owned by non-bumiputras would be encouraged to shift from import-substitution to export-oriented strategies (Perkins and Woo, 2000: p. 252).

Malaysia should continue to work on state industrial policies to include expiration dates for state subsidies and import protection as well as instituting a weeding-out process within its infant industry program in order to prevent high-cost inputs from undermining international competitiveness. This method, according to Perkins and Woo, will help protected firms to concentrate on improving productivity (Perkins and Woo, 2000: p. 253). Malaysia had taken an important step in that regard through the establishment of the National SME Development Council in 2004, courtesy of Bank Negara Malaysia. The Council represents the highest policy-making body that will chart the future direction and strategies of SME development in Malaysia, including improving SMEs financing, human resources development, training, as well as management (Bank Negara Malaysia Annual Report 2004, 2005: p. 4).

As far as finances are concerned, Malaysia's debt had risen to 47.2 percent of GDP at the end of 2002. The Government should be able to rationalize fiscal expenditures and augment tax revenue collection proceedings in order to reduce and manage the debt (Asian Development Outlook 2003, 2003: p. 80). Furthermore, Malaysia will continue with its efforts to restore market and investor confidence, as made indicative by the new stimulus package. As mentioned by the Malaysian Ministry of Finance in its nineteen-page report, the Malaysia's Package of New Strategies, passed in May of 2003, will do much to strengthen Malaysia's economic fundamentals that will ensure more sustainable growth in both the medium and long-term (ADO 2003, 2003: p. 80).

That Package, which by itself is quite far-reaching, includes initiatives aimed at raising government expenditures on infrastructural projects, promoting private investment (including FDI), developing SMEs so as improve their catalytic role in generating domestic investment, cleaning up lending practices, improving the nation's competitiveness and delivery systems, and developing new sources of growth (Asian Development Outlook 2003, 2003: p. 80). In the development of new sources of growth, Malaysia is seeking ways to become less dependent on external forces and engage in diversifying its new sources of growth in areas of construction, services, agriculture, and manufacturing. That idea, as with the Package itself, came about in the wake of a growing regional and global influence of China, among the major challenges facing Mr. Abdullah and his government. While China is recognized as a major source of growth and commerce in East Asia, Malaysia, as with other countries in Southeast Asia, is becoming concerned that China is attracting the most FDI in that region.

There are other concerns as well, though with Malaysia's strong economic fundamentals, these concerns are relatively less severe in comparison. SARS, the avian flu, fuel prices, and the geopolitical matters (the Iraqi War, the Middle East Crisis, and the lingering uncertainty in the global economic recovery) will continue to affect Malaysia's economy, let alone its trading performance. While Malaysia, being a net exporter of oil, continues to benefit from higher global oil prices, its trade-dependent economy is also vulnerable to secondary effects should those higher prices erode global economic growth (Asian Development Outlook 2006, 2006: p. 209). The government in 2005 provided RM 7.4 billion in direct subsidies for fuel consumption and tax exemptions on fuel cost an additional RM 7.9 billion in forgone revenues. This was offset by higher petroleum income tax receipts and royalty payments. According to the Asian Development Outlook report of 2006, as subsidies become phased down, Malaysia's fiscal posture will be made stronger (ADO 2006, 2006: p. 209). By achieving the GDP growth of 7.1 percent in 2004, Malaysia witnessed, according to the Malaysian Institute of Economic Research (MIER), marked improvements in its major economic indicators. Both exports and industrial production are growing at double-digit rates while export revenues improved due to an upswing in the electronics sector as well as higher commodity prices (MIER, 2004: p. 1). However, although the overall employment picture continues to improve, Malaysia needs to address perplexing and disturbing issues such as an estimated 450,000 illegal overseas workers, which continue to prompt concerns about potential labor shortages in plantations, building sites, and in factories. Furthermore, college and university graduates are still having trouble finding jobs, let alone careers. Therefore, as part of a long-term strategy, the educational system must be reformed to correct labor demand-supply mismatches especially among graduates (Asian Development Outlook 2005, 2005: p. 106).[20]

Even more so, the effectiveness of education and training systems in producing the skills and the expertise needed to assure the transition to a more technology-oriented and innovative economy must be looked upon also. Malaysia's enrollment performance in tertiary education is not in par with that in some newly industrialized countries. Schools in Malaysia, as in many other developing countries, tend to emphasize role learning, excessive pressure to pass exams, and uniformity rather than creativity, risk-taking, entrepreneurship, and adaptability, the attributes needed for an economy becoming more technologically oriented (Asian Development Outlook 2006, 2006: p. 212). Such a transition also requires the strengthening of language skills in English, and the government has already taken steps in that regard by, for instance, making mandatory for primary schools to teach mathematics and science using the universal language (ADO 2006, 2006: p. 212).

With a general improvement in the stock market, the recovery of private investment as of 2004 seems to be ongoing, albeit slowly and unevenly so. This rebound was due to both the pick up in domestic demand as well as a more conducive environment of accommodative monetary policy and fiscal expansion (Asian Development Outlook 2005, 2005: p. 106). As Japan and Europe are stabilizing to a steadier growth while China eases to a more modest growth to avoid overheating, Malaysia's hands-on approach in improving the overall economy and investment climate will more likely than not yield to consistent economic growth in 2007 and beyond. Indeed, Abdullah Badawi's administration's persistent fight against corruption and poverty (especially in rural areas) adds to the general goal for economic sustainability. The fight alone is a positive enough of an image Malaysia needs to continue to attract investments among foreigners and domestic residents, business and otherwise.

V.
Notes

1. In fact, agriculture attained 86 percent of the Plan's target, communications 82 percent, Public works, plant, and equipment 181 percent, transport 93 percent, utilities 111 percent, and commerce and industry, 77 percent (Cho, 1990: p. 54).
2. The pioneer firms were mainly new import-substituting manufacturing firms.
3. Although the Malaysian government began to promote export-oriented industrialization, it made no significant attempt to either reduce or remove the incentives provided during its active promotion of Import-substituting industrialization (Gomez & Jomo, 1999: pp. 15-16).
4. It must be noted, however, that domestic companies had fewer opportunities to benefit from the export-orientated industrialization than from the import-substitution industrialization (Gomez & Jomo, 1999: p. 18).
5. The weakness in the Third Malaysian Plan was that it placed a lesser emphasis on land development, deemed to be the key in combating poverty (Cho, 1990: p. 75).
6. Although there is no practice in consensus decision making in Japanese subsidiaries. Therefore, the sense of hierarchy is made more apparent relative to that of Japanese owned firms in Japan and abroad.
7. Fossil fuels and raw materials constituted 62 percent of Japan's total imports from Malaysia in 1993 (Lim Hua Sing, 1999: p. 28).
8. The Fourth Malaysian Plan (1981-1985) was an industrial strategy shifting Malaysia's industries from labor-intensive to capital-intensive, with emphasis of the development of heavy industrial projects (Lim Hua Sing, 1999: pp. 15 and 30).
9. The opposite was true in the case of Singapore as explained previously. Also, Japanese FDI in the branch offices and real estate in Malaysia has totally been negligible as compared to the Japanese FDI in Singapore in those service sectors (Lim Hua Sing, 1999: p. 37).
10. The NIEs included Korea, Taiwan, Hong Kong, and Singapore. Before becoming a second tier NIE, Malaysia was part of ASEAN which comprised of Thailand, Indonesia, and the Philippines.
1 'he ringgit was at 4.88 per dollar by January 7th of 1998 when the ringgit devalued against the dollar by roughly 50 percent (Athukorala, 1999: p. 29).
12. In comparison, the currencies of both Thailand and Korea showed signs of stabilizing at higher levels from March of 1998 and onwards (Athukorala, 1999: p. 29).
13. The property sector comprises of real estate, construction, and share trading.
14. Although Malaysia's hands-on policies were instrumental in shielding it from the severity of the Asian Financial Crisis of 1997-1998.
15. The debt service ratio (DSR) is an estimate of the ratio of debt payments to disposable personal income.
16. The top three FDI applicants for manufacturing projects during the period, based on investment value, were Germany, the United Kingdom, and the United States (Asian Development Outlook 2003, 2003: p. 79).
17. The inflows of FDI in 2004 were channelled mainly into services, manufacturing, as well as oil and gas sectors (Bank Negara Malaysia Annual Report 2004, 2005: p. 4).

18. The Basle minimal requirement of 8% was established in 1988 with the introduction of the Basle Accord. The Basle Accord, formulated by the Basle Committee on Bank Supervision (which is part of the Bank of International Settlement or BIS based in Basel, Switzerland), had two goals. The first goal was to improve the overall stability and soundness of the international banking system by encouraging banking organizations to boost their capital position. The second goal was to reduce competitive inequalities. The impact and successfulness of the Accord is still debatable (Basle Committee on Bank Supervision Working Papers, 1999: pp. 1-10).
19. The Industrial Coordination Act (ICA) was introduced by the government in 1995 to accelerate the rise of bumiputra ownership. The ICA required that all enterprises with equity over a certain limit must sell 30 percent of their shares to bumiputras. There was an important loophole however. Firms that exported over 80 percent of their output were not subject to the bumiputra ownership requirement (Perkins and Woo, 2000: p. 233).
20. In fact, the problem is quite as pervasive even in the West, such as, for examples, in France and in the United States.

Chapter Five
Thailand: From Economic Growth to and Beyond The Initial Point of the Domino Effect of Currency Devaluations

I.
Thailand's Sound Economy in the Pre-1997 Crisis

A. Introduction

Although Thailand's economy began to slow down during 1996, its GDP continued to grow at 6.4 percent per year until that point. While Thailand's investment ratio was at 41.7 percent, the rate of inflation was 5.6 percent. Output in the manufacturing sector increased by 7.3 percent while at the same time, output in construction rose by 8 percent. In February of 1996, the Bangkok stock market index was 1,400 points, an increase of 200 points since November of 1995 (Tan, 2000: pp. 60-61). But, there were various factors which led to Thailand's economic crisis of unprecedented severity, all of which will be explained later.

B. Explaining Thailand's Economic Growth and Sustainability

1. Import Substitution Industrialization and Efforts for Industrial and Economic Efficiency

Field Marshall Sarit Thanarat, who came to power in 1958, was instrumental in Thailand's economic growth. Although Sarit had no clear economic policies of his own, he realized the need to give control of macroeconomic agencies to technocrats who were allowed considerable leeway in policy making. It was this strategy that not only helped Sarit remained in power by undercutting his opponents, but it also created conditions crucial for Thailand's economic growth. Officials such as Dr. Puey Ungphakorn used this power to "promote macroeconomic stability and to gain control over the budgetary process" (Doner and Ramsay, 1999: p. 172).

Investors at first doubted that Thailand would be an economic success it eventually turned out to be. This was because Sarit ruled dictatorially for the next six years (Neher, 1991: p. 25). Furthermore, the industrial, commerce, and agricultural sectors remained heavily politicized and were used for patronage purposes (otherwise known as nepotism). However, as Doner and Ramsey state, "the implicit agreement between technocrats would not encroach on the sectoral and microeconomic mismanagement which benefits the political masters, while the latter would not allow the technocrats to keep control over the macroeconomy" (Doner and Ramsay, 1999: p. 172). Furthermore, Thailand's efforts in attracting new investors and clients were expanded, particularly due to its decision not to restrict new opportunities for entrepreneurs (as will be seen throughout this chapter).

Thailand's efforts in creating an economic environment for profitable private investment came in two aspects. *The first aspect* was microeconomic stability marked by low inflation rates, realistic exchange rates, cautious fiscal policies, and hard budget constraints for private enterprises. *The second aspect* was ensuring ethnic Chinese entrepreneurs that their property would not be confiscated (Doner and Ramsay, 1999: p. 173).[1] Entrepreneurs themselves could protect their property rights in two ways. *One way* in doing so was by finding patrons in the military and upper reaches of the civilian bureaucracy. Officials realized that by protecting entrepreneurs rather than "squeezing them dry," they themselves can reap profits and benefits from such connections such as protection should they lose out of the political struggles. *The other way* in protecting property rights was by creating joint ventures with foreign firms doing business with Thailand. Although they became less dependent upon patronage for protection and growth as they grew in size, such protection was critical in the early years of industrial and commercial growth (Doner and Ramsay, 1999: p. 173).

Sarat's penchant for efficiency, as exemplified by the institutional arrangements made after he came to power in 1958, created an atmosphere where economic growth and sustainability were even more possible. Firms, in particular, placed a heavy emphasis on efficiency by: 1) refusing to use state funds to bail out firms that got into predicaments, and 2) discouraging the creation of monopolies even though competitive clientelism was encouraging competition (Doner and Ramsay, 1999: p. 173). Competition, rather than creating monopolies, was encouraged because competition among patrons in the state elite, eager to obtain extra-bureaucratic funds, helped to facilitate a constant flow of new private sector entrants into markets. This was because intra-elite rivalries insured that aspiring entrepreneurs could always find patrons. As Doner and Ramsay further state, "Patrons in a range of agencies could satisfy particular groups of supporters because powers to grant licenses and permits were scattered throughout the bureaucracy. Five departments in three ministries influenced access to industrial permits and licenses" (Doner and Ramsay, 1999: p. 173). Consequently, firms prohibited from expanding due to excess capacity by the Industry Ministry, were able to expand under the incentives of the Board of Investment (BoI). Firms that believed at first that they could gain privileged market positions through the BoI's measures found themselves competing with firms supported by officials of other ministries (Doner and Ramsay, 1999: p. 173).

The Board of Investment was established in order for it to grant a wide range of incentives for investing in Thailand. For example, the BoI were bestowed: 1) the authority to guarantee the investors that the government would not nationalized a promoted firm or undertake any new activity that would compete with such a firm, and 2) the power to grant firms with a wide range of tax and tariff exemptions to encourage investment (Doner and Ramsay, 1999: p. 174). These incentives paved a way to a rapid growth of ISI in the 1960s.

2. Onto the Path of Export-Oriented Industrialization: Post 1970s

By the early 1970s, Thailand began to experience balance of payment problems caused by ISI and declining prices for raw material exports. In response to these macroeconomic problems, the BoI began to offer a series of export incentives to firms, such as rebates on import taxes, bonded warehouses, streamlined customs procedures, tax and tariff exemptions, and cuts in electricity costs. These incentives, which exemplified Thailand's shift towards export promotion, were made notwithstanding the rise of overall tariff levels during the 1970s onto the 1980s. For instance, the effective tariff rates rose from 30 percent in the 1970s to 52 percent in 1985 (Doner and Ramsay, 1999: p. 174).[2]

Notwithstanding the continued desires for protectionist trade incentives, exports for Thailand grew at a rapid pace due to the following reasons. *First,* producers of low-wage manufactured goods faced overcapacity in the 1970s and the 1980s because of: 1) the aggressive promotion of the BoI, 2) the smuggling of certain products, especially electronics, and 3) the Thai government's inability in impede new entrants (Doner and Ramsay, 1999: p. 174). As a result, the shift of comparative advantage went in favor towards firms producing labor-intensive products. What made Thailand more favorable to produce labor-intensive products was the rise of currencies of the Asian NICs, which made demands for these products too costly for these NICs to handle. Furthermore, the devaluation of the baht along with the rise of other major currencies after the Plaza Accords in 1985, gave Thailand's exports a major cost advantage over several other Asian exporters. *Second,* the tax incentive packages of the BoI, combined with low labor costs, made them highly attractive for MNCs such as Data General, Minibea, and Seagate to establish and carry out productions in that country (Doner and Ramsay, 1999: p. 174).

The *third and final* reason for the rise of Thailand's exports, other than the commitment to free-market discussed above, rested in Thailand's sagacious economic policies and institutional arrangements. Export-driven policies were carried out by highly trained and generally conservative technocrats. In comparisons to the officials in earlier periods and in neighboring countries, these new officials avoided the personal, clientele-oriented policies. They, instead, had carefully screened pending development projects to ensure that they will contribute to the overall economic growth (Neher, 1991: p. 40). Furthermore, the Thai state and private institutions possessed the capacities to resolve numerous collective action problems which accompanied the growth of industrial exports, such as sugar, rice, garments, textiles, tourism, and automobile parts.[3] For instance, the Board of Trade and the Ministry of Commerce, aided rice exporters by working collectively to set prices, share quotas, share risks, and maintaining rice export quality (Doner and Ramsay, 1999: p. 175). Budget allocations centered in Bangkok coincided with the resolutions of collective action problems. For example, the Bank of Bangkok helped to shift resources from agriculture to industry as the largest provider of credit to textile firms, while it served as a key player in linking firms with newly trained engineers (Doner and Ramsay, 1999: p. 175). However, collective action efforts were not without one important weakness: these efforts failed to devote more attention and resources to technological upgrading. Thailand had an over-reliance on cheap labor in industries such as garments and toys as well as foreign investment in industries of higher-valued products such as hard disk drives for its exports while allowing most domestic-oriented producers to enjoy the fruits of protection (Doner and Ramsay, 1999: p. 175).

3. Thailand's Economic Performance and Competitiveness after 1980: The Steps Thailand took for Economic Success and Ultimate Economic Failures

Before the 1990s, Thailand's financial system was highly regulated and well protected from both domestic and foreign competitions (Arphasil, 2001: p. 167). Its ability to sustain high economic growth in the past was due in part to its strong economic fundamentals, such as maintaining expansive foreign reserves, minimal or no foreign debt, current account surpluses, relatively strong banking systems, as well as sound and fiscal policies.[4] As you will see in Table 5.1, the macroeconomic indicators demonstrate the reasons why Thailand engaged in the series of financial deregulation and liberalization efforts.[5]

Due to Thailand's industrial and economic policies, coupled with its strong indicators, its exports grew up to the rate of 24.8 percent by 1995. However, by 1996, exports decreased to minus 1.9 percent due to the following reasons. *First*, as in the case of much of the Pacific-rim region, the global demand for electronic products decreased, as world trade slowed (Doner and Ramsay, 1999: p. 176). *Secondly,* Thailand experienced the appreciation of the baht as well as high domestic inflation and interest rates. *Lastly,* Thailand saw increased wages in the labor intensive industries, many of which were the most successful in exportation. These real wages increased by 70 percent, which in turn constituted the loss of competitiveness in the labor intensive export oriented industries of other countries of the region (Doner and Ramsay, 1999: p. 176). This kind of industry has been the basis for much of Thailand's growth since the 1970s.[6]

In addition to the aforementioned loss of competitiveness in the labor intensive export oriented industries, Thailand lacked the kind of import-competing coalition enjoyed by much of Latin America. This was due to the involvement of large banks in the export of raw materials and low-wage products (Doner and Ramsay, 1999: p. 176). *However, as you shall see, there were other factors that contributed to Thailand's weakness in higher valued products.*

Table 5.1
Thailand's Financial Indicators, 1985-1997

The Indicators	1985	1990	1995	1996	1997	1998
GDP Growth Rate	4.6	11.2	8.8	5.5	-0.4	-8.0
Inflation Rate	2.4	6.0	5.8	5.9	5.6	8.0
Current Account (% of GDP)	-4.0	-8.3	-7.8	-7.9	-2.9	11.0
Investment (% of GDP)	28.2	41.4	41.6	41.7	N/A	N/A
Savings (% of GDP)	24.4	33.0	34.9	33.2	N/A	N/A
Exports (% change)	10.5	15.1	24.8	-1.9	3.8	-3.1
Imports (% change)	4.6	29.8	31.9	0.6	-13.4	32.4
Balance of Payments (in US$)	0.5	3.8	7.2	2.2	-10.6	1.7
Foreign Exchange Reserve (in US$)	3.0	14.3	37.0	38.7	27.0	28.5
Fiscal Balance (in baht millions)	-38,978	107,046	134,965	34,118	-26,707	N/A
Exchange Rate (baht/$)	27.16	25.59	24.92	25.34	31.37	41.37

Source: Arphasil, Prakarn "Financial Liberalization and Financial Crisis: The Case of Thailand." *Financial Big Bang in Asia.* Masayoshi Tsurumi, editor. Singapore: Ashgate, 2001: p. 168.

The first reason was that the Finance Ministry, which contributed to Thailand's rapid growth from 1960 through 1995 and which proved to be especially important for industrial upgrading (as designer of the country's tariff policies), showed very little knowledge of, or interests in, particular industrial sectors (Doner and Ramsay, 1999: pp. 178-179). The Ministry was instrumental in insulating itself from rent seeking and politicization that has plagued other less developed countries. However, the Ministry of Finance did very little to offset the significant rise of import tariffs in the 1970s and the 1980s, despite years of strong opposition by firms which benefited from the lowered tariffs and their supporters in the Ministry of Industry and Commerce (Doner and Ramsay, 1999: p. 178-179). It was not until the early 1990s when the Ministry decided to lower the import tariffs when Thailand began to enjoy substantial budget surpluses. However, a cascading the tariff structure as well as the business tax system that encourage vertical integration rather than growth of local suppliers offset the Ministry's move and undermined any attempts to link local firms with firms that had greater experiences not only in producing higher-valued goods, but also in exporting those goods into the global market.[7] Furthermore, the Board of Investment (BoI) granted temporary measures such as surcharges. On the debit side, however, the BoI has led the way in providing a wide range of countervailing export incentives (Doner and Ramsay, 1999: p. 178-179).

The second reason for Thailand's weakness in higher valued products lied in the BoI. In a regime that was labeled "export-oriented protectionism," the BoI proved instrumental in simply grafting export-oriented measures on to continued protection for local firms producing for Thailand's domestic market. But, the BoI lacked sufficient knowledge about particular industries. Moreover, there were almost no incentives to engage in technological transfers from foreign investors to local firms. Instead, the trade liberalization prompted final assemblers to demand similar reductions in tariffs for raw materials and immediate inputs. The result was series of conflicts over tariffs, price making, and price control between upstream and downstream firms (Doner and Ramsay, 1999: p. 178-179).

The third reason for Thailand's weakness in higher valued products lies in the above-mentioned factors. These factors led to the complexities in establishing public or collective institutions to resolve collective action problems and to promote technological transfer and diffusion of technical knowledge (Doner and Ramsay, 1999: p. 179). However, Thailand's dualistic production structures added further murkiness to Thailand's overall economic picture despite the initial success story since the 1970s. While the country is credited to have a relatively deep base of supporting industries in metalworking, plastic parts, tool and die production, and electrical and electronics components, these industries lacked the linkages to the dynamic exporting sectors, especially in higher value-added products (Doner and Ramsay, 1999: p. 180). Consequently, these weaknesses made it difficult for Thailand to move to higher value-added production while the labor-intensive exports became increasingly vulnerable to competition from other countries, including China and India (Doner and Ramsay, 1999: p. 181). This vulnerability, along with the decrease in global trade in 1996, appreciation of the baht, and the resulting high domestic inflation rates, contributed to the slowdown of Thailand's rapid economic growth in 1996 (Doner and Ramsay, 1999: p. 181). However, as you shall see in the next section and beyond, there were other factors leading up to Thailand's financial and economic crisis beginning in July 2nd, 1997.

II.
The Origins of Thailand's Financial Crisis

A. Thailand's Political Inefficiencies and Fragmentation

Economic governance in Thailand did not decline with democratization; rather, its constitutional and electoral system produced serious problems for political leadership and policy-making. The political leadership in Thailand was seriously plagued with deepening indecisiveness resulted from the fragmentation of the political system and the tendency towards weak coalition governments. With parliamentary majorities constructed of half a dozen parties, each with internal weaknesses, the problems of cabinet instabilities became chronic (Haggard and MacIntyre, 2000: pp. 61-62). Meanwhile, the prime minister was proned to vulnerability due to policy blackmail by coalition partners "threatening to defect in pursuit of better deals in another alliance configuration; indeed, all democratically elected governments except the Chatichai government, which fell to a military coup, met their end in this fashion" (Haggard and MacIntyre, 2000: p. 62).

Thailand's combination of a parliamentary and a multi-member electoral system was the institutional root of these problems discussed above.[8] Thailand multi-member electoral system strongly encouraged candidates to campaign on the basis of individualized strategies, not on the basis of the party-based electoral strategies.[9] Consequently, not only did this practice create political parties with ill-discipline, but it also ensured that politicians strove to deliver selective benefits to voters in their electorate in order to differentiate themselves from their rivals of the same party. This "encouraged vote-buying and placed a premium on politicians being able to generate a flow of cash to cover costs while on office" (Haggard and MacIntyre, 2000: p. 62).

In September of 1996, Banharn Silapa-archa's government collapsed after key coalition partners deserted him. After the election, widely deemed as Thailand's most dirtiest in its history, Chavalit Yongchaiyudh's New Aspiration Party (NAP) narrowly emerged as the largest party in the parliament. Chavalit proceeded to construct a six-party coalition comprising most of the parties from the previous government. Whereas Banharn's government was looked upon as corrupt and inept, Chavalit's administration yielded much more promise in the eyes of many. Chavalit, who had strong military links, was supported by big businesses, and had the reputation as a skillful politician. He realized that these assets could be exploited by appointing a cabinet built around an "economic dream team" of highly respected technocrats, most notably Amnuay Viruwan as Finance Minister (Haggard and MacIntyre, 2000: pp. 63-64).

Amnuay Viruwan realized the scope of the problems and tried to persuade the coalition's leaders in cabinet to move onto more extensive financial sector reforms as well as budgetary cuts. The leaders refused to cooperate, and frustrated by this standstill and with no progress towards reforms in sight, Viruwan resigned in June 19th, 1997. The leaders of the "economic dream team" lasted for no more than seven months. His attempts at major economic and financial reforms were blocked by other parties within the government. As Haggard and MacIntyre point out:

> ...with the diverse coalition and massive debts incurred by all parties in order to win office, there was little prospect of the cabinet agreeing to take tough measures that might hurt the economic interests of ministers or their financial benefactors. Even if a majority was in favor of taking action, a minority could veto the action by threatening to walk out of the coalition (Haggard and MacIntyre, 2000: p. 66).

Thanong Bidaya became the next Finance Minister after the resignation of Amnuay Viruwan. Seeking to seize the initiative, Bidaya, on June 27th, 1997, announced the suspension of sixteen finance companies, not excluding seven of the original ten, while giving them thirty days to implement merger plans. Since the central bank lost its ability to sustain the exchange rate, it was announced, on July 2nd, 1997, that the baht was being cut loose. The baht fell immediately and lost 45 percent of its previous value by the end of the year (Haggard and MacIntyre, 2000: p. 66).

Like Viruwan, Bidaya faced debilitating obstacles. Although Bidaya won approval for the initiative, Chart Pattana leaders were able to block its implementation by: 1) blocking successfully the closure or forced merger of the sixteen finance companies, and 2) persuading the central bank to continue injecting liquidity into the institutions. In the midst of negotiating with the IMF to obtain a rescue package, it was revealed in late July of 1997 that the loans to these sixteen finance companies amounted to 430 billion baht.[10] It was a scandal the government desired to distance itself from: it forced the resignation of the central bank governor Remgchai Marakanonda as well as another senior and respected official (Haggard and MacIntyre, 2000: pp. 66-67).

In order to regain the initiative and to make the necessary policy prepayment on the IMF's rescue package, Bidaya announced on August 5th, 1997 that a further forty-two finance companies would be suspended due to their massive loan problems and their imminent insolvencies.[11] These companies were given a brief period to either meet new capital adequacy rules, merge with a stronger institution, or go out of business. In an effort to stem charges of corruption and cronyism, Virabhongsa Ramangkura, a respected technocrat, was appointed as deputy prime minister, who in turn appointed Amaret Sila-on, the respected leader of the Thai Stock Exchange (Haggard and MacIntyre, 2000: p. 67).

In early October of 1997, the Association of Finance Companies acted vigorously in its efforts to court Chart Pattana leader Chatichai Choonhavan and Prime Minister Chavalit to relax the criteria for the finance companies' rehabilitation efforts. The IMF publicly expressed a desire to have the independence of Amaret Sila-on's screening committee to not be undermined. On grounds that Amaret was being undercut by forces within the government, he resigned by mid-October. Further concessions were made to Chart Pattana and the finance companies. Meanwhile, Thanong extended the deadline for their restructuring, even after he announced the creation of two new independent agencies to handle the evaluation and processing of the finance companies: both the Asset Management Corporation (AMC) and the Financial Restructuring Agency (FRA).[12] Thanong also revealed that earlier loans to these finance companies by the central bank could be treated as equity (Haggard and MacIntyre, 2000: p. 67).

Thanong's moves were costly. By extending the restructuring deadline and allowing the loans from the central bank to be treated as equity, Thanong's concessions increased the probability that the public resources injected into the finance companies would never be recovered. Furthermore, Chart Pattana succeeded in "delaying cabinet approval of the plans for the two new agencies announced by Thanong until the decrees included text that specifically reversed their independence from the government" (Haggard and MacIntyre, 2000: p. 67). Governmental disintegration proved to be even more axiomatic after Finance Minister Thanong resigned on October 19th, 1997. Prime Minister Chavalit followed suit on November 3rd of that year (Haggard and MacIntyre, 2000: pp. 67-68).

A new government under Chuan Leekpai showed signs of promise by 1998. As well as committed itself to implement the IMF program, the government forged ahead with the closure of the financial institutions and some aspects of a broader process of restructuring. Unlike the previous administrations, the new government was able to make considerable progress because: 1) there was a clear, coherent sense of national emergency, 2) the new government's status as a transitional administration in the lead-up to the introduction of the newly appointed constitution, and 3) of the domestic bargaining leverage deriving from the IMF conditionality. However, as 1998 progressed, the new government began to be plagued by the same pressures that adversely affected the administrations that preceded it (Haggard and MacIntyre, 2000: p. 68). Therefore, the combination of weak parties and weak coalitions made strong, consistent action on policy issues (such as, for instance, exchange rate management) a rarity. The series of collective policy errors, capital misallocations, and moral hazard were indeed manifestations of Thailand's weak and fragmentary political structure as well as the lack of stability of the electoral system.

B. Financial Liberalization (1990-1993): The First Policy Error

Financial liberalization began in 1990 through the gradual abolition of ceiling interest rates. During that year, Thailand accepted Article VII of the International Monetary Fund (IMF), which removed all controls on foreign exchange transactions in the current account (Doner and Ramsay, 1999: p. 183). By increasing the number of financial institutions, Thailand was able to promote competition within the financial sectors. Furthermore, in order to establish Bangkok as a financial center in the region, capital controls were relaxed.[13] The Bangkok International Banking Facility (BIBF) was created in 1993 to lure foreign funds by providing tax incentives. Commercial banks were allowed to hold net foreign assets up to 25 percent, while the maximum percentage of net foreign liabilities was raised to 20 percent (Nidhiprabha, 1999: p. 68). Furthermore, forty-two licenses were granted to Thai and foreign commercial banks which allowed them to engage in a number of foreign exchange activities. Financial institutions were able to take deposits and loans from abroad and extending loans in the form of foreign currencies to local markets. Most of the business goals generated by the BIBF were to facilitate lending by foreigners to Thai firms, with the banks in the facility acting as intermediaries (Doner and Ramsay, 1999: p. 183).

Financial liberalization, which consisted of capital account opening and an easing up in global liquidity conditions, yielded much of a promise towards Thailand's economic growth. Thailand became the recipient of large inflows of international capital for much of the 1990s and the capital inflows fed a spurt in investment that helped to underpin strong economic growth. Such a growth was coupled with a widening current account deficit and an appreciation of the real effective exchange rate (Yoshihiro Iwasaki, 1999: p. 193). Portfolio investment experienced a six-fold increase, from 23.5 billion baht in 1992 to 138 billion baht in 1993 while short-term private borrowing was augmented during that period. Furthermore, the virtually fixed exchange rate constrained monetary policy, even though some economists pointed to the potentially de-stabilizing influence on short-term inflows (Lauridsen, 1998: p. 143).

However, the Thailand's economy became immensely overheated, due particularly to an unsustainable current account deficit and rising price levels. By 1996, the lending of the BIBF to domestic sectors amounted to 1.8 times the size of the monetary base as the ratio of accumulated short-term capital inflows to international reserves was rising at a rapid pace. The economy became vulnerable and, consequently, the process of gradual financial liberalization ended in 1995. The euphoria of the BIBF just simply evaporated (Nidhiprabha, 1999: p. 69).

The Bank of Thailand concluded that the *liberalization policy was indeed premature.* Although various capital control measures were introduced in order: 1) to increase the cost of short-term borrowing and 2) to increase the proportion of long-term capital flows, the measures were *simply too late* and not enough to reverse the damage caused by capital flows rampant during the liberalization policy. Thailand was blessed with low interest rate and high economic growth in the early 1990s. However, as Nidhiprabha points out, "*sound economic fundamentals alone were not sufficient to guarantee successful liberalization*" (Nidhiprabha, 1999: p. 69). This was especially true when prudential banking regulations and supervision were not adequate to deal with increasingly complex financial transactions financial liberalization permitted.

Nidhiprabha assertion is compelling yet true. As Yoshihiro Iwasaki puts it, "lurking beneath the surface of Thailand were structural weaknesses that not only frustrated the normal adjustment process, but which ultimately proved the undoing of Thailand's financial and corporate sectors" (Iwasaki, 1999: p. 193).

An important reason why foreign capital was attracted to Thailand was that it undertook significant steps to liberalize its banking and non-banking sectors. However, Thailand *failed to pursue measures to promote supervision, corporate governance, market discipline, and financial stability with commensurate vigor* (Iwasaki, 1999: p. 193).[14]

C. Maintaining High Interest Rates: The Second Policy Error

Although attempts were made to rely on the market mechanism to determine Thailand's interest rates, the rationale behind maintaining high interest rates was to limit aggregate demand and to keep inflation low, notwithstanding the fact that monetary policy was futile with the fixed exchange rates and open capital accounts. With high domestic interest rates, Thai business could borrow foreign loans at lower costs than they could domestically. Furthermore, the forty-two BIBF license holders could borrow dollars and still make profit re-lending the dollars to local customers at lower rates than those of baht loans (Doner and Ramsay, 1999: p. 183).[15] The Bank of Thailand responded to the overheated economy be rising the interest rates in 1995. However, that effort propelled further foreign borrowing: by the end of 1996, $31.2 billion were loaned, which made up of roughly a half of total private foreign debt. Most of the loans were short-term and most were not hedged against currency fluctuations (Doner and Ramsay, 1999: p. 183).

In essence, the expansion of credits from banks and finance companies became alarmingly large, especially since these institutions were able to borrow from international markets at relatively low interest rates.[16] Furthermore, those loans were channeled to non-productive sectors such as property and assets speculation. Thailand's financial system remained weak due to fundamental mismanagement via credit concentration, maturity and currencies mismatching, as well as insider loans (Nidhiprabha, 1999: pp. 67-69). By the end of 1996, Thailand's ninety-one finance companies (twenty-five were pure finance companies and sixty-six performed both finance and securities functions) accounted for nearly 25 percent of the total credit (Haggard and MacIntyre, 2000: p. 64).

D. Pegging the Baht to a Basket of Currencies with an Overbearing Dollar: The Third Policy Error

Thailand's economy, even today, is under the fixed exchange rate, which means that the effectiveness of the monetary policy is limited as long as capital mobility is perfect. Before July of 1997, the Bank of Thailand adhered at the fixation of the baht via a basket of currencies in which the U.S. dollar had a weight of more than 80 percent. However, that policy decision came with a huge price. As the dollar value rose in the mid-1990s, Thai exports became less competitive which contributed to export difficulties that plagued the country. Also, this policy led borrowers to assume that the Thai government would never leave them holding a bag under devaluation pressure. As Baopichitr Kirida states:

> Local firms thought they could safely borrow dollars, convert them into baht, and then pay off debts at the same exchange rate at which they had borrowed them. Foreign investors believed they could invest in the Thai stock market or in government bonds with the assurance that their investments could be changed into baht and back into dollars with little or no risk (Doner and Ramsay, 1999: pp. 183-184).

E. Capital Misallocations and Moral Hazard: The Fourth Policy Error

It was axiomatic that the usage of much of the capital which came into Thailand was anything but productive. In fact, much of the inflow of capital went into real estate and low-yielding commercial and industrial projects. Incremental output to capital ratio of Thailand's firms decreased from 0.5 in mid-1987 to 0.25 in 1996. Furthermore, the return on assets of all non-financial companies listed on the Thai stock market dropped from 7.5 percent in 1991 to 2.3 percent in 1996 (Doner and Ramsay, 1999: p. 184).

There are three reasons why capital misallocation took place in Thailand's economy. *First,* capital flowed into real estate because real estate could be used as collateral for bank loans (and financial institutions were more than ready to provide loans when land or real estate was put up as collateral). Most businesses remain family-owned and depended heavily upon bank borrowing for the capital needed to expand. Characteristically, the amount of loans provided was fewer in value than that of the collaterals. However, Thailand experienced its economic boom between 1988 and 1995, which meant that as land prices rose significantly, the investment in land and real estate paid off additionally in terms of the capacity to float more debt. Part of the increased debt was used to purchase more land, which caused prices to increase further (Doner and Ramsay, 1999: p. 184). In early 1997, one of the largest property developers, Samprasong Land, defaulted on interest payments on $3.1 billion foreign loan. Bangkok Land, another leading property firm, accumulated 33.5 billion baht in liabilities and 19.8 billion baht on an equity base (Tan, 2000: p. 65).

Secondly, the prolonged economic boom and large inflows of foreign funds played a huge part in inflation, which by itself provided the incentive to produce for domestic consumption: a rise in price could be done without fear of foreign competition. *Finally,* excessive lending of the financial institutions created inflation of asset prices, not of goods. As assets became overpriced, the financial condition of the intermediaries seems sounder than it was. The liabilities of commercial banks and other financial institutions were looked upon as having implicit government guarantee: *no question a moral hazard argument.* Also, this problem was made worse by globalization of the financial markets. With access to global capital markets possible, the asset bubble was allowed to grow larger than it would have otherwise (Doner and Ramsay, 1999: pp. 184-185).

Stephan Haggard's example of moral hazard surrounding Thailand mentioned in the introduction of this manuscript is particularly striking in its own right. Thailand's commercial banks have been politically powerful for decades and served as critical sources of funds and financing of commodity exports and industrial growth, undoubtedly very instrumental towards Thailand's economy and tax base. Therefore, the government has the incentives to protect the banks. However, even the World Bank in the mid-1980s had warned Thailand that it

> had too much of a tendency to protect the solvency and stability of existing banks and financial institutions, rather than to promote efficiency and competition broadly among all categories of institutions, or providing for orderly exit or reorganization of financial firms that became insolvent. As regulatory policies move toward greater freedom of entry and exit, Thai authorities will need to vigorously implement the power to force individual institutions to reorganize or disappear when necessary without damaging the confidence and stability in the financial system as a whole (Doner and Ramsay, 1999: p. 185).

Needless to say, the Thai government did not heed the World Bank's advice as Stephan Haggard effectively pointed out in his example. Bankers and finance companies continued to engage in financing risky projects, out of expectations that they would enjoy profits while the government would cover serious loses. Most of the bad loans of the Bank of Thailand, for example, were made to politicians from the Chat Thai political party who lacked sufficient collateral and thereafter used the loans to buy land (Doner and Ramsay, 1999: p. 185). Furthermore, not only were troubled banks and finance companies supported at the local level, but efforts were also made to protect the baht against attacks by foreign speculators in 1996 and 1997. But the efforts themselves proved to be immensely expensive. In fact, the Financial Institution Development Fund (FIDF) lent out more than one trillion baht in the efforts to "shore up weak finance companies" (Doner and Ramsay, 1999: p. 186).

Rather than defending the baht, the Bank of Thailand could have devalued this currency. That alternative, however, was not sought for two reasons: 1) The Bank of Thailand believed that the problems were short-term and could be overcome without devaluation and 2) there was never a good time to devalue because even in an unsettling economy, devaluation may induce further instability. Furthermore, even if the Bank of Thailand should decide to devalue the currency, it would have been very difficult politically to do so.[17] The devaluation in the late 1996 or early 1997 would have left many firms and banks in predicaments since they would have to pay back foreign loans in devalued bahts (Doner and Ramsay, 1999: p. 186).

By July of 1997, the Bank of Thailand had exhausted the foreign exchange reserve defending the baht and was compelled to announce a managed float of the currency by July 2nd of that year. As the baht began to sink rapidly in value, full consequences of large-scale borrowing began to take hold. Firms' debt dependence had grown quickly in the 1990s beyond expectations. Between 1994 and 1996, the average debt/equity ratio increased from 1.58 to 1.98 while their interest cover fell from 14.2 to 10.7 percent.[18] Non-bank companies in the private sector accrued a debt of $63 billion at the end of 1996 of which $29.2 billion were due in less than a year (Doner and Ramsay, 1999: p. 186).

Businesses continued to accrue debt out of expectation that the rapid economic growth would continue. However, the slowing of exports in 1996 was a sign that such a continuation of the economic growth would not be long-lasting. And in fact, it wasn't. Furthermore, large numbers of firms had borrowed dollars and had to pay back the loans in dollars, and yet their revenues were in baht. To make matters worse, most of the funds borrowed from abroad were not hedged. Firms had argued that because they were lulled into believing that the value of the baht would remain stable vis-à-vis the dollar, there was no reason to pay the hedging fees (Doner and Ramsay, 1999: p. 186). The baht suffered further decline in its value as borrowers scrambled to convert the baht into dollars before the baht continue to decline. Firms simply could not repay the loans to finance companies and banks. Consequently, this led to losses for the finance companies and banks, beginning a downward spiral of asset deflation and disintermediation (Krugman, 1998: pp. 9-10).

Thailand was forced to go to the IMF for help by August of 1997. The IMF organized a $17.2 billion package, which included standby credits of $4 billion. Of $17.2 billion, $14.5 billion came from contributions from other Asian countries and $2.7 billion came from structural adjustment loans from the World Bank and the Asian Development Bank (Doner and Ramsay, 1999: p. 187).

F. The Slowdown of Thailand's Export Growth

As mentioned before, especially in the introduction, Thailand and the rest of the countries in the Asia-Pacific region began to experience declines in exports by the mid-1990s and onwards. Whereas Thailand's growth of manufactured exports reached 50 percent in 1987, the export growth declined to 15 percent per annum by 1992. Although the export growth recovered noticeably for the next three years, the growth declined even more sharply, to -0.05 percent in 1996.

There were factors which contributed to the decline in exports. *First,* there was a growing over-supply in the world electronics market, aggravated by a downturn in the world demand for electronics products. For instance, whereas the orders of the U.S. electronics industry for components were growing at roughly 20 percent per annum, the orders declined to 2 percent per annum by mid-1996. Electronic components accounted for a tenth of Thailand's manufacturing output, and a fifth of its exports. The net profits of listed electronics companies on the Bangkok Stock Exchange fell from 177 percent in 1994 to 6 percent in 1996 (Tan, 2000: p. 61).

Second, the baht has been fixed to the U.S. dollar. As mentioned before, with the economic boom the United States experienced in the 1990s, the appreciation of the dollar between 1990 and 1996 caused the baht to appreciate as well.[19] Consequently, the baht was ten percent above its 1990 value relative to the dollar by 1996. This made Thai exports increasingly uncompetitive in the global markets. *Third,* as Thailand's economy continued to blossom, wages and other costs began to rise, which in turn eroded the country's comparative advantage in labor-intensive manufactured exports.[20] *Fourth,* Thailand began to suffer from severe infrastructural inefficiencies, such as long traffic jams, which made it unattractive to produce and transport finished products. *Finally,* Thailand's exports to its largest trading partners the United States and Japan respectively fell on average from 13 percent in 1991 to 0.9 percent in 1996 (Tan, 2000: p. 63).

III.
The Effects of Thailand's Economic and Financial Crises

A. The Contractionary Effects of Devaluation: The Financial Sector

The immediate effects of the currency depreciation, capital flight, the closures of fifty-eight finance companies, and budgetary cuts have been recessionary and resulted in a decline in imports, all of which improved Thailand's balance of trade. During the last quarter of 1997, Thailand had a current account surplus and that surplus was expected to exist in 1998 and 1999. During 1998, however, Thailand experienced a negative growth from -3.0 to -3.5 percent while gross fixed investments were expected to decline by 21 percent (Lauridsen, 1998: p. 153).[21]

The fifty-eight finance companies under suspension were experiencing restructuring through the Financial Restructuring Agency (FRA). While Thai small and medium-sized commercial banks have seen their deposits moving to both foreign and larger domestic commercial banks, some of the deposits have been taken over by state banks. For instance, the Development Bank of Singapore bought the Thai Danu Bank, while equity and nationalization of the four medium-sized banks with liquidity problems and relatively greater exposure to property loans have been written down. As the financial crisis tended to favor the top five commercial banks thus far, the Chuan Leekpai government promised the IMF that it will prepare a restructuring and privatization strategy for the four nationalized banks by June of 1998 (Lauridsen, 1998: p. 154).

However, restructuring the financial sector carries further disintermediation and huge public costs. While shareholder equities continued to be written off, the costs of financially restructuring loans in finance companies and banks were expected to be 12 to 15 percent of Thailand's GDP and were to be funded by the state budget as well as by banks through their higher contributions to the FIDF. As Lauridsen points out:

> Recapitalization of the financial sector will require $10-$25 billion over the next several years, and as local funds are tight, increased sale of equity to foreign financial institutions, even allowing foreign investors to take a majority stake, has been the strategy chosen (Lauridsen, 1999: p. 154). However, financial sector reform and recapitalization, debt restructuring, and the implementation of effective bankruptcy and foreclosure laws proceeded slowly than anticipated. Although a bankruptcy law was passed in February of 1998, the response to pressures from influential debtors proved to be ineffective (Flatters, 2000: p. 265).

Bounded by pressures especially from abroad, the Thai government and the IMF agreed on a major relaxation of monetary policies.[22] The goal was to "switch from exchange rate to monetary growth targets and thus to stimulate the real estate sector through lower interest rates. Lower interest rates were also seen as means of easing the loan payment burdens on debtors" (Flatters, 2000: p. 266). The plan worked. As consequences of the substantial and rapid fall of both lending and deposit rates, the stock market investment and the Stock Exchange of Thailand (SET) index in the fourth quarter experienced something of a resurgence. The baht was strengthened further, which the Bank of Thailand (BOT) attempted to restrain. Furthermore, FDI was beginning to return and was significantly higher than it was in 1997 (Flatters, 2000: p. 266).

This progress was encouraging and the SET index led some observers to suggest that Thailand's economic recovery was definitely on the horizon. On the debit side, however, most of the real economic indicators such as exports, imports, bank lending, manufacturing output, investment and employment still showed little signs of improvement (Flatters, 2000: p. 266). Furthermore, notwithstanding the efforts made to tighten the non-performing loan reporting rules and to phase in new loan provisioning requirements, the non-performing loans were still on a rise, from 40 percent of loans in the banking system in 1998 to 47 percent by early 1999. As non-performing loans continued to expand, full provisioning would effectively erase most, if not all, existing shareholders' equity, even for the more healthy of the remaining banks. Simply put, there were no real incentives for the banks to adjust (Flatters, 2000: pp. 266-267).

B. The Contractionary Effects of Devaluation: Consumption, Investment, and Trade

After the massive devaluation and the rising foreign debt in terms of baht, uncertainties about the future employment and gloomy sales resulted in a downward adjustment in permanent income and expected profit (Nidhiprabha, 2000: p. 73). Exports have not responded sufficiently to the large real depreciation of the baht. The baht failed to stimulate the economy despite abundant resources and a real wage cut because: 1) devaluations by Thailand's competitors have made Thai's products less attractive than anticipated, 2) the contagion effect on a global scale caused a slowdown in economic activity in major trading partners, 3) the reduction of imports from Thailand stemmed mainly from the income effect, which outweighed the substitution effects of the baht depreciation, and 4) exporters were denied access to export credit, especially since banks became more cautious in lending due to the rise of non-performing loans (Nidhiprabha, 2000: p. 73).

Furthermore, because the excess capacity built up over the boom years in Asian countries had placed downward pressure on the prices of manufactured goods, export prices in terms of the baht had not increased proportionately to the currency depreciation. Yet, import prices in terms of the baht did not rise as much as the depreciation rate of the baht, since foreign exporters may reduce their dollar prices so as to maintain market shares in Thailand. In essence, the substitution effect of the exchange rate depreciation on the trade balance may not yield much improvement on such a balance in the short run (Nidhiprabha, 2000: p. 73).

C. The Contractionary Effects of Devaluation: The Manufacturing Industry and Employment

Whereas the devaluation of the baht made Thai exports more competitive, the cost of imported components and raw materials had increased as well. Furthermore, the devaluation of the baht had a severe impact on the profits of large companies and conglomerates with un-hedged foreign loans. Companies in construction and petrochemicals such as the Thai Petrochemical Industry and the Siam Cement Company were the most vulnerable from the impact of foreign exchange losses on corporate earnings. As credits continued to dry up while liquidity problems remained both pervasive and persistent, the suspension and closure of fifty-eight finance companies had particular impinges on small and medium-sized enterprises (SMEs): those firms that had obtained their working capital from these sources (Lauridsen, 1998: p. 155).[23]

The social implications behind the currency devaluation could never have been more profound than it has since 1998. The number of the unemployed tripled from 1996 through the end of 1998, while there were major reductions both in hours worked and in nominal wages. Whereas the urban work force was among the hardest hit (the other being manufacturing especially in rural areas), agriculture benefited from depreciation-induced increases in domestic currency prices of tradable goods. The Consumer Price Index (CPI) inflation remained low, despite the large depreciation of the baht.

IV.
Epilogue
Thailand of Yesterday, Today, and Tomorrow: What Direction Thailand is Taking Given the Events of the Past and the Present?

A. Thailand's Classic Economic Growth: From Inwardness to Expanding From Within-A Recapitulation

Thailand's economic success story was marred at first by doubts expressed by investors who saw Sarit's dictatorship and heavily politicized sectors as impediments to investment and commercial activities. However, the Thai government under Sarit's leadership proved instrumental in not only limiting the power of the technocrats, but also attracting new investors and clients by expanding entrepreneurial opportunities. In doing so, the government created a favorable economic environment for profitable private investment. The steps taken in that regard involved microeconomic stability, emphasis on efficiency, as well as protection of property rights (particularly those of ethnic Chinese entrepreneurs). The protection of property rights proved essential during the early stages of Thailand's industrial and commercial growth. During the ISI stage, the BoI was created in order to provide a wide range of investment incentives; the incentives which involved a broad based tax and tariffs exemptions as well as the promise of the government to not nationalize a promoted firm or undertake any new activity that would compete with that enterprise. The incentives worked, for the ISI stage witnessed some accelerating growth in the latter half of the 1960s.

The incentives remained a decisive factor during the 1970s, when Thailand began exporting to abroad. The mechanisms behind the incentives included rebates on import taxes, bonded warehouses, streamlined customs procedures, tax and tariff exemptions, and lower electricity costs. Thailand, very much like Taiwan during this period, remained protectionist in its trade incentives. However, exports continued to grow at a rapid pace due to Thailand's visionary yet risk-taking economic policies, the BoI's tax incentive packages, and the shift of comparative advantage (or competitiveness) towards labor-intensive firms. Also, by the 1980s, Thailand's financial sector remained both well regulated and well protected. With strong GDP growth in 1990 strong trading performance, Thailand embarked on a series of financial deregulation and liberalization, although the move, at first successful, exposed Thailand's financial sector to rapid changes in the global market in the coming years. The political climate, partly due to its peculiar constitutional and electoral system, placed Thailand in a more precarious position during the Asian Financial Crisis of 1997-1998.

B. The Election of Thaksin Shinawatra, January of 2001

The election of Thailand's new leader, Thaksin Shinawatra took place in January of 2001. Although Thaksin's Thai Rak Thai party has won the biggest popular vote ever in Thailand's history, Thaksin Shinawatra was fully aware that the work shall be done in order to turn the economy around. After the election, Thaksin announced his intentions to continue with the restructuring process embarked by the Chuan Leekpai's administration. One of the ways to get the real economy moving again was, according to Thaksin, for Thailand to spend its way towards recovery. For Thaksin, it was imperative to "generate a consumer boom at all levels of society by giving money to the rural sector in particular, funds being distributed to villages around the country, and by means of a tax moratorium for farmers themselves" (BBC World Service, 2001: pp. 1-2).

Among the key endeavors undertaken by the prime minister was his four day visit to India, which took place in November of that year. His goals during the visit were to strengthen economic and political ties with India as well as to construct a regional highway, linking Thailand and India via Burma (BBC News, 11/26/2001: pp. 1-4).[24] As a governmental official puts it, "Trade, investment, and technological cooperation are the primary concerns on this trip" (BBC News, 11/26/2001: pp. 1-4). While Thaksin Shinawatra's goal was to increase trade and investment in the short-run, he was keen in exploring the possibility of developing a free-trade pact with India in the longer-run (BBC News, 11/26/2001: pp. 1-4).[25]

The government's economic advisors had a more far-reaching idea, however. They believed that although Thaksin Shinawatra's focus on India was an euphonious idea, his free trade agreement should've been complimented by negotiating with China as part of a regional arrangement with Beijing. Supachai Panitchpakdi, Thailand's former deputy prime minister and the then general-director of the WTO, believed on focusing on India instead on China. Thaksin seemed to concur, and focused in developing Thailand as a knowledge-based economy and then sharing the information technology sector with that of India (BBC News, 11/26/2001: pp. 1-4).

C. Thailand's Economy under Strong Recovery, though Picture remains Murky

1. The Overall Economic Picture (1999-2003)

Despite the effects of the currency devaluation and financial disarrays, there are continuing hints that the economy is beginning its' turnaround for the better. By late 1999, most indicators show that the Thai economy has finally bottomed out and has begun its road to recovery. GDP growth of 0.8 percent in the first quarter of 1999 increased to 3.5 percent by the second quarter. As you will see in Table 5.2, GDP grew at 4.6 percent in 2000, only to decrease to a 1.9 percent growth the following year.

Meanwhile, the growth of manufacturing production turned positive in January of 1999 and has gradually accelerated since then. As the rate of decline of consumption slowed noticeably throughout the year, both imports and exports started their growths in May and in June respectively. Furthermore, even though private investment was still failing as of August of 1999, there were signs that some of the levels of investments are coming back to Thailand. Although high levels of excess capacity in manufacturing and real estate meant that the short-term recovery will not be investment-led, it did connote that rapid growth could be achieved at relatively low costs (Flatters, 2000: p. 269).

Thailand's economy continues to improve since 2002, with the growth of 5.2 percent in GDP (again, see Table 5.2). The overall improvement of the economy was due to a series of accommodative policies as well as mechanisms aimed towards growth as well as stability. The budget deficit for 2002 was 116.6 billion baht, or rather 2.2 percent of GDP, which was a significant decrease from the targeted rate of 3.8 percent of GDP. This was due primarily to the buoyant tax receipts that accrued from higher than anticipated economic growth. The government's revenue spending, which showed a ten percent increase in 2002 from the previous year, remained instrumental in giving the economy its needed stimulus (The Asian Development Outlook 2003, 2003: p. 94). Meanwhile, the inflation rate remained subdued in 2002, with consumer price inflation that averaged 0.7 percent while "core" inflation (excluding food and energy items) stayed at its 0.4 percent average. Notwithstanding the rise in global oil prices, the underlying inflationary pressures remained weak thanks to the excess capacity in many sectors (ADO 2003, 2003: p. 94). The baht was also stabled, with its reference rate averaging 43.0 to the dollar in 2002 (a 1.5 decrease from the 44.5 rate of 2001). As exports and strong economic expansion continues to be positive attributes of Thailand recovering economy, the baht was set to be strengthened in 2003 and beyond (ADO 2003, 2003: p. 94). With the GDP growth of 6.7 percent in 2003, it did.

Table 5.2
Thailand's Economic Indicators (2000-2005)

The Indicators *(in percentage)*	**2000**	**2001**	**2002**	**2003**	**2004**	**2005**
GDP Growth	4.6	2.1	5.2	**6.7**	6.1	4.1
Gross domestic investment/GDP	22.7	24.1	23.9	25.2	27.1	31.7
Gross domestic savings/GDP	31.0	30.0	30.5	28.7	29.6	n/a.
Inflation rate (consumer price index)	1.6	1.6	0.7	1.8	2.7	4.5
Money Supply (M2) growth	2.2	4.2	2.6	4.9	5.4	n/a.
Fiscal balance/GDP	-2.4	-2.1	-2.2	0.6	0.3	0.1
Merchandise export growth	19.5	-7.1	4.8	18.6	23.0	15.0
Merchandise import growth	31.3	-2.8	4.6	17.1	26.9	26.0
Current account balance/GDP	7.6	5.4	5.5	5.6	4.5	-2.1
Debt service ratio	15.4	20.8	19.6	16.0	8.4	<16.0
Unemployment rate	3.7	3.9	2.9	2.2	1.5	1.4

Sources: 1) The Asian Development Outlook 2003, 2004, 2005, and 2006. ***Website:*** www.adb.org
2) IndexMundi (on the unemployment rate and gross investment for 2005).
Website: www.indexmundi.com

Notes: According to BBC News, Thailand's GDP achieved a 6.7 percent growth in 2003 **(in bold).**
*Website: **http://news.bbc.co.uk/1/hi/business/3543945.stm***

And in fact, the Thai economy witnessed a more accelerated growth of 6.7 percent in 2003, despite the SARS scare and the bird flu crisis. This tremendous growth was due, in a large part, to a vast improvement in the production sector (particularly in non-agricultural sectors such as industry, trade, and construction). The improvement in global trade, though it remains gradual and uneven at best, is playing a part in Thailand's improving economic picture. The 2003 growth was such an upbeat news that the government forecasted a stronger growth between 7 to 8 percent for 2004 (BBC News, 03/08/2004: pp. 1-2).

2. Thailand's Economic Picture in 2004

In fact, despite the forecasted 7-8 percent GDP growth, the GDP instead reported a 6.1 percent growth in 2004 (a slight decrease from 6.7 percent in 2003).

This was due to a prolonged drought, the Avian bird flu, rising oil prices, and persistent unrests in the southern provinces, all which proved damaging to consumer and investor confidence (Asian Development Outlook 2005, 2005: p. 118). Despite this broader trend, investment continued to accelerate, rising by 16.1 percent and contributing 3.6 percentage points to the overall growth. The chief factor to such acceleration was the 11.7 percent surge in public investment (after its 0.8 percent fall in 2003). Meanwhile, private investment grew by 15.3 percent in 2004, slowing a bit from 17.5 percent a year earlier. Furthermore, although consumption grew by 5.4 percent and contributed 3.4 percentage points to GDP growth, the rise of private consumption decelerated from 6.4 percent in 2003 to 5.6 percent in 2004 (ADO 2005, 2005: p. 118).

The drought, Avian bird flu, and a reduced export demand for shrimps due to antidumping measures of the United States had adverse affects on the production side of the agricultural sector: its growth of 8.7 percent in 2003 was sharply reduced to 4.4 percent in 2004 (Asian Development Outlook 2005, 2005: p. 118). Manufacturing overall likewise eased from 10.4 percent to 8.3 percent and light manufacturing industries such as food and beverages, declined due to the drought and the Avian flu, even though it recovered in the third quarter (ADO 2005, 2005: p. 118). The production of chemicals was strong, thanks largely to the high demand from China. But, capital goods and technology industries continued to slow in 2004 due to the declining in the demand for motor vehicles thanks to higher oil prices and the revisions to excise taxes (which caused some consumers to delay purchases until after July when the revisions took effect) (ADO 2005, 2005: p. 118).

The services sector showed improvement overall in 2004. Although growth in wholesale and retail trade slowed a bit, hotels and catering services in general recovered nicely from the SARS outbreak of 2003 to 12.4 percent growth in 2004. Hotel occupancy rates improved from 57 percent in 2003 to 64 percent a year later while tourism showed its convalescence by 17.3 percent (to 11.7 million) during the same period (Asian Development Outlook 2005, 2005: p. 119). Other sectors such as financial, construction, and transport and communications likewise improved, with the 14.2 percent growth of the financial sector that was recorded in 2004 (although it was a two percentage points lower than its 2003 growth rate) (ADO 2005, 2005: p. 118).

Thailand's fiscal position and the overall economic well-being remained sound for the most part in 2004. The governmental budget registered a surplus of B17.2 billion (0.3 percent of GDP) even with a non-budgetary deficit of B2.2 billion. The surplus was recorded even as government revenues and expenditures both increased by roughly 17 percent in FY2004 (Asian Development Outlook 2005, 2005: p. 119). In addition, prices overall increased largely due to higher costs in farm and oil products. Consumer price inflation reached 2.7 percent in 2004 (from 1.8 percent in 2003) while core inflation remained fairly constant at 0.4 percent (as in 2002 but decreased slightly to 0.2 in 2003). In fact, core inflation stayed within the target range set by the Bank of Thailand (BOT) (Asian Development Outlook 2005, 2005: p. 119). In 2002, the goal of the BOT was set towards inflation targeting, with the goal of keeping stable at a range of 0 percent to 3.5 percent. Unsure of the rate of Thailand's economic recovery, the BOT cut its benchmark 14-day repurchase rate by nearly twenty-five basis points to 1.75 percent (The Asian Development Outlook 2003, 2003: p. 94). Two years later, the BOT raised the benchmark on three occasions in the second half of 2004 by a total of seventy-five basis points to 2.0 percent for the sake of leaning against inflationary pressures. That benchmark was increased by another twenty-five basis points to 2.25 percent not just due to the aforementioned pressures, but also due to rising global rates and a lessened need for low rates in Thailand (Asian Development Outlook 2005, 2005: pp. 119-120).

The financial sector altogether was performing not too poorly in 2004. Although the ratio of NPLs in Thai commercial banks improved from 14 percent to 12 percent in 2004, commercial bank deposits increased to merely 2.6 percent during that year (from a 4.4 percent growth in 2003) (Asian Development Outlook 2005, 2005: p. 119). Also, commercial bank private credits expanded at a rate of 6.8 percent, almost twice as much as they did in 2003 (at 3.6 percent). On the reverse side of the financial sector's performance picture, the Stock Exchange of Thailand Index declined by 16 percent in 2004, after making large gains a year before (Asian Development Outlook 2005, 2005: p. 119).

Notwithstanding some uneven growth in Thailand's financial sector, its trading performance continued to be strong in 2004. Merchandise exports jumped from 18.6 percent in 2003 to 23.0 percent (or to $96.1 billion) in 2004, mainly due to higher shipments of products to the European Union, ASEAN member countries, and Japan. However, exports were outperformed by merchandise imports, which grew from 17.1 percent in 2003 to 26.9 percent a year later. The surge in imports was influenced decidedly by higher oil prices and imports of intermediate products and capital goods (Asian Development Outlook 2005, 2005: p. 119).

Thailand's economic fundamentals remained quite sound in 2004, with a trade surplus of 1.7 billion dollars, a current account surplus that reached $7.3 billion (or 4.5 percent of GDP), and the rise of gross international reserves from $42.1 billion in 2003 to $49.8 billion in 2004. In addition, external debt fell from $51.8 billion to $50.6 billion while the debt service ratio fell from 16.0 percent to 8.4 percent (Asian Development Outlook 2005, 2005: p. 119).

With those positive developments in mind, the government strengthened its position in Parliament in the February 2005 elections by ensuring the country: 1) of its continuing commitment to its dual track policy of building the economic fundamentals even further and 2) by enhancing Thailand's links to the global markets through international trade, investment, and financial cooperation (Asian Development Outlook 2005, 2005: p. 119). Furthermore, the government is expected to continue with its programs such as, for instance, the Village Fund, a program that provides loans to communities as well as assistance to SMEs. The noticeable reduction of poverty during that time was attributed to two reasons. *One reason* was high crop prices, which significantly led to increases in farm income by 28.5 percent in 2003 and 15.4 percent in 2004. *The other reason* was due to government programs that injected funds into the rural communities. However, despite achieving much of the Millennium Development Goals, income disparities among different regions and groups remain problematic (Asian Development Outlook 2005, 2005: pp. 119-120).[26]

Investment plans are likewise well in the works. The government and the State-owned enterprises (SOEs) had drawn up such plans with the aim to spend up to B2.7 trillion ($69 billion) mainly on infrastructural projects in transport and energy for the fiscal years 2005 through 2008. The planned funding was projected to come from sources such as the government budget (36 percent), domestic loans (25 percent), international loans (24 percent), and income from SOEs (15 percent) (Asian Development Outlook 2005, 2005: p. 120). The investment, according to the Ministry of Finance, was expected to raise GDP growth by roughly 0.2 percentage point per year during the investment period. However, it must be mentioned that although infrastructural spending would boost economic competitiveness, debt sustainability and macroeconomic stability shall not be overlooked (ADO 2005, 2005: p. 120).

Private investment is being looked upon also, with tax breaks provided by the government in hopes of spurring such a venture. For instance, in the first months of 2005, the corporate tax income tax rate on the first B1 million of profit was reduced for businesses with registered capital not exceeding B5 million. This reduction took place as consumer confidence was in a downward trend during that period (Asian Development Outlook 2005, 2005: p. 120).

3. Thailand's 2005 Economic Performances

In 2005, the GDP growth cooled noticeably to 4.5 percent due to factors such as drought, higher prices of oil on a global scale, the political unrests in the southern provinces of Thailand, as well as the aftermath of the December, 2004 tsunami (Asian Development Outlook 2006, 2006: p. 225). The tsunami factor was particularly important because of the deleterious effects it had on the tourism industry. And the seemingly chronic severe drought affected output from agriculture, which remains an important export sector. However, matters improved as the year went along, as both agricultural and tourism sectors made strong recoveries. High external demand was particularly helpful in Thailand's recovery in the remaining quarters of 2005. Also a healthy expansion of exports of manufactured and agricultural products (like electronics, meat, and fisheries) benefited the economy as a result (ADO 2006, 2006: p. 225). Therefore, second-half GDP growth at 5.0 percent was roughly one percentage point higher than in the first half.

However, higher energy costs and rising interest rates damped private consumption and investment. Consumption, a major GDP growth contributor, added 3.4 percentage points while investment added 2.9 (Asian Development Outlook 2006, 2006: p. 225). Net exports, however, suffered a contraction of -2.1 percentage points. Furthermore, with rising retail oil prices catapulting both transport and energy prices as well as with increases in wages, consumer inflation rose to 4.5 percent in 2005, which happened to be the highest rate in seven years (ADO 2006, 2006: p. 225). Among the reasons for the rise in retail oil prices were due to a series of governmental policy initiatives, which gradually removed fuel subsidies in the first half of 2005 and then completely abolished it in July. As a result, retail prices of both diesel and gasoline jumped by 57 percent and 33 percent respectively (ADO 2006, 2006: p. 225).

The rise in oil prices percolated to other prices. Core inflation, for instance, accelerated although it remained subdued at 1.6 percent in 2005. Out of concerns over both rising inflationary pressures and interest rate differentials with the United States, the Bank of Thailand lifted its fourteen-day repurchase interest rate in stages to 4.00 percent by December 2005 and again to 4.50 percent in March 2006 (Asian Development Outlook 2006, 2006: p. 225). Meanwhile the fiscal position remained quite as strong in 2005 as it was a year before. This was made possible by not only the government's realistic spending (which remained within its original budget target), but also by the government's revenue collection, which expanded to 13.3 percent (ADO 2006, 2006: p. 226).

The government initiated $42.0 billion in the Megaprojects Investment Program aimed at improving physical and social infrastructure for the 2005 through 2009 fiscal years (the amount, by the way, that's projected to be equal to about 5.0 percent of GDP for each of those year) (Asian Development Outlook 2006, 2006: p. 226). The program seems to be a revision from the plans drawn up earlier and targets substantial investments in mass transit (in the proposed amount of $10.5 billion), transport ($7.8 billion), housing ($8.2 billion), water resources ($5.1 billion), education ($2.4 billion), health ($2.3 billion), and others ($7.5 billion). While some expenditures on the program were made under the 2005 budget, they had no significant effects on the government's outlay; the impact of the program is expected to be felt beginning in 2007 (ADO 2006, 2006: p. 226).

Like the GDP, trading performances were marred by the drought, the aftermath of the tsunami, and high oil prices and the first quarter marked a considerable slow start for the year as a result. However, matters improved in the remaining three quarters of the year, and consequently, merchandise exports reached a 15.0% growth (ADO 2006, 2006: p. 226). Not only did agricultural exports improved in the final three quarters of 2005, meat and fisheries, high-technology products, chemicals, automobiles, plastics, and rubber likewise rose robustly (ADO 2006, 2006: p. 226). Of all total exports made by Thailand during 2005, machinery and mechanical appliances constituted 14.7%, electrical apparatus for circuits 11.4%, Computers and parts 8.1%, and, finally, electrical appliances, at 7.5% (Economist.com, 2006: p. 2). On the other hand, due to rising cost of oil imports and buoyant demand for capital goods as capital utilization increased after a prolonged period of low business investment in manufacturing, merchandise imports recorded a 26.0% growth (ADO 2006, 2006: p. 226). Such a growth is by itself a good economic indicator of Thailand's continual economic recovery from the Crisis of 1997-1998. Yet, for the first time in several years, the overall trading performance of 2005 yielded a current account deficit of 2.1% of GDP (or by $3.7 billion) (ADO 2006, 2006: p. 226). Fortunately, capital inflows remained strong and it, therefore, ensured a comfortable overall balance of payments outcome. Due to this development, along with the narrow interest rate differential with the U.S. dollar rates, the baht strengthened toward the end of 2005. Also, international reserves rose to $52.1 billion, almost twice their level of 1997 (ADO 2006, 2006: p. 226).

D. Thaksin Shinawatra: His Vision, His Troubles, and His Uncertain Political Future

1. Thaksin's Economic Agenda and its Uniqueness.

Since Prime Minister Thaksin Shinawatra entered office in January 2001, his vision was quite clear: to propel Thailand to economic performing predominance in the eyes and recognition of the global community. As mentioned previously in this chapter, among the key steps he took early in his tenure was visiting India to strengthen ties between the countries. Three years later, the legislative piece, the White Paper "Facing the Challenge: Economic Policy and Strategy" (published in August 2004), spells out Thaksin's economic agenda he set forth since 2001. The agenda includes: 1) balancing past excessive dependence on external demand, 2) balancing urban-based mass manufacturing and unproductive asset building with structural development in domestic demand, traditional sectors (like, for examples, agriculture, SMBs, and rural households), as well as enterprises, and 3) improving Thailand's pricing power of its goods and services (Asian Development Outlook 2005, 2005: p. 41). In other words, the intention, as laid out by Prime Minister Thaksin, was to revive both domestic demand (by boosting private consumption and developing traditional sectors) as well as exports. It is, in short, a *dual-track strategy*, in contrast to a *single-track model* which one-dimensionally focuses on production mainly for exports. Thailand is in many ways unique for it follows the former whereas many countries in the Pacific region focus primarily on improving their exporting performances (ADO 2005, 2005: p. 41).

The dual-track strategy is five-pronged. *First,* in Thailand's continual economic revitalization is the bolstering of growth at the grassroots level. The saying "one tampon (village) one product" embodies the notion of developing villages throughout the country through mechanisms such as farmers' debt suspension, SME loans, asset capitalization, venture capital, and entrepreneur promotion. *Secondly,* key sectors are being jump-started, especially in relation to demand levels on certain products produced by those sectors. For example, the government has set up a new Entrepreneurs Promotion Board (EPB) to create 50,000 new SMBs in order to boost the manufacturing sector (Asian Development Outlook 2005, 2005: p. 41). *Thirdly,* greater economic efficiency and long-term competitiveness are still being targeted and enhanced through identifying a series of industries to promote them (such as, for instances, automobiles, tourism, hospitality, and health care services). *Fourth,* Thailand is providing a stable and supportive macroeconomic environment to facilitate growth while maintaining and even enhancing the overall economic fundamentals and policy discipline like debt servicing and trade. *Lastly,* the goal remains to promote the external sector through market expansion while fostering financial stability through regional and global cooperation (thus, the dual-track model) (Asian Development Outlook 2005, 2005: p. 41).

The dual-track strategy is simultaneous both by nature and by design, for the reliance on external demand (first track) is coupled with the development of domestic demand and supporting domestic enterprises (second track) (Asian Development Outlook 2005, 2005: p. 40). In many ways, this model evokes the economic development strategies of the late 1950s through the 1970s through its inward-lookingness for the sake of self-evaluation for better economic performances within the Thai borders and beyond. The admirable growth rates in recent years seem to vindicate this honest-seeking type of an approach.

2. The Troubles

Prime Minister Thaksin Shinawatra had won wide support and praise for tackling poverty especially among farmers while propelling the economy to new heights. Unfortunately, the business move he made in January 2006, changed the political atmosphere for the worst, however. On January 23rd, Thaksin sold 49.6 percent stake in Shin Corp for $1.9 billion in a move aimed at freeing him from allegations of conflict of interests. The buyer? Temasek, which happens to be Singapore's state-owned investment company. Temasek agreed to buy the stake as it looked to tap and benefit from the growing Thai demand for mobile phones and services. The move happened to be Thailand's biggest corporate takeover ever in its history (BBC News, 01/23/2006: pp. 1-2).[27]

The business move turned out to be disastrous from a political point of view. Many people saw the selling of an important national asset to a foreign firm as a betrayal while they've increasingly accused Thaksin Shinawatra of corruption (tax dodging particularly) and incompetence. The matter had gotten so worse that Cultural Minister, Uraiwan Thienthong, resigned on February 3rd out of concerns for the "ethics of good governance" (BBC News, 02/03/2006: pp. 1-2).

3. Thaksin's Uncertain Political Future: Its Implications on Thai Politics and the Economy

The mounting political crisis had made the Prime Minister to consider the possibility of stepping down temporarily to ease the tension that was plaguing the country. He made such an indication on March 14th, 2006 amidst the heated protests that had occurred for some time: during that same day, roughly 50,000 protesters blockaded his office and demanded that he step down over corruption allegations (BBC News, 03/15/2006: pp. 1-2). Thaksin called for a snap election for April 2nd to regain his authority, even though the opposition announced a boycott against the poll. In support of his consideration to temporarily step aside, he promoted Justice Minister Chidchai Vanasatidya to become his number two. However, as Sihasak Phuaungketkeow, a spokesperson for the Thai Foreign Ministry states, "the recent moves made by Prime Minister Thaksin do not mean that he's talking about resigning" (BBC News, 03/15/2006: pp. 1-2).

Thaksin has remained adamant (even now) that he committed no wrongdoing and has spent much of his time campaigning in rural communities in the spring of 2006, where their support remains high in comparison to urban areas like Bangkok (BBC News, 03/15/2006: pp. 1-2). However, the matter continued to worsen to the point that protest leaders (like Chamlong Srimuang, among Thailand's most powerful opponents and member-leader of the Buddhist Santi Asoke sect) asked King Bhumibol Adulyadej to intervene on March 25th. The protests, loud, noisy, yet relatively peaceful, remained ongoing throughout the coming months of 2006 (CNN.com, 03/26/2006: pp. 1-3).

Crestfallen by the results of his proposed April 2nd, 2006 snap election, Prime Minister Thaksin Shinawatra decided to step down as his country's leader, despite his claims that he had garnered over 50 percent of the votes.[28] His announcement to step down came shortly after his meeting with King Adulyadej and declared that he would remain in a caretaker role until parliament meet and a successor would be chosen (MSNBC.com, 04/05/2006: p. 2). In fact, in less than twenty-four hours after he announced his resignation, he had already appointed Deputy Prime Minister Chitchai Wannasathit as head of state, who at that time was not a member of the parliament (MSNBC.com, 04/05/2006: p. 2).

A month later, on May 8th of 2006, however, Thailand's Constitutional Court voted 8 to 6 that the inconclusive April 2nd election was unconstitutional and voted 9 to 5 that a new election should be held (The New York Times.com, 05/08/2006: p. 1). After a prolonged period of recess in the aftermath of the snap election, Thaksin resumed his duties as Prime Minister on May 23rd, attending the weekly cabinet meeting. His appointment of Chitchai Wannasathit was revoked later that day. However, the election left a considerable constitutional mess. The parliament was dissolved and Thailand has had a caretaker government during Thaksin's absence (CNN.com, 05/23/2006: pp. 1-2). On May 30th, Thailand announced that it would re-run an annulled general election on October

15th, but the aforementioned constitutional mess has yet to be untangled (Wong-Anan, 05/30/2006: p. 1).

The Election Commission came under considerable heat during May. On the 9th, Thailand's Supreme Court had asked five members of the Commission to resign for failing to stop abuses during April's snap election (BBC News, 05/09/2006: p. 1). The three remaining members of the Commission held firm and the main opposition parties refused to talk to the body. Furthermore, an opposition politician filed a lawsuit with the Bangkok Criminal Court against the commissioners alleging that they held the April 2nd snap election unlawfully. The trial was set for June 19th (Wong-Anan, 05/30/2006: p. 1). Since then, members of that commission were removed and jailed by a court for malfeasance and a new commission declared that the election would be delayed, a definite setback to Thaksin and his party (Mydans and Fuller, 09/20/2006: p. 1).

Meanwhile Thaksin Shinawatra was fighting back with a series of defamation lawsuits. One lawsuit was against a newspaper of former business partner Sondhi Limthongkul, who started the street campaign against him. Also Thaksin was planning to file two additional criminal libel lawsuits on June 2nd against a group of academics and a group of senators. In all, a $26 million civil libel case was being planned against the groups according to his lawyer, Thana Benjathikul (Wong-Anan, 05/30/2006: pp. 1-2).

However, the political landscape has become even more precarious despite recent developments that went in Thaksin's favor. On September 20th, 2006, leaders of the Thai armed forces staged a bloodless coup by seizing control of Bangkok and suspending the constitution. Martial law was declared and houses of parliament, the cabinet, as well as the constitutional court were 'terminated' (Mydans and Fuller, 09/20/2006: p. 1). General Sondhi Boonyaratkalin, the chief of the armed forces who was named acting prime minister, led the coup. During the overnight hours on September 20th, General Sondhi appeared on television in an audience with King Adulyadej, a clear yet striking indication that the monarch endorsed the move (Mydans and Fuller, 09/20/2006: p. 1).

Prime Minister Thaksin was effectively ousted while he was attending a meeting at the United Nations in New York. During the coup, he declared a state of emergency on television, but was cut off at mid-speech (Mydans and Fuller, 09/20/2006: p. 1). While he was on a leave of absence, Thailand's new military government announced on September 24th that a new commission was set up to investigate claims of corruption under Thaksin's leadership. In addition, the leaders of the military coup have been discussing the appointment of a new civilian prime minister to commence within a couple of weeks. Among the possible candidates for prime minister include Supachai Panitchpakdi (former WTO chief), Chatumongol Sonakul (former central bank chief), Pridiyathorn Devakula (central bank chief), and Ackaratorn Chularat (president of the Supreme Administrative Court). The fresh elections, according to the military, will be held in October of 2007 (BBC News, 09/24/2006: pp. 1-2).

Protests and oppositions were expected to continue throughout the rest of 2006 and even beyond as the constitutional crisis is far from being resolved. The 'termination' of the parliament is quite huge and the ongoing battle with the Election Commission is not offering hopes for a foreseeable resolution. The economy is likely to be adversely affected by the turmoil as the investment climate continues to be threatened. Moreover, the Thaiksin debacle symbolizes a deep and sharp social divide. Thaksin's Thai Rak Thai party has won three elections by landslides: in 2001, 2005, and April of 2006 thanks mostly to rural voters, who benefited from Thaksin's populist policies. However, opposition to Thaksin has swelled among the elite, primarily of those living in Bangkok (Mydans and Fuller, 09/20/2006: p. 1). Whether the opposition is at all fuller justifiable remains a source of debate. But, what makes this entire situation even more symbolic is an increasing awareness and vigilance of the population at large that grew wary over the effects of the 1997-1998 Crisis and the factors leading to it. The government of Thailand, and indeed leadership in much of the global community, are increasingly under the watchful eyes of the public speaking out for greater transparency and greater efforts against corruption. That alone will be examined further in the final chapter of this book.

E. Outlook in 2004 and Beyond

1. With Strong Economic Recovery, Policy Recommendations Remains crucial

As Kiat Sitteamorn, Deputy Secretary General of Thailand's Board of Trade, suggested, there must be other ways to finance SMEs, especially those at their infancy stage. The SMEs continue to be harmed because of the closure of fifty-eight finance companies, the chief sources of credit and financing (BBC World Service, 2000: p. 2). Other policies recommendations include the following. *First,* Thailand must [continue] with its fiscal expansionism in order to rejuvenate stagnant domestic demands. Additional spending should include providing financial resources for the corporate sector and alleviating the social impact from the Crisis through: 1) public employment, 2) skill-demand based training, and 3) maintaining current social security and public welfare. *Secondly,* Thailand should enhance credit expansion of specialized financial institutions (SFIs). The SFIs must not only provide credits for their current customers, but must also expand their coverage for those seeking liquidity and investments. *Thirdly,* Thailand must continue with its financial reforms *accompanying by financial restructuring.* Whereas the government should continue its full support for the existing recapitalization measures to further credit expansion, the supervisory and regulatory framework should be strengthened to enhance financial stability, transparency, accountability, and efficient provision of financial services. *Fourth,* Thailand should continue in facilitating corporate debt restructuring procedure in order to eliminate the likelihood of moral hazard. *Finally,* long-term competitiveness enhancement measures should be supported and set up with respect to the four following criteria: 1) technological development, 2) human resource development, 3) infrastructure investments, and 4) tariff reform (Fiscal Policy Office and the Office of Industrial Economics, Bangkok, Thailand. 2000: pp. 233-234).

2. Thailand's Mechanisms to Assure Continual Recovery and Growth

The recommendations of the Fiscal Policy and the Office of Industrial Economics are not wholly without merit. However, it must be point out that Thailand are taking steps in meeting with at least some of the aforementioned recommendations, especially with the implementation of the aforementioned dual-track strategy set forth since 2001. *For one thing,* the unemployment rate, once a chief concern during the onset of the Asian Financial Crisis, continues its downward trend since 2001. Whereas the unemployment rate was 3.3 percent in 2001, it went further down to 2.4 percent in 2002. By December of that year, the rate dropped to a five-year low of 1.4 percent (The Asian Development Outlook 2003, 2003: p. 94). As shown in Table 5.2, the unemployment rate remained low at 1.5 percent in 2004 and 1.4 percent in 2005. Poverty remains a chief concern however. But with the Millennium Development Goals in place, Thailand is taking steps to combat poverty and income inequality.

Secondly, the Thai government continues on with its accommodative monetary and fiscal policies. Deficit spending measures included a public health program, a village and urban revolving fund, a debt suspension program for farmers, as well as housing credit support for government officials (The Asian Development Outlook 2003, 2003: p. 96). Thus, expenditures rose by 11.1 percent overall in 2002. In addition, tax breaks were provided for home purchases, business start-ups, and stock exchange growth. However, when looking at an overall picture of stronger than expected economic growth, it cannot be argued that buoyant tax and non-tax revenues helped stabilize the actual deficit (ADO 2003, 2003: p. 96). Tax breaks are still being provided as of 2004 and investment towards mainly infrastructure projects continue to climb out of expectation that the economy will be more competitive (The Asian Development Outlook 2005, 2005: p. 120). The aforementioned Megaprojects Program has generated considerable uncertainty especially in the first quarter of 2006 as far as its speed and magnitude of implementation are concerned. The call made by the government for a more open and wider international bidding process for constituent projects will delay the beginning of some of the Program's activities. However, as mentioned before, the effects of the Program will likely be felt beginning in 2007 when expenditures are expected to accelerate (The Asian Development Outlook 2006, 2006: p. 227).

Thirdly, the Thai government continues to work towards the creation of greater financial and fiscal transparency, among the hot issues when discussing the Asian Financial Crisis and the lessons to be learned from that historical event. In 2002, arrangements were worked out for the amortization (or liquidation) and servicing the debts of the Financial Institution Development Fund (FIDF) through the use of BOT's profits. Such an endeavor may take two or three decades to accomplish the write-offs, however (The Asian Development Outlook 2003, 2003: p. 96).

Fourth, the budget for the 2003 fiscal year signals a shift towards fiscal consolidation. This, at least from the standpoint of the Thai government, was necessary since: 1) the ratio of public sector debt to GDP increased from 16 percent in 1996 to 54 percent in November of 2002 and 2) this consolidation was not as pressing at previously thought since the external environment is expecting to be continually supportive. The government's plan as of 2003 was to pare the total public sector deficit with the public enterprise financing needs by 1.4 percent of GDP relative to 2002's outcome (The Asian Development Outlook 2003, 2003: p. 96). By using this mechanism, the government hoped for the 55 percent reduction of the public debt ratio (ADO 2003, 2003: p. 96). As mentioned before, the overall debt (such as external debt and debt service ratio) continues to show regression by 2004 (The Asian Development Outlook 2005, 2005: p. 119).

Fifth, Thailand is taking steps to stimulate credit expansion, including some relaxation of loan provisioning as well as loosening classification requirements for banks (The Asian Development Outlook 2003, 2003: p. 96). Credit card usage and home mortgage market showed signs of revival, even to the point of issuing limitations on credit card cash advances and reintroduction of minimum income requirements on credit card issuance. These measures were aimed to not only take some of the heat away from consumer credit expansion, but to also prevent the rise of personal debt as much as possible (ADO 2003, 2003: p. 96). However, credit expansion has become too excessive and debt levels (of households and property investment particularly) are becoming areas of concerns (The Asian Development Outlook 2005, 2005: p. 121).

Sixth, the Thai government is still working on increasing both public as well as private investment. In its effort to lift the latter, the officials are offering tax incentives for re-investment for a period of three years from the current year of 2006. Furthermore, incentives are being offered to companies to add value to output, such as, for instance, processing agricultural produce. With the dual-track development policy well in place, spending on rural programs will continue to be substantial. In fact, 30,000 villages received $B_{9.4}$billion in 2005 and the budgeted amount to be spent on such rural programs for 2006 has been raised to B_{19} billion (Asian Development Outlook 2006, 2006: p. 229).

Lastly, Thailand remains well aware that re-structuring and improving its banking and corporate sector is a very crucial enterprise for the sake of a recovery of business investment and a continuation of its economic resurgency and growth. The Thailand Asset Management Corporation (AMC) had acquired $17 billion on NPLs by 2003, largely from public sector banks (and $11 billion of these NPLs were resolved the year before) (The Asian Development Outlook 2003, 2003: p. 96). The Corporation, which acquired assets at an average cost of 33 percent of their book value, aimed to recover 45 percent from repayments by debtors. Eyes are now turned towards acquisitions of debts of less than 20 million in baht from state-owned financial institutions as well as debts from the Industrial Finance Corporation of Thailand (ADO 2003, 2003: p. 96.). As stated previously, the ratio of NPLs in Thai commercial banks are showing signs of improvement, decreasing from 12 percent in December 2004 from 14 percent a year before (The Asian Development Outlook 2005, 2005: p. 120).

3. Thailand Beyond 2006: What to Look For?

With the slowing of growth from 6.7 percent in 2003 to 4.5 percent in 2005, accompanied by lower unemployment and yet higher than expected inflation rates, the policies towards stimulating credit expansion, restructuring of the banking and corporate sector and accommodating fiscal and monetary policies, Thailand should be expected to continue its economic expansion beyond 2006. Because Thailand is aiming towards financial and fiscal transparency, it can be looked upon as a model for economic discipline and accountability for years to come, especially since the future remains fairly murky as far as global financial restructuring is concerned. Also, the government is still responding to the aftermath of the tsunami disaster. It announced that the expected expenditures for emergency and rehabilitation assistance could be about 10 billion bahts (of which 50 percent will be used to immediate programs such as direct assistance to families, support for industries, and low-interest loans for businesses. Furthermore, the BOT announced that it will provide funding for commercial banks to lend at low rates to businesses located in tsunami affected areas (The Asian Development Outlook 2005, 2005: p. 120).

However, there are both internal and external issues that shall not be ignored. The protests and the eventual coup against the now ousted Prime Minister Thaksin Shinawatra are undoubtedly posing harm to the Thai economy as investor and consumer confidence continues to fall (BBC News, 03/15/2006: p. 3). The overall political picture remains uncertain as the climate continues to heat up. Furthermore, issues such as global trading performance and conditions, SARS, the Avian bird flu, the ongoing high oil prices, and the geopolitical conflicts and insurgencies mainly in southern Thailand (which claimed over nine-hundred lives by Fall of 2005), will continue to affect the trading-dependent country.[29] Thailand must also pay attention to excessive credit expansion and private debt levels due to rising property investment and household debts, which will increase the vulnerability of the national economy as a whole (especially as interest rates will rise in response to the alarming rate of credit expansion) (The Asian Development Outlook 2005, 2005: p. 121).

Furthermore, Thailand's new listings of major companies in hopes that they would give a boost to the stock market are already facing obstacles. For example, an initial public offering of EGAT's shares was suspended in November of 2005 by the supreme administrative court out of constitutional concerns (The Asian Development Outlook 2006, 2006: p. 226). This problem surrounding EGAT, the state electricity generation authority, is one of a number of concerns facing the government's efforts to improve its stock market. Thai Beverage, a major privately owned liquor company, postponed a listing in Thailand due to opposition from anti-alcohol groups. Instead, it proposed to list in Singapore (ADO 2006, 2006: p. 226). Also, Thailand's privatization program is likewise facing hurdles. Among the chief goals of Asian countries in their recoveries from the Asian Financial Crisis of 1997-1998 include privatization. Its importance lie in the fact that it helps the countries develop capital markets, assists them in infrastructure investment, and aids them in enhancing investor confidence. Thailand embarked on it as one of its structural reforms and a privatization master plan was drafted, with several committees formed to oversee, implement, and audit the sale process. In fact, two major companies, the PTT (the state petroleum company) and the AOT (the airport authority) were already privatized and listed. However, the privatization program is being attacked and protested by employees and consumer groups out of concerns over, for instances, regulatory deficiencies and transparency of share offerings (The Asian Development Outlook 2006, 2006: pp. 226-229).

Notwithstanding these setbacks, improving the capital markets continues to be a top priority for the government. In January 2006, a capital market development master plan was finalized and includes measures to increase supply of high quality stock, strengthen domestic securities companies, and encourage participation of institutional investors in the stock market (ADO 2006, 2006: pp. 226-227). But, the Megaprojects program continues to be a lingering concern. The uncertainties surrounding it and the consequent delay of the program are already well known. However, should the program faces further delays and uncertainties in 2007 and beyond, the baseline outlook for growth, investment, and capital market development would be significantly eroded and may undo much of the progress Thailand made after the 1997-1998 Crisis (The Asian Development Outlook 2006, 2006: p. 227). Clearly, this is one topic that cannot be overlooked.

What Thailand must also do is to continue its focus on higher education, in terms of quality and accessibility for the sake of the longer term. A larger pool of trained employees, particularly in technical fields, is essential should the economy remain competitive (The Asian Development Outlook 2005, 2005: p.

121). But despite the concerns of today, Thailand is overall on the right track with its relatively strong economic fundamentals (robust export growths, lowering national debts, healthy fiscal condition, and a comfortable level of external reserves). With the aforementioned flexible and accommodative approaches Thailand continues to undertake, the conditions for investment, private consumption, sound economic fundamentals (including lower debt levels) are expected to remain positive and promising if not without some cautions and concerns here and there (especially with the ongoing political unsteadiness even as we speak).

V.
Notes

1. The ethnic Chinese entrepreneurs were politically vulnerable at the time (Doner and Ramsay, 1999: p. 173).
2. Efforts in restructuring tariffs in the late 1980s were made difficult by import-competing industries and their allies in the Ministries of Industry and Commerce. Furthermore, the Ministry of Finance expressed its reluctance to lose revenues generated by tariffs, thus a further incentive to keep the tariff rates at high levels (Doner and Ramsay, 1999: p. 174).
3. Among the collective action problems included setting export quotas, resolving conflicts in regards to pricing, establishing the ability and the willingness to share risks, and maintaining the quality of exports (Doner and Ramsay, 1999: p. 175).
4. Current account surplus occurs when a country exports more than it imports, as opposed to a current account deficit.
5. Thailand's move towards deregulation and financial liberalization enjoyed steady process and yielded much of a promise towards its economic growth. However, as you will see, such a move exposed Thai's financial sector to rapid changes in the global financial market (Arphasil, 2001: p. 167).
6. Competition among these industries of developing countries was on the rise during this period.
7. Vertical integration occurs when one firm (the "upstream" firm) produces a product that is used as an input for another firm (the "downstream" firm). This process is problematic for: 1) if each firm has a monopolistic position, price formalations and control will likely to result in conflicts and 2) if demand or supply is uncertain, than problems of coordination can arise, especially since price fluctuations can be excessively risky for either party (Krugman and Obstfeld, 2000: p. 173).
8. To Haggard and MacIntyre, parliamentary structure is one in which government rests on party cohesion. However, the multi-member electoral system undermined such cohesion (Haggard and MacIntyre, 2000: p. 62).
9. There were incentives of the candidates to differentiate themselves from competitors of the same party.
10. It was the amount that exceeded the total capital of the finance companies and equalled roughly 10 percent of GDP (Haggard and MacIntyre, 2000: p. 66).
11. A total of fifty-eight finance companies, two-thirds of Thailand's finance companies, were suspended during June and August of 1997 (Haggard and MacIntyre, 2000: p. 67).

12. The two agencies created were: 1) the Finance Restructuring Agency (FRA), responsible for supervising the suspended finance companies and to evaluate the rehabilitation plans submitted by the finance companies before the end of October of 1997, and 2) the Asset Management Corporation (AMC), responsible for buying, managing, restructuring, and then selling bad assets under FRA's direction (Lauridsen, 1998: p. 150).
13. Capital controls were relaxed on grounds that Thailand would be able to attract foreign capital should capital mobility prevail (Nidhiprabha, 1999: p. 68).
14. Japan likewise failed to be aggressive in maintaining and even enhancing financial and industrial supervisions, corporate governance, market discipline, and financial stability since the First Oil Shock of 1973. However, the New Economic Plan created in March of 2001 may be a turning point in reversing this predicament. As of 2006, Japan's economy is showing signs of improvement.
15. The real incentive behind this practice was that interest rates on those dollar loans were 4 to 6 percent lower than the baht loans (Doner and Ramsay, 1999: p. 183).
16. In 1994-1995, credit from banks and financial companies expansion to over 30 percent, partially because the fixed exchange rate was perceived as a guarantee for low foreign exchange risks (Nidhiprabha, 1999: p. 69).
17. The Bank of Thailand and other macroeconomic agencies did not have the political autonomy they have enjoyed since the 1960s.
18. Interest cover is earnings divided by liabilities before taxes and interest payments.
19. Regional currencies also appreciated, which in part caused a sharp in world export growth (Tan, 2000: p. 62).
20. The erosion of Thailand's comparative advantage (that is, competitiveness) of labor-intensive manufacturing was compounded by the implementation of economic reforms in China, Vietnam, Laos, and Bangladesh, where wages were much lower compared to Thailand (Tan, 2000: p. 62).
21. Capital outflow of $12 to $14 billion was forecast for that same year (Lauridsen, 1998: p. 153).
22. The strict monetary policies were perceived as a major cause of the alarming contraction of the real estate sector and continuing growth of non-performing loans (Flatters, 2000: p. 266).
23. The SMEs accounted for 98 percent of the total enterprises in Thailand (Fiscal Policy Office and the Office of Industrial Economics, Bangkok, Thailand. 2000: p. 233).
24. The road linking India with Rangoon had already commenced, with financial backing courtesy primarily of India (BBC News, 11/26/2001: pp. 1-4).
25. Thailand's interests in improving its political and economic ties with India were not new. For several years, Thailand pushed for a regional cooperation with South Asia through BIMST-EC, which includes Bangladesh, Sri Lanka, Myanmar, with India and Thailand as an economic cooperation group (BBC News, 11/26/2001: pp. 1-4).
26. The Millennium Development Goals (or MDG) is a set of policy initiatives designed to fight poverty, do away with gender discrimination through empowering women especially as voters, improving education, and to deal with the HIV/AIDS crisis. It is being promoted by the United Nations Development Programme (UNDP). The deadline in meeting the goals in accordance to agreements with the United Nations is 2015.

    Source: The UNDP (http://www.undp.or.th/mdg/index.html).

27. Shin Corp, an empire founded by Thaksin, has businesses covering telecommunications, satellite, airline, and media industries. After he became prime minister in 2001, he stepped down from Shin Corp and transferred share holdings. His family members still had key roles in the firm and controlled the equity stakes. According to the prime minister, his children decided to sell after expressing their desire for their father to focus on politics and to avoid public criticism about [possible] conflict of interests (BBC News, 01/23/2006: pp. 1-2).
28. According to the preliminary results, Thaksin's party won 57 percent of the votes in the April 2nd election, although about 37 percent of voters showed their disapproval of Thaksin by casting abstention votes (MSNBC.com, 04/05/2006: pp. 3-4).
29. The Avian Bird Flu has claimed the lives of at least 14 people in Thailand (including a five-year-old boy) and about 70 people in Asia as of December 9th, 2005. The problem has worsened since its outbreak in 2003 and there are fears of a pandemic if the virus mutates to pass between humans (BBC News, 12/09/2005: pp. 1-2).

Chapter Six
Indonesia: Its Rise to Commercial Power and Factors Leading to the Instabilities of the 1990s

I.
Introduction: Indonesia's Success Story (1970-1997)

A. Indonesia before 1970

Before the New Order government led by Suharto came to power in 1966, in the wake of massive social and political upheavals generated by the Communist Party of Indonesia (PKI) in its attempted coup d'etat, Indonesia's economy was in a perilous state.[1] Its economy was barely functioning due to its annualised inflation rate at roughly 1,000 percent. The foreign exchange rate was dangerously weak while physical capital remained in disrepair (Brown, 1998: p. 180). There were reasons why Indonesia's economic conditions were severely lacking until Suharto came into power.

For one thing, Indonesia could not quite shake off the legacy of colonialism under the Dutch, which led to an almost complete destruction of the indigenous Indonesian merchant and trading classes (Brown, 1998: p. 181). While the merchants and traders were successfully active in markets involving China and the Indian sub-continent in the first 1,000 years, they found themselves overwhelmed by the level of international trade and investment by Dutch commercial power as well as by the immigration of the Chinese to the Indies during the eighteenth and nineteenth centuries: the immigration which was encouraged by the Dutch (Brown, 1998: p. 181).

Secondly, after Indonesia gained independence from the Dutch in 1945, liberal democracy did not flourish. One serious attempt to establish democracy was done during the period of 1950 through 1957. During that time, multiple political parties and a parliamentary government were featured. However, Indonesia's step towards that direction was marred by the series of great political unrests during that time (Neher, 1991: p. 94). Sukarno, who was Indonesia's first president during the transition (1945-1966), paid scant attention to the daily administrative tasks. While the collapse of the economy and infrastructure were contributing factors to the fragile democratic system, Sukarno's notion of a unique, indigenous form of democracy was readily embraced as the most appropriate form of politics for the country (Neher, 1991: p. 94).

As far as Sukarno was concerned, a "fifty percent-plus-one" Western parliamentary practices worsened problems rather than solving them. He, therefore, advocated a "democratic practice" of the villages of Indonesia, where "deliberations were held until consensus emerges, in the spirit of gotong rojong with himself as the trusted elder" (Neher, 1991: p. 94). It was this concept of democracy that resembled closely to the traditional Javanese value systems where power was given to one person, typically a sultan. Indonesia's political system was hierarchical and authoritarian, with opposition and independent gathering of power resources that were cracked down and prohibited (Neher, 1991: p. 94).

While Indonesians welcomed guided democracy as the most effective way to make policy, the West (and those who cherished Western democratic ideals), saw guided democracy as assured perpetuation of Sukarno's power at the expense of openness and liberties under liberal democratic countries. They did not see real democracy as a philosophy destroyed by traditional values, but rather by corruption and a leader's yearning for power and authoritarianism. Therefore, once Suharto emerged to power in 1966, his New Order was viewed as an archetypical authoritarian administration that practices dictatorship rather than the virtues of democracy. Many, especially officials who supported Suharto, argued that during Suharto's reign as president, Indonesia has evolved to where Indonesian-styled democracy can begin to be meaningful. Besides, with a country with virtually no experience in practicing Western-style democracy, sustaining it would pose difficulty (Neher, 1991: p. 94). And it did.

The third reason why Indonesia's economy failed to flourish until the era of Suharto lied in its substantial population, which was multi-ethnic in composition. While it can be argued that whereas this population can represent a huge potential resource and a potential market, it can also be a huge potential drain on those natural resources. Therefore, providing physical and social needs in areas such as education, health, infrastructure, employment, and transportation would be a difficult yet a politically crucial task (Brown, 1998: p. 182). Also, even though there has been a great dispersion of wealth within the Sino-Indonesian community as within the Indonesian community as large, the latter community continues its resentment of the former for the extent of economic power they believed they're having and the wealth they clearly control (Brown, 1998: p. 182).

The Fourth reason is that the Indonesian economy was deeply along fault lines, with a clear geographical divide between Java and Bali and the rest of the country, otherwise called the Outer Islands. The lack of coordination is apparent, for Java and Bali continue to be most heavily populated regions, with its consumptions of the bulk of Indonesia's economic wealth (Brown, 1998: pp. 182-183). However, the Outer Islands were the main sources of that wealth (especially of export earnings). Java's economic interests rested on the demands and needs of consumers and importers while the Outer Islands' economic policies were influenced by the demands of producers and exporters (Brown, 1998: p. 183).[2]

Finally, Sukarno's government practiced *economic nationalism*, which was primarily concerned with exercising clear indigenous control over the national economy, including ownership of major industrial enterprises. This principle argued for economic autarky, with emphasis placed on both import-substitution industrialization and the protective measures that were involved: those measures that included tariffs as well as non-tariff barriers like subsidies. Foreign participation was curtailed while favoritism given to certain industrial and financial sectors became commonplace (Brown, 1998: p. 183). Sukarno's revolutionary economic system under his guided democracy was, as Clark D. Neher states, "isolationist and xenophobic and was skewed to meet ideological goals rather than the needs of the citizenry" (Neher, 1991: p. 95).

Since Suharto took over as president in 1966, he shaped governmental economic policies to reflect *economic rationalism*, the principle that placed more emphasis on the achievement of economic efficiency (hence the word technocracy, or technocrats, who practiced less state intervention while arguing that less protectionism and more export-oriented policies and industries would be mediated through the government) (Brown, 1998: p. 183).

Suharto's government was located chiefly in the State Planning Bureau, Bappenas. While the government aimed to restore economic stability while maximizing economic growth, there was little concern placed on the distributional or the equitable effects of such growth (Brown, 1998: p. 183). This growth was to be produced by encouraging export-oriented industries, the industries whose development depended heavily on a substantial and continuing inflow of foreign capital from countries such as the United States, Japan, and Australia and creditors such as the IMF and the International Banking for Reconstruction and Development (IBRD). Indonesia major creditor nations altogether formed the Inter Governmental Group on Indonesia (IGGI) for the purpose of coordinating the flow of foreign aid and loans to the country (Brown, 1998: p. 184).

B. Indonesia and its Road Toward Commercial and Economic Strengths (1970-1997)

From 1970 until 1997, the Indonesian economy experienced a growth rate of 7 percent of its GDP annually, which was among the best in the developing world. The structure of the economy has become diversified as dependency on the oil sector has declined in favor of the emergence of an export-oriented manufacturing base. This economic and industrial turn-around was led by a dynamic private sector and fueled by high domestic savings and large inflows of FDI (Harvie, 2000: p. 95).

To support this aforementioned fact, the manufacturing sector grew at twice the rate of industry as a whole and made a sizeable contribution to exports (Brown, 1998: p. 195). Manufactured exports grew from $501 million in 1980, to $2.5 billion in 1986, and to $16.1 billion in 1992. According to the National Development Information Office, manufactured exports grew to $29.4 billion by 1995. Whereas oil and gas exports decreased from 41 percent of export revenues in 1988 to 23 percent in 1995, electrical goods produced increased from $105 million in export revenues by 1988 to $3.2 billion by 1996. The shift from Indonesia's reliance in oil to its reliance upon non-oil products was important, for it substantially reduced the vulnerability of its balance of payments to changes in the terms of trade (Brown, 1998: p. 195).[3] However, the ultimate key to this success has been a consistent adherence to prudent macroeconomic policies, high investment and saving rates, as well as market-oriented trade and exchange regimes (Harvie, 2000: p. 95).

Indonesia, as with Thailand, became a favorite yet a major assembly area. The country, consequently, served as a factor for the great increases of foreign investments from Hong Kong, South Korea, Taiwan, Singapore, and to lesser extents, the United States and Japan. Unlike Singapore and Taiwan, Indonesia's production was labor-intensive in nature, with low-valued goods produced such as footwear, clothing, toys, sporting goods, electronics, textiles, food canning, and wood processing (Neher, 1991: p. 96). Indonesia's comparatively lower wages attracted entrepreneurs from higher-wage countries. Also, the Chinese, who became active in the Indonesian economy, have been given greater leeway in return for their support of Golkar, a "government party" of Indonesia which was dominated by the military and administered by officials at every governmental level. An acronym for *golangan karya* (or Functioning Group), Golkar developed a national apparatus (Neher, 1991: p. 89). The Chinese business executives were bestowed with protection and favorable legislation from officials and military officers, while receiving capital and access to profits from the Chinese themselves (Neher, 1991: pp. 96-97). Known as *cukong* (or boss), the Chinese civilians were a source of resentment from the Indonesian population who viewed them as corrupt and exclusive (Neher, 1991: p. 97).

Macroeconomic fundamentals and policies were sound: balance of payment was maintained, inflation has been contained at relatively low levels, current account deficits were kept at moderate levels, and international reserves were admirably maintain at comfortable levels. Furthermore, broad-based labor-intensive growth, together with sustained improvements in basic education and health services, has drastically reduced poverty levels, from 58 percent in 1972 to 11 percent in 1997 (Harvie, 2000: p. 95). Quality of life and life expectancy also improved as infant mortality decreased considerably. Therefore, it is hardly surprising that on May 30th, 1996, Indonesia was ranked fifteenth in economic competitiveness by the World Economic Forum, slightly outranking China and Thailand (Sadli, 1999: p.16).[4] Indonesia competitiveness was improved due to the importance of oil exports, financial liberalization, and the series of deregulation packages since the 1980s.

The importance of oil to the Indonesian economy was demonstrated by the fact that by the early 1980s, oil exports accounted for 78 percent of export earnings while oil revenues accounted for 70 percent of Indonesia's income.[5] This was accomplished notwithstanding the bankruptcy of Pertamina, which was the government-owned oil industry (Neher, 1991: p. 96).[6] From 1973 through 1989, development projects grew 2,000 percent as a result of oil revenues. On the debit side, however, oil prices dropped precipitously from $34.00 per gallon in 1981 to $8.00 per gallon in the mid-1980s, thanks chiefly to the Oil Crisis of 1982. As a result, economic growth fell and the decade of greatly increased government outlays for education, infrastructure, and, communication had ended. Oil, no longer the largest share of exports, was a replaced manufactured item in this capacity. Oil revenues were less relied upon as Suharto mobilized his technocrats not only to bring about order to the economy, but also to force austerity in budget expenditures in order to reduce the deficit (Neher, 1991: p. 96).

A series of reform measures was initiated to not only open the economy to foreign investment and joint ventures, but to essentially clean-up the financial sector as well. To be seen below, these reforms included, in brevity, the establishment of duty-free zones, liberal investment laws, and less bureaucratic red tape (Neher, 1991: p. 96). These reforms were not without success, since foreign investment commitments rose from $1.4 billion in 1987 to $4.7 billion in 1989. But, Indonesia's foreign debt increased to roughly $50 billion in 1989, the largest in Asia. Furthermore, the debt service ratio by 1989 reached 38 percent and debt servicing became at that point a major part of Indonesia's national budget (Neher, 1991: p. 96).

The reforms of the 1980s were designed to lessen abuses in the banking system through liberalization, competition, reduced credit subsidies, and a significantly reduced role for state banks. The reforms also included prudential measures covering limits on loans to individual borrowers or business groups, limits on related-party lending, capital requirements, prohibition on underwriting by commercial banks, and prohibition on ownership of non-financial companies by the banks. From 1991 and beyond, new prudential regulations included the phased introduction of increased capital adequacy ratios, risk management systems, and guidelines on asset quality. Efforts were made to step up training sessions for banking industry personnel and supervisors (Hamilton-Hart, 2000: pp. 122-123).

The Oil Crisis of 1982, characterized by the decline in oil prices, created the spark for Indonesia's liberalization of its domestic financial sector. This program included: 1) abolition of the credit ceiling system as means of monetary control while indirect monetary instrument were introduced, 2) reductions of liquidity coming into the market through liquidity credits of the central bank, and 3) permission granted to state-owned banks to fix their own interest rates and encouraged all banks to mobilize deposits from the public sector and to extend credits (Montes & Abdusalamov, 1998: p. 165).

The program yielded new resources coming into the economy. Whereas private banks took more risky projects and used the flexibility to extend credit rapidly, state banks, hampered by cumbersome procedures in granting loans, were more successful in attracting deposits[7] (Montes & Abdusalamov, 1998: p. 165). Unlike private banks, state banks were constantly enjoying surplus of funds, which resulted in the dynamic development of the inter-bank money market, and with initially high fluctuating interest rates. Higher interest and deposit rates: 1) encouraged foreign currency inflows, including banks' repatriated foreign exchange, which affected the amount of funds being exchanged in the inter-bank market and 2) contributed to the overall confidence in the stability of the rupiah. In 1984, Indonesia's Central Bank introduced the Sertifikat Bank Indonesia (SBI), which was a short-term liability of the bank designed to manage the overall liquidity. The Surat Berharga Pasar Uang (SBPU), also introduced in 1984, was a banker's acceptance instrument which could be sold to Bank Indonesia at a discount (Montes & Abdusalamov, 1998: pp. 165-166).

Indonesia's most ambitious financial reform effort was the October 1988 package (known as PAKTO 27, 1988). In order to foster competition, the package included the following measures: 1) the removal of most restrictions upon entry of foreign banks into Indonesia's economy and the establishment of branches of domestic banks, 2) allowing non-bank financial institutions (NBFIs) to issue certificates of deposit, 3) allowing public sector entities to place up to 50 percent of their deposits outside state banks, 4) permitting banks and NBFIs to issue certificates of deposit, 5) easing entry to leasing, insurance, venture capital, consumer finance, factoring and securities activities, 6) drastically reducing bank reserve requirements from 15 percent to 2 percent, 7) introducing improvement in other aspects of the banking sector, not excluding its policies and requirements, and 8) providing for the setting up of a privately-owned parallel stock market with less strict listing requirements, and with permission, in principle, for the establishment of other private stock exchanges (Montes & Abdusalamov, 1998: p. 166).

That package, part of Indonesia's financial liberalization efforts, caused an unprecedented growth in the bank and its branches after 1988. The number of banks increased from 124 in 1988 (with 2,044 branches) to 158 a year later. By 1994, there were 244 banks with 6,090 branches. As competition increased due to the package, added competitive pressures compelled each of Indonesia's large private conglomerates to own at least one bank while pension funds of state-owned enterprises established their own banks as well. The weakening of differentiation by function in the financial sector encouraged every NBFI to become full-fledged commercial banks by 1993. *However, the growth of banks and their branches did not go without concerns: prudential regulations even at their minimal levels were increasingly on the minds of many by the early 1990s* (Montes & Abdusalamov, 1998: p. 166).

Indonesia, by September of 1989, granted foreigners the right to buy up to 49 percent of all issued securities of firms listed on the stock exchanges. While domestic banks were permitted to operate more actively in foreign exchange and to open branches abroad, foreign banks enjoyed eased entry into the Indonesian economy. Foreign banks were instrumental in the continuing growth of Indonesian economy. Besides increasing their activities in buying issued securities of firms listed in the stock exchange, foreign banks also increased their activities in arranging private sector loans to both government and domestic firms. Additionally, these banks served as conduits for official development assistance from their own governments and multi-lateral institutions to the government. Ceilings on offshore borrowings were effectively replaced by a system of Net Open Positions (NOPs) and limitations placed on inflows of foreign direct investments were abolished.[8] The Banking Law of 1992 unified the regulations governing the banking system and further deregulated ownership restrictions in the financial sector. The Law permitted commercial banks to issue shares through stock exchanges and allowed foreigners to purchase up to 49 percent of the shares of commercial banks at the stock exchange (Montes & Abdusalamov, 1998: pp. 166-168).

The success of Indonesia's financial liberalization was axiomatic due to the fact that financial intermediation increased noticeably. The repatriation of the banks or any other inflow from abroad coupled with the easing of reserve requirements, led to an enormity in the size of funds intermediated in the financial system, an amount called TAFI.[9] The increases in the number of banks and NBFIs as well as the growth of M1 and M2 led to the rise of the concentration of assets in financial institutions and the level of intermediation by them in the system.[10] *Table 6.1 below supports this notion of the importance of banks in the economic and financial growths of Indonesia after 1970.*

Table 6.1
Indonesia: Ratios of M2 and TAFI to GDP and to Each Other, 1970-1991 (years selected)

The Ratios	1970	Growth(%)	1982	Growth (%)	1988	Growth (%)	1991
M2/GDP	0.10	47	0.19	36	0.30	25	0.40
TAFI/GDP	0.26	50	0.52	35	0.81	21	1.03
M2/TAFI	0.38	(0.02)	0.37	0	0.37	0.05	0.39

Source: Cole & Slade, 1996.

Table 6.1 provides a revelation of Indonesia's economic growth since 1970, thanks to the increasingly important role of the banks. It is worth noting that the slow growth in the TAFI/GDP ratio suggests that banks continue to possess a significantly larger portion of the total financial system, proved by the decrease in the M2/TAFI ratio between 1970 and 1982. The M2/TAFI ratio represents the share of the financial system controlled by institutions other than banks. That ratio hardly grew since 1988 (Montes & Abdusalamov, 1998: p. 169).

II.
The Coming of the Indonesian Financial Crisis

A. Poor Lending Practices and the Vulnerability of the Financial Sector

Notwithstanding the success in the financial sector caused by Indonesia's financial liberalization, such a success led to a greater vulnerability in domestic financial and capital markets. Like Thailand, Indonesia after financial liberalization engaged in excessive lending for property development and other endeavors. The end result was an increasing proportion of bad loans (non-performing loans), a weakened banking system, and domestic capital markets that "would be highly vulnerable to falls in the international value of the rupiah in its wake" (Montes & Abdusalamov, 1998: p. 169). The government failed to develop the regulatory and supervisory capacities needed to ensure strong and sustainable financial development, while basic prudential banking standards were never enforced (Radelet & Wing Thye Woo, 2000: p. 171).

Although financial liberalization was also designed to reduce problems inherent in the state-dominated financial system, poor lending practices did not subside. In 1993, the Minister of Finance, Mar'ie Muhammad, discovered that six of seven banks were technically insolvent and urgently in need of recapitalization up to 8 percent pursuant to the 1991 prudential regulations. Seven banks were reduced to three due to a merger program completed on July 31st, 1998: Bank Dagang Negara, Bank Bumi Daya, Bank Ekspor Impor Indonesia, and Bapindo were merged into a single bank; the Bank Tabungan Negara (BTN) became a subsidiary of one of the others: while the last of the seven state-owned banks, Bank Rakyat Indonesia, was to continue as before. Bank BNI was the only state bank listed on the stock exchange (McLeod, 1999: p. 220).

Furthermore, state-owned banks accounted for 72 percent of all bad debts in the banking sector in 1995, though that percentage subsided slightly to 65.9 percent by 1996. Because 5.08 percent of total credit of state-owned banks and 5.82 percent of the total credit of private non-foreign banks were non-performing by 1995, this meant that banks would have needed a margin of roughly 6 percent on their loans in order to absorb the losses on their existing loans. However, financial liberalization compelled banks to compete for deposits as the deposit rates increased in value and costs. In addition, the high interest rates gave domestic corporation incentives to borrow from abroad, placing a cap on the interest rates that could be charged on the lending side (Montes & Abdusalamov, 1998: p. 171).

B. The Contagion Effect

Whereas the origins of the Indonesian Financial Crisis were due to crony capitalism, weak financial structures, and inept macroeconomic policies, the contagion process triggered by a shift in market sentiment (the external factor) played much to the origins of the Crisis as well. The contagion factor, emanating from sudden changes in market sentiment in the Pacific Rim region, led to a shock in the currency markets of that region.[11] Entrepreneurs and investors panicked as a result, selling local currencies for dollars in haste. The change in market sentiment was demonstrated by the rapid downgrading process in the region's sovereign credit ratings. As J. Soedradjad Djiwandono points out:

> But, the most telling was the Institute of International Finance's publication on capital flows for Thailand, Malaysia, Indonesia, the Philippines, and South Korea, which showed a dramatic shift from inflows of $93 billion in 1996 to outflows of $12 billion in 1997, or a change of capital flows of $105 billion in a single year. For Indonesia, the reversed capital flows of last year [1997] were estimated to reach $22 billion, from inflows of $10 billion to outflows of $12 billion (J. Soedradjad Djiwandono, 1999: p. 116).

Confronted with the contagion effects, the Indonesian economy could not cope with the shock. The weakening of the rupiah was pervasive and had an adverse affect upon the financial sectors and the real sectors of the national economy. The combination of severe external shocks, along with the financial real sector structural weaknesses and vulnerability, had caused contagion effects that ultimately damaged Indonesia's economy severely (J. Soedradjad Djiwandono, 1999: p. 116).

C. Crony Capitalism and Political Ineffectiveness

Indonesian politics was shaped by President Suharto, who took control of Indonesia after his supportive attempted coup that overthrew President Sukarno in March of 1966. Suharto strove for authoritarianism, where political parties were marginalized and their inputs channeled into state sponsored activities. Although Indonesian politics under Suharto could never be deemed as open or democratic, that changed in the late 1980s when the government briefly signaled a political opening, especially with the introduction of PAKTO 27 of 1988 discussed above. However, the general elections of 1992 and Suharto's indirect elections of March of 1993 signaled a turning back to authoritarianism, with Suharto centralizing power within both the government and the ruling Golkar. The military was severely purged under Suharto's orders while promoting loyalists, including Suharto's son-in-law Prabowo Subianto. One of two opposition parties, the Indonesian Democratic Party (PDI) was allowed to function. However, its alluring leader, Megawati Sukarnoputri and her followers, were likewise purged. As increased labor activism (including forming a new political party) was met with repression, Tempo, Indonesia's most respected independent publication, was effectively shut down (Haggard, 2000: p. 115).

The fact that institutions were under centralized control had created uncertainties amongst economists and investors. Such uncertainties grew due to participations of the Suharto's family in Indonesia's business activities. By the late 1980s and the early 1990s, the Suharto family (not excluding his children) and the family's closest allies, expanded their businesses rapidly. The children became involved in a growing range of entrepreneurial activities, beginning with resource-based ventures, then in manufacturing for the domestic market, and later in financial services, construction, and toll road operation. Suharto's family business operations were met with little restraints, especially in the early 1990s. Cronyism and corruption were not at all new in Indonesia; substantial economic activity has been channeled to the military and a small circle of private business personnel were close to Suharto. What made matters worse was that during the Crisis of 1997, although Suharto was willing to make tough decisions that required some sacrifice by those chosen entities, he did nothing of the sort when his children's business interests were at stake (Radelet & Woo, 2000: p. 171). Suharto's failing health after the mid-1990s, the uncertainty of Suharto's future leadership, clashes within the military, and speculations of his successors did not help matters in the increasing volatile political and economical situations.

Suharto's repressive policies did not, however, prevent to coming of social and political protests after 1998, all of which were followed by riots. The long-term causes of the unrests which ultimately led to Suharto's downfall were the economic downslide characterized by increasing unemployment and the rise in poverty level, as well as corruption and political uncertainties. Unlike Malaysia, Suharto's Indonesia failed to control the scope of the protests; most of them participated by students. The spark of Suharto's downfall came on May 12th, 1999, when four students were killed outside Triskati University. The protests following this tragedy placed a seal on Suharto's thirty-three year reign: he resigned on May 21st after growing opposition especially from B.J. Habibie, who became Suharto's successor by October of 1999 as interim president (Haggard, 2000: pp. 115-116).

B.J. Habibie earned a reputation as an advocate for industrialization based on high-tech sectors. His close economic advisor, Adi Sasono, advocated for an economy based cooperative ownership. However, such advocacies helped to undermine the efficacy of various market oriented reform programs already implemented. What's more was that from August of 1999 and onwards, Habibie's management of the economy was met with greater difficulties when foreign aid was suspended. The suspension came due to Indonesia's military suppression upon East Timorese's efforts for independence in the elections supervised by the United Nations (Radelet and Woo, 2000: p. 168).

The election of Abdurrahman Wahid to the presidency was met with surprise, especially since the election was the result in the formation of a large cabinet that encompassed the wide range of interests that the coalition partners represented. Kwik Kian Gie, the head of the economic team, was from the Partai Demokrasi Indonesia-Perjuangan (PDI-P), the party led by Megawati Sukarnoputri and which received 34 percent of popular votes in the parliamentary elections. However, because many important ministers within the economic team were from parties opposed to a Megawati presidency, Kwik Kian Gie found it difficult to assert leadership in economy policy, to coordinate the work of the various economic ministries, and to formulate a coherent development strategy out of disparate economic programs (Radelet and Woo, 2000: p. 168). The political structure of Indonesia is almost as clustered and clouded as that of Thailand.

However, Ms. Megawati Sukarnoputri, the daughter of the late Sukarno who died in 1970, took over as president in July, 2001. Immensely popular among many ordinary Indonesians, she won the election after the period of erratic governance of Wahid's administration (along with his isolationism) (BBC News, 06/02/2004: pp. 2-4). Entering politics in 1987 at age forty, she became a symbol of popular resistance against Suharto, partially due to her parentage, but also due to Suharto's attempts to oust her as leader of the PDI-P. During her tenure as president, her government oversaw the country's gradual economic growth and continued recovery, although she was still contending with high unemployment and corruption. Furthermore, her political style, characterized by her reluctance to give interviews and make speeches, were seen as cunning by some and a sign of weakness by others (BBC News, 06/02/2004: pp. 2-4).

III.
Indonesia and the Asian Financial Crisis: The Scope, The Nature, and the Actions Taken

A. The Crisis Unfolded

Despite poor quality bank loans and pressures on monetary policy due to large inflows of capital prior to 1997, optimism about the financial sector was high. Deregulatory reforms were considered successful, the stock market was buoyant (though on occasion yielding towards turbulence), and the bank stocks were particularly favored. Indonesia's macroeconomic fundamentals were deemed as sound while the Jakarta Stock Exchange index continued to rise until July 8th, 1997 (Hamilton-Hart, 2000: pp. 111-112).

In essence, the Indonesian financial crisis originated from an ordinary currency problem, when the rupiah suffered from sudden pressure in July of 1997 after the Thai baht floated. However, the policy responses of the Indonesian government and the reaction from the market contributed more to the currency problem in unprecedented severity. As the rupiah underwent market pressure as part of the contagion effects, the government, based on its exchange rate management policy of a managed float with creeping depreciation that relied on the mechanism of interventionist bands adjusted continuously since 1994, decided to widen the bands from eight percent to twelve percent on July 11th, 1997.[12] Furthermore, the widening of Bank Indonesia's intervention bands led to a rapid depreciation of the rupiah. When the spot rate crossed the Bank Indonesia selling rate, some intervention in the currency market was exercised. However, as the intervention began with the forward sales of dollars in the beginning, and later progressed to spot sales, the pressure on the currency was not abating. Intervention in both the forward and spot markets resumed after Bank Indonesia floated the rupiah on August 14th, 1997. To support the currency intervention, monetary tightening was conducted through drastic increases in interest rates and fiscal tightening (J. Soedradjad Djiwandono, 1999: pp. 117-118).

However, after Bank Indonesia intervened in the market several times and exercised monetary tightening, the problems became pervasive in the banking sector and the sector began to experience distress. Despite the rise of interest rates, the rupiah continued to slide and, consequently, confidence from bank depositors and creditors began to dissipate. The closure of sixteen insolvent banks, as part of the IMF supported package, made matters worse and despite the efforts to fix the weakening economy, the rupiah remained relatively weak (J. Soedradjad Djiwandono, 1999: pp. 118-119).[13]

Indonesia began its negotiations with the IMF, with which it reached an agreement on October 31st, 1997. Meanwhile, the central bank, in cooperation with the Monetary Authority of Singapore and the Bank of Japan, intervene to support the rupiah in the first week of November (Hamilton-Hart, 2000: p. 112). Indonesia requested a three-year standby loan from the IMF, which was processed through an emergency procedure. The loan was SDR (Special Drawing Right) $7.3 billion, and together with those provided by the World Bank and the Asian Development Bank (ADB), the total amount was $18 billion. Indonesia's own reserves set aside for balance of payment support, added $5 billion to the overall amount to be drawn. Together with bilateral participation in a second line of defense, the total amount of the package reached $43 billion (J. Soedradjad Djiwandono, 1999: p. 123). The measures led to the stabilization of the rupiah at roughly 3200 to the dollar, down from 2400 during the early months of 1997 (Hamilton-Hart, 2000: p. 112).

However, the success was anything but long-lasting. The rupiah fell steeply in December of 1997, reaching Rp 16,500 to the dollar by January the following year. Although the currency showed some recovery in March and April, it crashed once again to nearly 16,000 to the dollar in June. There was no doubt that the real currency devaluation met with unprecedented severity. Furthermore, the stock market had lost 60 percent of its July 1997 value (91 percent in U.S. dollar terms). Even though both the stock and currency values improved towards the end of the year, the banking system remained effectively bankrupt (Hamilton-Hart, 2000: p. 112).

Indonesia's financial system in effect approached the 1997-1998 Asian Financial Crisis with banks in heavy need of recapitalization in anticipation of write-offs on non-performing loans. Furthermore, the private corporate sector and the banking system had heavy un-hedged external liabilities most denominated in U.S. dollars.[14] The decline in the value of the rupiah resulted in a severe imposition of debt servicing difficulties upon corporate and banking sectors (Montes & Abdusalamov, 1998: p. 171). The economy contracted by around 14 percent as unemployment increased and by March of 1999, the central bank classified 59 percent of all bank loans in Indonesia as non-performing (Hamilton-Hart, 2000: p. 112). On March 13th, the government announced the closure of thirty-eight insolvent banks, nationalization of seven domestic banks, and recapitalization of nine banks (Tan, 2000: p. 114). The announcement was an immediate foretaste for what was to come: by April of 1999, private bank claims on the private sector had been written down to Rp134 trillion, a decrease from Rp202 trillion a year previous (Hamilton-Hart, 2000: p. 112).

By 1998, Indonesia witnessed a 36 percent collapse in real fixed investment and a 21 percent drop by 1999. There was no doubt that Indonesia's financial status was in a terrible disarray, as Radelet and Sachs point out:

> ...the seven banks that dominated the financial system before the crisis are now insolvent. The corporate sector is mired in debt, and owners of bankrupt firms are reluctant to embrace formal bankruptcy or to engage in debt-equity swaps because of the possible loss of control over the firms. The hope is that the rupiah will appreciate when political stability is restored; thence the debt-servicing problem will be greatly diminished. However, without a marked improvement in the economy, and with it the generation of economic rents to co-opt political opposition, it unlikely that political normalcy will return any time soon (Radelet and Woo, 2000: p. 165).

Indonesian corporations and to some extent, the banks, borrowed extensively from foreign creditors utilizing loans with short maturity structures. Short-term foreign debt outstanding increased rapidly from $19 billion in 1994 to $35 billion in June of 1997. The latter figure exceeded greater than $20 billion in foreign exchange reserves available at the time to meet these obligations. Had much of the debt hedged against the risk of exchange rate movements, the hedging alone, according to the World Bank, would have added six percentage points to the cost of borrowing (Radelet and Woo, 1997: pp. 171-172). Table 6.2 shows debt outstanding to foreign commercial banks by sector.

Table 6.2
Debt outstanding to foreign commercial banks by sector (in billions of $)

Dates	Total:	Banks:	Public:	Non-Bank private:	Short-term debt:	Foreign reserves (excluding gold):
June 1997	58.7	12.4	6.5	39.7	34.7	20.3
Dec. 1997	58.4	11.7	6.9	39.7	35.4	16.6
June 1998	50.3	7.1	7.6	35.5	27.7	17.9

Source: Radelet, Steven C. & Wing Thye Woo. "Indonesia: A Troubled Beginning." *The Asian Financial Crisis: Lessons for a Resilient Asia.* Wing Thye Woo, Jeffrey Sachs, and Klaus Schwab, editors. Cambridge, Massachusetts: The MIT Press, 2000: p. 172.

Real GDP fell from 8.5 percent in 1997 to -17.7 in 1998 (fourth quarter), although it recovered to -8.0 percent in 1999 (first quarter) and then to 3.1 percent in the second quarter. Despite the noticeable recovery of the GDP, various sectors underwent severe losses. The construction sector alone experienced a 40 percent drop in activity level. Likewise, both financial and business services fell by 26 percent, trade, hotel, and restaurants fell by 18 percent, and transport as well as communication fell by 15 percent. Due to over-devaluation, the export sector grew by 11 percent. Nevertheless, the decline in activity levels demonstrated the widespread economic distress that had translated into rising formal sector unemployment, a great concentration of employment in informal activities, and falling of real wages. According to the World Bank, it was estimated that real wages declined by 50 percent and consequently, the number of Indonesian below the poverty level rose sharply (Radelet and Woo, 2000: pp. 176-177).[15]

B. The International Monetary Fund (IMF) and the Restructuring Process

According to the IMF Executive Board, efforts to strengthen the banking system should be guided by the following principles. *First,* the soundness of a bank was first and foremost the responsibility of its owners and managers, yet the soundness of a banking system is a public policy concern. *Second,* bank soundness was crucially linked to sound macroeconomic policies. *Third,* a framework for sound banking must include structures to support internal governance and market discipline, as well as official regulation and supervision. *Lastly,* the International Cupertino and coordination can play an important role, not only in strengthening the global financial system, but also in improving the soundness of the national banking system (J. Soedradjad Djiwandono, 1999: p. 122). However, as previously mentioned, the soundness of the banking system was never achieved due to ill-discipline in both borrowing and lending. The lack of market discipline, regulation, and supervision all led to the contagion effect and the ultimate closures of thirty-eight insolvent banks.

The October 1997 agreement between the IMF and Indonesia was aimed at trade liberalization, the deregulation of monopolies, and privatization in order to enhance competition. Competition was to be enhanced by leveling the playing field for foreign investors, lifting restrictions on foreign-owned banks, and establishing foreign ownership of local banks (Hamilton-Hart, 2000: p. 118).

The financial restructuring program, put together with the technical assistance from the IMF, the World Bank, and the ADB, to restore public confidence in the financial system, consisted of five components, namely: 1) the closure of sixteen insolvent banks, which commenced on November 1st, 1997, 2) the establishment of proper procedures and policies to deal promptly with weak but viable financial institutions for the sake of recovery, whereas some banks were placed under intensive supervision of Bank Indonesia, 3) the resolution of specific problems of state and regional development banks, 4) the strengthening of the institutional, legal, and regulatory frameworks for banking operations to ensure the emergence of a sound and efficient financial system, not excluding modification of Central Bank Law, the Law on Bank Liquidation, and Bankruptcy Law, and 5) the establishment of Indonesia Bank Restructuring Agency (IBRA) after the second letter of intent (J. Soedradjad Djiwandono, 1999: pp. 123-124).

IBRA was created on January 27th, 1998 to oversee the bank restructuring process. It has the authority to close, manage, or oversee troubled banks, and to transfer assets of closed banks to its own Asset Management Unit (AMU) for eventual disposal. In the beginning, IBRA focused on recovering liquidity credits that Bank Indonesia had lent to support ailing banks that were eventually frozen. Since banks such as Bank Central Asia (BCA), Bank Danamon, and Bank Dagang Nasional Indonesia could not repay their liquidity credits, they agreed to swab the debts for shares in a "plethora of affiliated companies" (Radelet and Woo, 2000: p. 179). During the next year, IBRA had fifty-four banks, representing 40 percent of the banking assets under supervision. IBRA also took over most of Indonesia's large private banks such as Bank Central Asia and announced on July 1999 that it had assets worth Rp 600 trillion under management (Hamilton-Hart, 2000: p. 115).

In December of 1998, the Indonesian government completed an audit to separate the levels of "soundness" among banks and to classify them in accordance to their capital asset ratios (CAR).

Table 6.3
The Healthiness of Banks in Categories According to CAR

Banks in Category	CAR	Healthiness of banks
Category A banks:	CAR > 4%	Sound banks
Category B banks:	-25%<CAR<4%	Salvageable banks
Category C banks:	CAR< -25%	Bad banks

Source: Radelet, Steven C. & Wing Thye Woo. "Indonesia: A Troubled Beginning." *The Asian Financial Crisis: Lessons for a Resilient Asia* .Wing Thye Woo, Jeffrey Sachs, and Klaus Schwab, editors. Cambridge, Massachusetts: The MIT Press, 2000: p. 179.

There were seventy-four banks in category A while seven state banks that dominated the banking sector prior to 1998 were in category C. The government stipulated that banks in category B would be eligible to participate in a state-sponsored recapitalization program. However, private banks in category C would be closed unless they could raise enough capital to upgrade themselves to a category B status (Radelet and Woo, 2000: p. 179). After the completion of the audit, the Indonesian government announced that most state banks were to be merged into a new entity, Bank Mandiri, as a prelude to privatization (Hamilton-Hart, 2000: p. 118).

Foreign banks acquired controlling stakes in two Indonesian banks and one-third was under heavy foreign management by mid-1999. However, the reduction of government ownership as a goal was utterly reversed by the recapitalization program, which, theoretically, made the government the majority owner of all Indonesia's major banks. Furthermore, the government established a new export financing bank to provide subsidized export credits, guarantees, and working capital facilities for exporters. Whereas the privatization of state-owned banks is still on the works, the privatization of Bank Mandiri remains uncertain. Furthermore, the plan to sell the major nationalized banks by the end of 1999 continues to be behind schedule. Full divestment is unlikely to take place unless these banks are sold much less than the cost of governmental rescuing efforts (Hamilton-Hart, 2000: p. 118).

As part of the IMF conditionality, Indonesia engaged in policy reform in order to improve prudential regulation. Banking capital requirements were reduced in the April 1998 IMF agreement, which "nonetheless set them higher than they had been prior to the crisis" (Hamilton-Hart, 2000: p. 118). An amendment to the Banking Law to: 1) eliminate restrictions of foreign investment in listed banks, 2) amend bank secrecy laws, and 3) enable state bank mergers and privatization, was submitted to parliament on schedule on August of 1998. Shortly thereafter, Indonesia passed a new banking law: 1) to increase disclosure requirements and 2) to rationalize prudential regulations and penalties. However, the conditions of Indonesia's banking and corporate sectors made capital requirements and meaningful prudential regulation almost impossible. It was reported that Bank Indonesia monitoring efforts showed no signs of improvement (Hamilton-Hart, 2000: p. 118).

Indonesia also established a better capital account monitoring system. As Hamilton-Hart reminds us, "before the crisis, Indonesian authorities imposed minimal reporting requirements on capital transactions and private foreign liabilities later proved much higher than officially reported. Plans to remedy that deficiency first surfaced in Indonesia's October 1998 letter of intent to the IMF, which envisaged IMF advice on procedures for monitoring capital flows" (Hamilton-Hart, 2000: p. 119). However, the new capital account monitoring system has yet to work in practice. The government did not decide on the minimum transaction size that would be subject to reporting requirements. Overcoming the underlying reasons for poor monitoring will be crucial to the success of the new monitoring regime, especially since banks would have partial authority to investigate foreign liabilities of Indonesian companies. However, such an authority may be ineffective, because the policy may not be actively enforced or its effects may be severely limited due to intrusion and abuse in the system. The message behind this situation is that successful policy reform, like crisis management, depends on underlying institutional capacities (Hamilton-Hart, 2000: p. 119).

The role of the IMF was well-intentioned but severely lacked realistic vision and an adequate understanding of the scope of Indonesia's financial crisis. Instead of turning the tides against the crisis, the IMF played a major role in the deepening of its severity. Instead of keeping resources fully employed, the IMF attached higher priority to stabilizing the rupiah. The closure of banks and financial institutions required in the IMF rescue package resulted in panics and outcries by connected and influential owners of the closed-down institutions in the country. Furthermore, macroeconomic reforms insisted by the IMF had very little to do with the Crisis (McLeod, 1999: p. 229). For instance, IMF's requirement for the removal of government subsidies on food, medicine, fertilizer, cattle feed, and poultry, led to sudden price hikes and consequent riots in many provinces in the country (Tran Van Hoa, 2000: p. 22). Knowing that the first package yielded in little favorable results, the IMF pointed to the failure of the government to abide by its commitments and then multiplied the list of demands for reforms several times over (McLeod, 1999: p. 229). Had the IMF reexamined the nature and the impact of the first package, its' understanding on the crisis would have been even more secured and, at least arguably, Indonesia would've had a rate of recovery similar to that of Thailand and perhaps Malaysia.

IV.
Epilogue
Indonesia Then and Now: The Areas of Concerns Indonesia Must Continue to Face

A. Indonesia's Economic Story-A Recapitulation

Prior to the Asian Financial Crisis of 1997-1998, Indonesia became one of the fastest growing economic forces in the developing world. As dependency on oil gave way to the emergence of an export-oriented manufacturing base, the structure of Indonesia's economy has become diversified. Such a turn-around was led by not only a dynamic private sector, but also by high domestic savings and large inflows of FDI which fueled the sector in the first place. Furthermore, the Oil Crisis of 1982, characterized by a decrease in oil prices, played a role in the turn-around as well as the creation of the financial liberalization programs. However, although much praises shall be given to Indonesia's economic and financial performances per se, the government remained, at least for the most part, consistently adherent to its prudent macroeconomic policies, high investment and savings rates, and market-oriented trade and exchange rate regimes.

Indonesia's macroeconomic policies were sound and exemplary: balance of payments was maintained, inflation remained low, current account deficits were kept at moderate levels, and international reserves were well maintained. Furthermore, broad-based labor-intensive growth, along with sustained improvements in basic education and health services reduced the poverty rate drastically during the twenty-five year growth period (1972-1997). Indonesia clearly became a very competitive nation by 1996, primarily due to both its financial liberalization as well as a series of deregulation packages of the 1980s.

These abovementioned reforms of the 1980s were designed to eliminate as much as possible the abuses in the financial sector through liberalization, competition, reduced credit subsidies, and a significantly reduced role of state banks. At first, the reforms were successful, for they yielded new resources for the economy. State banks became very successful in attracting deposits and enjoyed their surplus of funds. PAKTO 27, 1988, a reform package passed in October, 1988 for the sake of fostering competition, led to unprecedented growth in the financial sector, as the creation of the banks nearly doubled in a six year span, from 1988 to 1994. Foreign investors and foreign banks were granted easier entry in the Indonesian economy, as restrictions "loosened up" thanks to those reforms, not excluding the PAKTO 27, 1988.

Although the financial liberalization was a success, it did not, however, prevent poor lending practices and the vulnerability of the financial sector. As with the case of Thailand, Indonesia engaged in excessive lending for property development and other endeavors. The end results of this practice were the escalations of NPLs, a weakened banking system, and a weakened rupiah. The government, although prudent in its macroeconomic policies, was less so in developing regulatory and supervisory policies and mechanisms needed to sustain strong financial development. Basic prudential banking practices and standards were never enforced and crony capitalism resulted.

With the emergence of the Asian Financial Crisis, Indonesia suffered from its contagion effects. The effects were caused by external shocks, financial real sector structural weaknesses and vulnerability, and political instability. Along with Suharto's repressive policies and the ensuing social protests, Indonesia had to cope with rising unemployment and poverty rate, as well as a loss of confidence among domestic and foreign consumers and investors. Although Indonesia engaged in policy reforms at part of IMF's conditionality to improve prudential regulation, the problems remained institutional and persistent.

In this era after the Asian Financial Crisis, Indonesia's economic growth and recovery remained the most modest in comparison with the other countries examined in this book (as with Hong Kong and Korea). As you shall see, Indonesia's recovery from the Crisis was at first precarious, with the surge of rates of unemployment and poverty. However, since 2000, the growth and recovery of the Indonesian economy became steadier though uneven. Its growth remains, however, despite the growing concerns of social conditions that even politicians were facing for the 2004 elections.

B. After the Asian Financial Crisis, Indonesia's Recovery was, at first Precarious

Indonesia is barely recovering from its economy which contracted by 16 percent during the peak of the Crisis in 1998 through 1999. The good news was that the economy grew by more than five percent in the fourth quarter of 1999. However, unemployment had surged from 20 million in 1997 to 35 million by 2000. Twenty percent of the population was living below the poverty level and the negative economic growth has a profound adverse impact upon the middle class. Mark Baird, representative of the bank's Jakarta, contended that the crisis was not generalized, since the people in urban areas were worst off in comparison to those in rural settings. The rural areas had better support systems than did cities, with less than three percent of children who dropped out of school (BBC World Service, 2000: pp. 1-4).

C. Indonesia's Uneven Growth and Recovery since 2000

1. Introduction

As shown in Table 6.4, although Indonesia's GDP growth continues to grow, albeit modestly, it is still being confronted with its fiscal imbalances. Although not seen in this table, the year 2003 was something of a watershed in Indonesia's recovery, though not without some pressing concerns such as unemployment, lacklustre growth, and rising prices especially of oil.

Table 6.4
Indonesia's Economic Performances, 2000-2005

The Indicators *(in percentage)*	**2000**	**2001**	**2002**	**2003**	**2004**	**2005**
GDP growth	4.8	3.8	4.3	5.0	4.9	5.6
Gross domestic investment/GDP	15.8	17.8	15.7	16.0	21.3	21.5
Gross domestic savings/GDP	25.1	24.9	21.1	20.1	24.0	26.0
Inflation rate (consumer price index)	3.7	11.5	11.9	6.6	6.2	16.5
Money supply (M2) growth	15.6	13.0	4.7	8.1	8.1	n/a.
Fiscal balance/ GDP	-1.6	-2.3	-1.7	-2.1	-1.3	-0.5
Merchandise export growth	27.6	-12.3	3.1	7.2	9.4	20.0
Merchandise import growth	31.9	-14.1	2.8	9.4	13.3	26.0
Current account balance/GDP	5.0	4.8	4.5	3.7	2.6	1.1
The unemployment rate	-	8.0	10.6	9.3	9.2	10.9

Sources: 1) The Asian development Outlook 2003, 2004, 2005, and 2006.
Website: www.adb.org
2) IndexMundi (on the unemployment rate, the 2005 inflation rate).
Website www.indexmundi.com

Note: The latest and revised GDP growth figures from 2001 through 2004 are from the Asian Development Outlook 2006

2. The Years 2002 and 2003

Through 2002, the Indonesian economic growth was sustained, driven primarily by private consumption spending and the government's progress in improving both macroeconomic stability as well as fiscal sustainability. Furthermore, bank credit expanded, large formal sector wage increased, and both the currency and stock market strengthened. However, the growth remained modest due to declining investment and limited advances in overcoming the underlying impediments to investor confidence, which robbed the economy of its near-term growth potential (The Asian Development Outlook 2003, 2003: p. 68). In addition, although the Bali terrorist attacks in October of 2002 concerned the economists and investors alike, the impact of that tragic event was generally contained (BBC News, 02/17/2003: p. 1). Notwithstanding the economy remaining on track, not everyone is that excited over this prospect. According to the World Bank, Indonesia should be aiming at a growth rate of 5 percent to 6 percent if "it was serious about reducing its debts" (BBC News, 02/17/2003: p. 1). As you shall see in greater details below, although GDP growth remained modest at 5.0 percent in 2003, it grew to 5.6 percent in 2005 (Asian Development Outlook 2006, 2006: p. 198).

Manufacturing grew 3.7 percent in 2002, a number that was modest by any means due to the floods early in that year as well as less than ideal investment spending. Agriculture grew much better, at 2.3 percent from the recent 0.7 percent annual growth trend, a remarkable achievement given the meteorological concerns of the recent past (The Asian Development Outlook 2003, 2003: p. 68). However, the major stimulus to GDP growth came from a strong growth of private and government spending, with the former relatively stronger than income growth overall. Private spending, which was an equivalence to more than 70 percent of GDP, grew by 4.7 percent in 2002 while public spending rose by 12.8 percent (ADO 2003, 2003: p. 68). In 2005, however, both manufacturing and agricultural sectors declined after showing improvements in 2004.[16] Notwithstanding this problem, mining, construction, and services sectors were improving, with construction and services which accounted for about one-half of the economy (Asian Development Outlook 2006, 2006: pp. 198-199).

3. The "White Paper" of 2003 and Consequent Legislations

Indonesia's economy at the end of 2003 grew at about 4 percent, as inflation fell to a record low of below 5 percent. Whereas foreign exchange reserves reached a record high above $35 billion, monthly exports had reached the pre-crisis level of $5 billion. The inflows of direct investment showed improvement as portfolio investment broke record highs. Consequently, virtually every credit rating agencies upgraded Indonesia's own rating (Indonesian Embassy's News

& Views, 2003: p. 1).

The "White Paper," a program of economic measures passed on September 15th, 2003, was a result of the government's goal to graduate from the Extended Fund Facility arrangement with the IMF at the end of that year. The policy objective went in line the People's Consultative Assembly decree which recommended cessation of such an arrangement without creating instability (Indonesian Embassy's News & Views, 2003: pp. 2-4). The "White Paper" program has three key policy goals (or rather, three Economic Packages).

The first goal is to continue with Indonesia's macroeconomic stability through fiscal sustainability, low inflation, strong foreign exchange reserves with an efficient national payment system, and stability of the rupiah. After the parliament approved the budget goal for 2004, with the deficit reduced from 1.9 percent in 2003 to 1.2 percent in 2004, this First Package is geared towards macroeconomic stability through prudent fiscal management. Debt repayment remains an issue, however, and the government is facing challenges of raising additional revenues to deal with that issue. Through the "White Paper" program, the government focuses on key areas to raise revenue, namely tax and customs reforms and improved debt management. A move has been made to re-organize the Ministry of Finance and improve its budget and debt management. In regards to tax reforms, the Directorate General of Tax worked on drafting new Tax Law, drawing up and expanding the list of eligible tax payers for rebate qualifications. Also, the Directorate General is expanding the operation of Large Tax Payers Offices (LTOs) to regions (Indonesian Embassy's News & Views, 2003: pp. 2-4).

The second goal is to remain committed in restructuring and reforming the bank and non-bank financial sectors, including improving anti-money laundering policies and enforcement as well as improving the operations and governance of state-owned enterprises (SOEs) (Indonesian Embassy's News & Views, 2003: pp. 2-4). With this goal in place, the government and Bank Indonesia are jointly addressing the key issue of putting forth a variety of safety net measures designed to eventually replace the current "blanket deposit" guarantee with a more sustainable instrument. Furthermore, in the government's efforts to improve the soundness and the vibrancy of the non-bank financial institutions, the Capital Market Supervisory Agency (or BAPEPAM) was strengthened in its supervisory and enforcement capacities. By the end of 2003, BAPEPAM was holding consultation with the mutual fund industry to improve its regulations and supervision. In the meantime, the Center for Financial Transaction Analysis, the PPATK has been formalized through the issuance of presidential decrees. The Center, which entered into several cooperative arrangements with BAPEPAM, Bank Indonesia, and Directorate Generals to inspect money transactions, has also engaged in a nation-wide program to educate people and investors on potential money laundering ventures (Indonesian Embassy's News & Views, 2003: pp. 2-4).

The third and final goal is to increase the level of investment, exports, and employment by improving the investment climate, labor relations, industry and trade facilitation, legal reforms, as well as security and governance (Indonesian Embassy's News & Views, 2003: pp. 2-4). Among the measures under this goal includes the provision of equal treatment between foreign and domestic investment as well as streamlining licensing approval and guidelines on incentives. A National Team on Investment and Exports Promotion was set up through a presidential decree to deal with inter-ministerial issues that concern existing and potential investors. In addition to that, a series of measures has been introduced and passed in order to deal with improving trade facilitation and eliminating corruption. The Business Solution Center in Ministry of Industry and Trade is being strengthened to provide more effective intervention on commerce issues and to eliminate smuggling. At the same time, the government is accelerating the program of infrastructure development in energy, telecoms, transport, and water resources to issue land certificates in order to allow SMEs' access to credit resources. As far as fighting corruption is concerned, Indonesia's parliament had completed its selection process of commissioners to the independent Anti-Corruption Commissions (Indonesian Embassy's News & Views, 2003: pp. 2-4).

4. Indonesia in 2004 and beyond

Since 2001, Indonesia's GDP growth continues to climb upwards, reaching a 5.6 growth level for 2005. What's impressive about this growth is that it was achieved despite: 1) the major earthquake and tsunami of December of 2004 (which severely affected the Aceh province and Nias islands), 2) changes in budgetary procedures, which led to a slowdown in the release of development funding, 3) a sharp increase in domestic fuel prices, 4) a considerable elevation in both inflation and interest rates, and 5) a slump in the rupiah (Asian Development Outlook 2006, 2006: p. 198).[17] Due in large part to the legislations passed in 2003 (the White Paper in particular), the investment climate is improving.

Other indicators are showing improvements as well. The fiscal deficit has narrowed to less than 1 percent of GDP and public debt declined to 52 percent of GDP (down to nearly 30 percentage points over four years) (Asian Development Outlook 2006, 2006: p. 198). However, higher inflation and interest rates slowed both private consumption and investment spending, with the growth of the former slowed by one percentage point to 4.0 percent (it increased to 4.9 percent in 2004) (Asian Development Outlook 2006, 2006: p. 198). Fixed investment likewise slowed after showing signs of improvement in years past. In 2005, investment was dawdling by roughly 4.0 percentage points to 9.9 percent (ADO 2006, 2006: p. 198). Even though private consumption lost steam somewhat, the saving rate paradoxically declined between 2001 and 2004, signifying personal consumption as an engine for growth during those years. In 2005 however, the savings rate picked up slightly (from roughly 24.0 percent in 2004 to about 26.0 percent in 2005) thanks in part to higher inflation and interest rates (ADO 2006, 2006: p. 198).

The higher interest rates posed harm to the banking sector. Loan growth slowed during 2005 while the net NPL ratio rose from 1.9 percent to 5.0 percent during that year (Asian Development Outlook 2006, 2006: p. 200). Furthermore, banks' capital-adequacy ratio declined from 21.7 percent to 19.6 percent while state-owned commercial banks posted NPL ratios at around 15 percent, raising concerns about their governance and risk management. The inflation rate, which rose to 18 percent between March and October of last year, had considerable impact on the poor. In response to the situation, the government announced an unconditional cash transfer program to provide subsistence support of about $10 a month for one year to roughly 1.5 million households (to a total amount of $480 million in 2005) (Asian Development Outlook 2006, 2006: p. 199). In addition, the cut in subsidies, which gave the government conserved fiscal resources, yielded to a $1.4 billion spending program to upgrade education and health facilities as well as village infrastructure in 2005-2006 (Asian Development Outlook 2006, 2006: p. 199). The rise in inflation rate helped strengthen the rupiah and foreign reserves recovered consequently from $30 billion in September to $35 billion in December. The aforementioned trends continued throughout the first quarter of 2006 (Asian Development Outlook 2006, 2006: p. 199).

Private investment accelerated in 2005 while trading performances improved considerably. FDI in sectors other than oil, gas, and finance almost doubled from $4.6 billion in 2004 to $8.9 billion in 2005 (Asian Development Outlook 2006, 2006: p. 199). Even though the growth in FDI remained a far-cry from its $39.7 billion peak in 1995, the recovery, however slow, is evident, especially for the medium term. Likewise, realized domestic investment more than doubled to $3.2 billion. But, a slowdown in public investment outweighed the recovery in private investment, resulting in reduced fixed capital formation (which rose to 15.7 percent in 2004) (Asian Development Outlook 2006, 2006: p. 199). The exporting picture has become quite ideal, with total merchandise exports increasing to 20.0 percent in 2005 from 9.4 percent in 2004 (and non-oil and gas has increased around the same rate). In terms of volume, however, exports moved little despite currency depreciation in mid-2005 and Indonesia has lost market share in some major exports since 1998. Merchandise imports likewise improved, from 13.5 percent in 2004 to 26.0 percent a year later (ADO 2006, 2006: p. 199).

The oil debacle handicapped the Indonesian government during the second and third quarters of 2005 (please see endnote below). However, the government took bold measures in doubling fuel prices to slash the cost of subsidies. Meanwhile, Bank Indonesia took a complimentary step in raising its one-month policy interest rate by four percentage points to 12.75 percent between September and December to support the rupiah and damp down the inflation. The moves worked, for investor confidence was restored, but not without a price: inflation was vamped up while consumer spending slowed (Asian Development Outlook 2006, 2006: p. 199).

The economy overall is improving, with budget deficit declining from 2.4 percent in 2001 to 0.5 percent in 2005. Fiscal consolidation, a hallmark of Indonesia's economic policy since 1997, is indeed working by far. While the budget deficit shows improvement, so is the ratio of external debt to GDP, which decreased from 45 percent in 2000 to 27 percent in 2005. The Paris Club's decision to reschedule Indonesia's debt in 2005, which allowed the government to defer $2.5 billion in debt repayment until 2006, helped Indonesia in its debt management (Asian Development Outlook 2006, 2006: p. 201).

The employment picture is a major concern, however. The unemployment rate continues to climb for five strait years, reaching a 10.9 percent level in 2005, with 2.5 million annual entrants not able to find work. The poverty rate has fallen, from 23 percent in 1999 to 16 percent in 2005. But, about 53 percent of the population lived on less than $2 a day by that year. Furthermore, the rise in the cost for cooking fuel worsen the situation for the poor, although the aggressive programs the government has launched (the reduction in regressive fuel subsidy as well as the reorientation of fiscal resources in helping the poor) should be highly effective in fighting poverty in the future (Asian Development Outlook 2006, 2006: p. 201).

D. Despite the overall improvement of Indonesia's economy, Concerns Still Remain

1. The Social, Political and Economic Concerns

As mentioned before, the year 2003 was a watershed in some respects, not only due to the overall brighter economic picture, but also due the government's arguably resilient steps in improving and maintaining Indonesia's economic performance and well-being, with the "White Paper" program particularly instrumental in achieving this far-reaching endeavor. Also, Indonesia finished its IMF program in December of 2003. Despite that, Indonesia receives roughly $43 billion in aid from the Consultative Group on Indonesia (CGI) as well as from Non-governmental organizations (NGOs) since 2004 (CIA Factbook, 2006: pp. 10-11). However, there remain some lurking socio-economic problems.

First, as mentioned before, the employment picture remains highly worrisome. As seen in Table 6.2, the unemployment rate since 2001 remains roughly 9.5 percent on average. In 2003 for instance, with poverty as among the chief concerns, the rise of unemployment reached 9.3 percent with over 66 percent of the 40 million jobless in the age group of 15-24 (Guerin, 2004: p. 1). That unemployment figure worsened two years later, reaching a five year high of 10.9 percent.

Secondly, the investment climate continues to yield uncertainty, despite the government's efforts to improve consumers and investors confidence by being more transparent, especially in fighting corruption and mismanagement. The Manulife case of 2002, which involved a promising insurance company threatened by corruption in the judicial system, gained widespread attention and served as one of a number of examples of weak governance (Asian Development Outlook 2003, 2003: p. 68). Although the case happened a year before the "White Paper" program, the memory of it still lingers. In addition, fraudulent activities were disclosed in 2004 at three large state banks (Bank Mandiri, Bank Negara Indonesia, and Bank Rakyat Indonesia), reflecting the fact that risk remains in the banking sector. Bank Indonesia responded by suspending regular banking operations of Bank Global and placed Bank Persyerikatan Muhammadiyah under surveillance (Asian Development Outlook 2005, 2005: p. 97). The government, especially the Anti-Corruption Commission, took decisive action in fighting the scandals and corruption overall. But, more must be done and with greater clarity should Indonesia emerge further from the Asian Financial Crisis of 1997-1998.

Thirdly, the weakening of the rupiah along with the rises in oil prices has resulted in stronger inflationary pressures (Guerin, 2003: p. 1). *Fourth,* the debt repayment, which comprised one-third of Indonesia's budget, posed a fundamental problem to the country with massive deficits to begin with. The debt, which stood at $130 billion, with over $70 billion owed by the government, runs the risk of giving Indonesia its legacy of inflation in the coming years while stifling its future developmental goals (Guerin, 2003: p. 1). The deficits and debt levels are improving as mentioned above (especially with the IMF obligations out of the way). But the issue remains viable and relevant in the overall economic picture of the present and for the future. In fact, by 2005, Indonesia's external debt was about $135 billion by 2005 with $54.3 billion in revenues (CIA Factbook, 2006: pp. 9-10)

Lastly, although export performance overall has improved decidedly in 2005, it still needs revamping. Traditionally, Indonesia has had a comparative advantage in sectors that include furniture, palm oil, textiles, rubber, and footwear. That advantage helped to propel the Indonesian economy after the 1960s. In recent years, however, the growth of exports in those sector slowed significantly (in some cases the decline was absolute). As a matter of fact, the average growth rate for non-oil and gas exports has been at roughly 13 percent in years after the Asian Financial Crisis. Before then, the rate was 17 percent (Asian Development Outlook 2006, 2006: p. 200). The cause of this drop was due to rising labor costs, high inflation, and a relatively stronger currency, all which have hampered the economy's ability to compete in the export markets (Asian Development Outlook 2006, 2006: p. 200).

2. The Issues of Corruption and Lack of Transparency still Linger

Despite Megawati's continuing economic reforms (like her Five Point Agenda proposal for instance), the economic picture remains somewhat promising yet confusing, particularly since corruption remains a chief concern. On June 1st, 2004, Ms. Sidney Jones, the director of Indonesian branch of the Brussels-based International Crisis Group (ICG), was issued an expulsion order. During her work with Indonesia over the past twenty-five years, she emerged as one of the leading analyst of Indonesia, with a particular expertise in the country's terrorists groups such as, for instance, the Jemahh Islamiyah (Perlez, 2004: p. 1). During the past few months, Ms. Jones had been aware that her detailed reports submitted to the ICG drew some heavy criticisms from the director of Indonesia's intelligence agency, General A.M. Hendropriyono. Although the reason for the expulsion was given as visa violations, Ms. Jones contended that the expulsion may have been caused by her recent criticism of Indonesia's army and intelligence agencies (BBC News, 06/02/2004: pp. 1-2). This move proved damaging to Megawati's administration, which went to the very heart of the accountability issue that has plagued this country. Mr. Yudhoyono, greatly aware of the situation, called for greater specificity for the reason behind the expulsion determination (BBC News, 06/02/2004: pp. 1-2).

E. The Political Climate of 2004

The political climate became heated and intriguing for first the April legislative elections and then the July 5th presidential election, even to the point of dubbing the election year "the year of voting frequently." The votes, as Rachel Harvey points out, "look set to be crucial tests of Indonesia's democratic and reformist credentials" (Harvey, 2004: p. 1). The economy was clearly the key issue for that election year. After December of 2003, five candidates had vied for the presidential office: Rachmawati and Sukmawati Sukarnoputri (Megawati's younger sisters), Mr. Akbar Tanjung (Golkar's former chairperson), General Wiranto (former military chief), Mr. Amien Rais (leader of the National Mandate Party (PAN)), and Mr. Susilo Bambang Yudhoyono (former senior political and security minister) (Harvey, 2004: p. 1).[18]

The presidential run of Rachmawati and Sukmawati Sukarnoputri suggested not only a bitter rivalry with Megawati, but also a vulnerability of Megawati and the PDI-P, as the economy continues to be perceived by many as stagnating rather than as stable. In addition, the separatist movements in the Indonesian islands of Aceh and Papua persistently add to the threat of terrorism in the country (Harvey, 01/19/2004: p. 1). Moreover, the uncertainty many people were facing led to a growing nostalgia for the authoritarian rule of President Suharto, which could benefit the Golkar Party and its candidates, Akbar Tanjung and General Wiranto. Like General Wiranto, Tanjung found himself in political trouble; he was convicted of corruption charges in September of 2002. However, General Wiranto had troubles of his own. In 1999, he was indicted for war crimes in connection with the 1999 violence which marred East Timor's strive for independence. Amien Rais, who was one of the leading figures of the reform movement at the time of President Suharto's fall from power, was himself waning in popularity (Harvey, 01/19/2004: p. 1).[19]

The fifth candidate, who posed the most serious presidential challenge to Megawati, was Susilo Bambang Yudhoyono. A former senior political and security minister, he continues to be widely known and admired for his leading role in Indonesia's fight against terrorism in the immediate aftermath of the Bali bombings of 2002 (Harvey, 05/18/2004: p. 1). His speech, made in the anniversary commemorating the attacks, was looked upon as one of the strongest speeches delivered by any Indonesia leader on a topic especially sensitive. Mr. Yudhoyono's image is that of integrity, a strong communicator, and a firm leader in times of crises. Although he at times is deemed as indecisive, for he tends to consider all perspectives and opinions before making a decision, he is looked upon more positively as a thoughtful leader. With a long military background, Mr. Yudhoyono is especially remembered for refusing to declare a state of emergency during the time when former President Wahid was facing impeachment. He lost his position for his choice, but yet known and admired for his relentless stance for the sake of principles and values which he unwaveringly believes (Harvey, 05/18/2004: p. 1).

Knowing the difficult challenges Megawati faced, she unveiled her *Five Point Agenda* on June, 2004. The six-page populist manifesto, the *Agenda* listed five plans in fighting the uneven economic recovery: 1) to create 12.7 million new jobs and appoint 500,000 new teachers within the next five years, 2) to improve infrastructure including new roads and better irrigation, as well as providing subsidies for rice and fuel, 3) to expand railway infrastructure, 4) to improve family planning and local medical clinics, and 5) to provide clean water to 55 percent of those living in towns and 30 percent to those in villages within the next five years (Guerin, 06/08/2004: p. 1).

Megawati clearly had her hands full. The preliminary results one day after the July 5th election showed Susilo Bambang Yudhoyono with 33 percent of the votes, Megawati Sukarnoputri with 26 percent, Gen Wiranto with 23 percent, Amien Rais with 14 percent, and Hamzah Haz with 3 percent. The system predicted the election results by counting roughly one-half a million votes from 2,500 selected voting stations, with a margin of error of 1.1 percent (NY Times, 07/06/2004: p. 1). By that early summer, 17 million of the 155 million ballots were counted. In a number of ways, the event proved to be historical, for the occasion happened to be massive and a giant leap forward for the Indonesians' transition to true democracy in the world's largest Muslim country. This is especially a milestone because prior to this election, presidents in the past were selected by legislature acting as an electoral college. The 155-eligible voter spread has reached across 13,000 islands and three time zones. Unsurprisingly, the election results took close to two weeks before they became official (NY Times, 07/06/2004: p. 1). The preliminary results showed, however, that there was no candidate with at least fifty percent of the vote, which meant that a runoff between the two top vote-getters would have to be held on September 20th, 2004.

The September 20th election resulted in Susilo Bambang Yudhoyono's landslide victory over former President Megawati. He won 60.6 percent of the votes while Megawati gained 39.4 percent (New York Times, 10/04/2004: pp. 1-3). He was sworn in on October 20th although Megawati refused to congratulate him on his victory (BBC News, 10/20/2004: pp. 1-3). Josuf Kalla, the current leader of the Golkar Party after Tanjung, was sworn in as Indonesia's Vice President. With concerns of security, corruption, and the economy still lingering, President Yudhoyono and his administration have huge barriers to climb and overcome. However, there is at least hope and some optimism especially among foreign leaders. Prime Minister John Howard of Australia praised Susilo Bambang Yudhoyono in saying that "the new president has a very strong commitment to the relationship, as I do. I wanted by my presence at his inauguration to signal not only great personal goodwill, but also the great importance that Australia attaches to the relationship" (BBC News, 10/20/2004: pp. 1-3).

F. Indonesia's Path Towards Recovery: The Steps Needed to Continue its Financial, Political, and Macroeconomic Reforms

Among the recovery efforts Indonesia must continue to pursue are the following. *First,* Indonesia must continue its efforts in restoring confidence in private domestic and foreign investors in the economy. This shall be done: 1) through the establishment of stable macroeconomic framework not excluding low inflation and 2) through the creation of transparent investment regime that provides equal treatment of foreign and domestic investors and the removal of all impediments to investment, such as corruption and crony capitalism. The restoration of confidence will therefore restore both aggregate demand and new investment, crucial in reversing idle yet excess productive capacity that is plaguing Indonesia even as we speak (National Development Planning Agency (BAPPENAS), 2000: pp. 155-156).

Second, Indonesia must continue to ensure entrepreneurs and investors that impediments to resource allocation are removed so that firms can quickly shift to new markets. This goal should be accomplished by removing an extensive web of regulations, permits, and approvals companies must undergo in order to establish and operate businesses at all levels of government. Such a set of policies raises cost of doing business and impedes resource mobilization in the economy. *Third,* Indonesia must correct problems associated with customs administration and port facilities in order to ensure that resources can shift quickly to profitable sectors such as exports (National Development Planning Agency (BAPPENAS), 2000: pp. 155-156).

Fourth, Indonesia's trade and industry sectors have undergone substantial deregulation during 1999 through 2000 and beyond. The deregulation efforts included the elimination of statutory basis of several remaining monopolies and cartels, and a commitment to accelerate trade policy reforms, bankruptcy law, and a competition law. Furthermore, the government removed all subsidies given to fertilizer producers and removed quantitative restrictions on urea imports. However, the government should be persistent in reviewing other distortions in the economy, including the remaining fiscal incentives such as tax holidays. *Finally,* Indonesia must continue to recapitalize the banks in order to resuscitate the banking sector and to stimulate renewed lending to the corporate sector (National Development Planning Agency (BAPPENAS), 2000: pp. 155-156).

With new leadership now in question during Indonesia's 2004 election year, these recommendations and concerns must continue to be of paramount importance, for the future of Indonesia remains at stake. In addition to the economic reforms Indonesia must continue to undertake, it cannot rid itself of the issues surrounding corruption and crony capitalism. With the decision to expel Sidney Jones, Indonesia's political credentials and credibility are likely to be stained for quite some time to come. This is a very crucial prospect, for among the key moves Indonesia must continue to make is improving the investment environment in order to win back the confidence of both domestic and foreign investors. Furthermore, part of engaging in that endeavor will be to further engage in steps in fighting unemployment and poverty. Megawati's *Five Point Agenda* may likely be a good enough start in that regard.

V.
Notes

1. The PKI was crushed by a coalition of forces led by the military under the then General Suharto (Brown, 1998: p. 181).
2. Because political leaders from Java dominated the Indonesian government since 1945, Indonesia's economic policies tended to favor consumers and importers over producers and exporters (Brown, 1998: p. 183).
3. Terms of trade is defined by the price of a country's exports divided by the price of its imports (P_e/P_i) on a nation's welfare. Colloquially speaking, in discussing the welfare effect of changes in the Terms of Trade, it's a concept that spells out a country's capacity to trade relative to another country (or countries). Thus, a rise in P_e/P_i means that country exporting a good like oil is made better off (its national welfare improving), with a fall of P_i/P_e. It is only when the opposite occurs will a country be worse off (Krugman & Obstfeld, 2000: pp. 93-97). Think of it in terms of current account surplus verses a current account deficit.

4. Dr. Jeffrey Sachs, then chief adviser of the World Economic Forum, is Director of the Earth Institute of Columbia University and Special Advisor to the United Nations' Secretary-General, Kofi Annan.
5. By 1969, oil revenues accounted for only 19 percent of Indonesia's revenues (Neher, 1991: p. 96).
6. Pertamina, led by Suharto's colleague, General Ibnu Sutowo, accrued huge debts from lavish spending on fruitless projects (Neher, 1991: p. 96).
7. State banks were deemed as less risky by the public and had better developed and widespread networks of branches (Montes & Abdusalamov, 1998: p. 165).
8. NOP requirements stipulated that commercial banks must keep long and short positions in different currencies within 20 percent of their equities (Montes & Abdusalamov, 1998: p. 180).
9. TAFI stands for Total Assets of all types of Financial Institutions, and is a measurement of all financial assets, though excluding assets of the central bank or capital market instruments held by non-financial institutions (Montes & Abdusalamov, 1998: p. 180).
10. M1 is currency and demand deposits. M2 is M1 plus savings deposits.
11. Suharto's tenure as President since 1966 was perceived as less democratic than Thailand and Korea, the countries which experienced changes in government. Hence, Thailand and Korea were deemed as more stable in the longer run as compared to Indonesia (Sadli, 1999: p. 19).
12. Bands are ranges within which the government can set the exchange rate it desires, thus leaving room for some flexibility. Around this chosen fixed exchange rate is called the par value (sometimes called the central value) (Pugel & Lindert, 2000: pp. 425-426).
13. The closures of sixteen insolvent banks were originally designed to boost confidence in the banking system (J. Soedradjad Djiwandono, 1999: p. 123).
14. In less than ten years, the private sector, corporate, and banking, had borrowed some $80 billion, mostly un-hedged and unsecured (Sadli, 1999: p. 18).
15. Indonesian nominal per capita income declined by 65 percent between 1997 and 1998 with the inflation rate running at 47 percent in 1998. Indonesia's Misery Index increased from 7 percent in 1997 to 96.5 percent in 1998 as the costs of living became almost unbearable due to the Crisis (Tan, 2000: p. 118).
16. Manufacturing declined from 6.2 percent in 2004 to 4.6 percent in 2005 due to higher production costs while agriculture slowed from a 4.0 percent to a 2.5 percent growth due to changes in crop mix and a shift in land use, which caused a smaller harvest (Asian Development Outlook 2006, 2006: p. 198).
17. Fuel subsidies became a critical issue in 2005 due to the rise of global oil prices, which placed heavy burden on the budget (the subsidies cost alone came to about $10 billion or 3.5 percent of GDP). In response to this predicament, the government raised administrative prices of petroleum products by 29 percent in March. However, this was done in absence of a strong signal on future policy direction, and as a result, strong demand and soaring prices pushed oil imports higher. Consequently, current account reached a deficit in the second quarter of 2005 and due to reactions to this by the finance market, the rupiah slumped, the stock market weakened, foreign exchange reserves dropped (to over $5 billion in the second and third quarters of 2005), and private capital outflow accelerated (Asian Development Outlook 2006, 2006: p. 199).

18. Hamzah Haz, then Indonesia's Vice President, became the fifth candidate running for the presidency. Both Rachmawati and Sukmawati Sukarnoputri dropped out of the race. This revelation came from the latest election report from BBC News, July 5th, 2004.
Website: http://news.bbc.co.uk/1/hi/world/asia-pacific/3865557.stm
19. By May 26th, 2004, General Wiranto won the backing of the National Awakening Party (PKB), which was deemed as a major lift for Wiranto, his running mate Salahuddin Wahid (younger brother of former President Abdurrahman Wahid), and the Golkar Party itself (BBC News, 05/26/2004: pp. 1-2).

Chapter Seven
The Asia of Today and Beyond: The Lessons to be Learned from the Asian Experience

I.
The Overall Asian Economic Picture after the Asian Financial Crisis of 1997-1998

A. Asia's Road Towards Recovery Were Slow and Uneven

As Vasan Shridharan puts it quite aptly when talking about the recovery from the Asian Financial Crisis, "the restructuring has been excruciating." An economist at HSBC Singapore, he notes that "many of the companies that looked to be fundamentally strong were unmasked by the Asian Crisis" (Ryan, 2002: p. 3). As Table 7.1 shows, GDP growths in the first quarter of 2002 were quite varied in countries of East Asia, partially due to Japan's electronics slump and its impact on Malaysia and, to some extent, the Philippines, Singapore, as well as Vietnam.[1]

Table 7.1
GDP Growth of 2002 (first quarter)

Countries	GDP Growth (%)
South Korea	5.7%
Thailand	3.9%
Indonesia	2.5%
Taiwan	0.9%
Singapore	-1.7%
China	7.6%
Malaysia	1.1%

Source: Ryan, Orla. "Asia Still Scarred by Crisis." *BBC News* 2nd July, 2002: pp. 1-5. ***http://www.news.bbc.co.uk/1/hi/business/2077575.stm***

After the Crisis, the mindset for the large part, changed. Families that believed in keeping outsiders out are now realizing the importance of having other investors involved in their business endeavors. As Claudio Piron, head of Standard Chartered's foreign exchange strategy, points out, "we have [since the Crisis] also seen second and third generation families thinking that for the long term success of the company, we need to consider flotation...bringing in other investors" (Ryan, 2002: p. 3).

However, Piron's next statement is very revealing for its poignancy. As he states, "in any crisis, it is hard to see any clear winner. Everyone feels very much the loser" (Ryan, 2002: p. 3). Even after the Crisis, there are still losses to cope with during the restructuring phase. Unlike South Korea, the region in general was experiencing higher unemployment rate than the average rate of the previous decade. Although the employment picture improves overall in the region, poverty remains a hot issue in countries such as Indonesia. Even when a recovery phase in Korea seemed the strongest in the region, there was a rather pervasive perception among many Koreans that a lot of foreign investors were sitting on substantially higher gains, but at their expense (Ryan, 2002: p. 3).

The policies generated after the Crisis yield higher hopes and greater promises. Although the end results of those policies cause fundamental issues such as employment, job creation, confidence, and discipline, the policies shall be looked upon as visionary in their own rights (like Indonesia's "White Paper" initiative). How visionary depends upon who you're asking, but in general, the policies created positive containment in fiscal deficits. Furthermore, monetary policies remain accommodative, and they've created more favorable conditions for corporate and banking sector reforms and made debt servicing easier. Despite the internal problems the East Asian countries are facing, the region, according to the Asian Development Bank, will remain the fastest growing region of the world economy in 2003 and 2004, excluding Japan (BBC News, 12/11/2003: p. 1). The reasons for this pace? China's rapid growth, stronger consumer spending, and greater regional trading.

In fact, China's economic performance is only part of the reasons why East Asia and Southeast Asia are performing very well in recent years. Asia recorded a robust aggregate GDP growth of 7.4 percent in 2005, just 0.4 percent down from the 7.8 percent expansion a year earlier. The growth was made possible by favorable conditions in the global economy, by full-bodied global trade, and by continuing progress on domestic reform issues. Furthermore, developing Asia has been largely resilient to high oil prices and for the most part, consumers in the region were shielded against the rising prices through direct and indirect subsidies (ADO 2006, 2006: p. iii). Comparatively speaking, GDP growth in Southeast Asian economies was more modest at 5.5 percent in 2005 (ADO 2006, 2006: p. 31). However, investment, especially FDI as with consumption, continue to benefit countries of that region such as Vietnam, Indonesia, and Malaysia. The incessant push towards reform (to be seen below) plays an important part in the region's ongoing recovery after the Asian Crisis of 1997-1998.

B. The Steps Created to Assure Recovery and Growth

1. The Chiang Mai Initiative

The need to prevent another crisis especially of the magnitude of the previous one remains the paramount goal of the region as a whole. As mentioned in the introduction, a meeting in Manila (the capital of the Philippines) took place on November 19th, 1997 in order to adopt a number of principles in solving the Asian Financial Crisis. Indeed, the international community was fully aware of the Crisis. These principles were endorsed by the Southeast Asian finance ministers in December of that year in Kuala Lumpur to develop plans for improved surveillance of their economies to avoid the recurrences of the Crisis. The principles were also created in order to set up an early warning system to spot problems before they reach a crisis level, to call on the IMF to speed up plans for increasing its revenues, and to establish a "new quick disbursing short-term facility" (Tran Van Hoa, 2000: p. 18).

The countries in the Asia-Pacific region continue to work together in efforts to reverse the devastating effects of the Crisis and to prevent the re-occurrences of it. During the week of April 4th, 2001, members of the Association of South East Asian Nations (ASEAN) met in Kuala Lumpur, Malaysia to "come up with an agreement to create a Southeast Asian web of currency swaps to protect currencies in times of financial distress" (CNN.com, 2001: p. 1). This scheme is called the *Chiang Mai Initiative* after the Thai city where it was conceived in May of 2000. The objective of the Initiative is to link international reserves of the ten member countries of ASEAN with those of China, South Korea (an NIC), and Japan, as a form of facility to $1 billion that can be tapped in a financial crisis. Potential creditor nations, especially Japan, have stressed that the swaps would not be activated until the IMF programs were already in place or were at the point of being finalized. Only in cases where a member country was deemed to be suffering a passing cash crunch could the swap deal be triggered without a link to an IMF program. In such a case, a country could borrow no more than ten percent of the swap line. However, the scheme is met with a serious obstacle. Malaysia, one of the few countries in the region that did not turn to the IMF for financial and macroeconomic help during the Crisis, refused to give the IMF a key role in the arrangement as proposed by Japan (CNN.com, 2001: pp. 2-3).

Inevitably, the question is whether the proposed swap agreement is a sign of efforts towards recovery or a sign of a deeper financial and economic weakening in these countries. For the most part, this proposed agreement is a clear sign of the former and suggests that further meetings between the countries are forthcoming: the increase comparability among these countries that would prove instrumental towards regional recovery and reform.

2. The Bali Concord II

The ten ASEAN countries met in Bali, Indonesia on October 6th, 2003 to sign an accord that would establish an EU-style free trade zone by the year 2020 (CNN.com, 10/07/2003: p. 1). The Bali Concord II, as it is called, focuses on economic cooperation and is designed to counter the growing economic and financial clout of both China and India. The Concord also called for greater security cooperation and the promotion of greater social and cultural integration. President Megawati Sukaroputri, who hosted the ASEAN summit in Bali on October 6th, called the event "the watershed in the history of ASEAN." Megawati went on to declare that "[the concord] will make it possible for our children and their children to live in a state of enduring peace, stability, and shared prosperity." While several group members urged for a more faster integration, should the region keep up with the rest of the world, the goal of ASEAN when signing the accord remains far-reaching; to encourage investment in the region while creating a single market of 500 million people (CNN.com, 10/07/2003: p. 1).

With its aim to create the ASEAN Economic Community by 2020, the accord set deadlines for lowering tariffs and travel restrictions in the ASEAN region which has a trade totaling $720 billion per year. ASEAN also have China in mind, proposing to create a free trade agreement with it that would form a market of 1.7 billion consumers with a combined GDP of $2 trillion, which would be the biggest free trade zone in terms of population (CNN.com, 10/07/2003: p. 2). India, South Korea, and Japan expressed hopes of signing free trade agreements with ASEAN within the next decade (CNN.com, 10/07/2003: p. 2).

3. The Anti-Corruption Conference, 2003

With economic and security cooperation in mind, another paramount issue East Asia continues to deal with is corruption. Acknowledging that corruption was a key cause for the Crisis of 1997-1998 and realizing the need to curb it for the sake of continual recovery of the region, the fourth regional anti-corruption conference was held in Kuala Lumpur, Malaysia on December 3rd through the 5th, 2003 (OECD, 11/28/2003: p. 1). Senior policy makers from thirty-five nations as well as representatives of the private sector, civil society, and the international donor community gathered for the event to discuss progress made by countries in the region in implementing the Anti-Corruption Action Plan. The conference was organized by both the Asian Development Bank (ADB) and the Organization for Economic Cooperation and Development (OECD), in cooperation with the Anti-Corruption Agency of Malaysia (OECD, 11/28/2003: p. 1).

The ADB/OECD Initiative was first launched at a workshop in Manila, the Philippines in October, 1999. Endorsed by twenty-one countries, the Initiative's main instrument is the Action Plan, the Plan which contains legally non-binding principles and standards for strengthening both national and regional anti-corruption efforts. The countries under the agreement have made commitments in combating bribery, money laundering, and to promote public sector integrity (OECD, 11/28/2003: p. 1). The Initiative's regional anti-corruption conferences are important for three additional reasons: 1) they foster exchange of experience and cooperation among participants of the Initiative, 2) they provide countries with an opportunity to evaluate progress made in curbing corruption and the problems associated with that process, and 3) they increase knowledge on specific key themes in anti-corruption and identify and then discuss tools in fighting corruption (OECD, 10/02/2003: p. 1).

The fourth conference of December, 2003 was aimed at fostering the exchange of experience in such a fight. However, the conference also sought to: 1) benchmark the current legal and institutional anti-corruption framework in the region in order to facilitate future evaluation of progress and good practices, 2) discuss key areas identified by the endorsing members as challenges to their regional as well as national efforts in eliminating corruption, and 3) encourage additional countries to join the Action Plan. The outcomes of the conference were expected to be both comprehensive and comparative in their overall assessments in the fight against corruption (OECD, 10/02/2003: p. 1). With corruption a key issue in the region's restructuring phase after the 1997-1998 Asian Financial Crisis, the Initiative can (and should) be looked upon as an instrumental mechanism in assuring honesty and transparency in reforming the financial and economic frameworks of East Asia. Thus, it is safe to say that such an aggressive front to better the economic picture of the region while assuring promise and prosperity to its population should be a major influence to other countries particularly of the West in restructuring the financial sector on a global scale.

C. The Growing Influence of the Republic of China

1. Introduction

The Bali Concord II, created on October 6th, 2003, demonstrated Southeast Asia's awareness of the growing financial, economic, and trading influences of both China and India. The accord sought not to avoid the emerging countries, essentially because it would be feasible not to do so, but to become an effective mechanism and weathering the influences China and India possess while developing creative ways in working with them without too much concessions. Thailand's former president, Thaksin Shinawatra, understood this well during his visit to India in 2001. Yet, at the same time, it is becoming clear that Asian countries are looking at China as the increasingly vital regional power, political, and business leader in Asia as a whole. As Jane Perlez reports,

> The United States' two most important strategic Asian allies, Japan and South Korea, are particularly benefiting from China's growth. Last year for the first time, Japan's imports from China surpassed those from the United States. At the same time, Japanese exports to China surged by 39.3 percent. China has now become South Korea's largest trading partner (Perlez, 10/18/2003, p. 1).

2. China Then v. Now

China, the "Japan's heir as Asia's rising star," is becoming a major economic challenge to the global trading community. The openness that China embraced since 1978 has now led to a rush of MNCs and foreign investment. The news per se is not quite surprising, for China became the leading source of FDI during the 1980s. But the picture during the decade was different, and vastly so. During the 1980s, Japan's economy was vibrant, providing FDI enormously in countries in Southeast Asia and becoming a major influence in the region's continued economic growth and sustainability. China, in the meantime, was gradually developing its economy into producing higher-valued goods from simplistic ones. Today, as Japan's economic recovery from the prolonged stagnation remains gradual at best, China's economy is exploding to the point of talks of how to prevent it from overheating.[2] In fact, the Central Bank of China raised interest rates on a number of occasions in 2005 and 2006 alone for that very reason. Furthermore, its huge markets as well as cheap work force are simply attracting Western business executives, which add to the dynamics of the Chinese economy and the global response it elicits (Bradsher, 03/02/2004: p. 1).

3. China's Economic Zenith: Some History

A brief history of China's economic emergence is necessary to explain the zenith of its current economic power and influence. Since 1978, thanks to the initiatives of the late president, Deng Xiaoping, China achieved a stronger agricultural output and productivity, higher rates of saving and investment, higher literacy rate, lower income inequality, and a rapid growth of manufactured exports (Lardy, 1994: pp. 18-23). China therefore became a high-performing economy and the reforms continue to be responsible for China's transformation into a major international economic force. Thus, such an improvement in its economic and trading performances increased interdependence between China and its trading partners. So thought Michalski, Miller, and Stevens, who aptly point out that:

> In just a decade and a half, China has transformed itself from a dormant, introspective giant, into a dynamic powerhouse of major potential significance to the economy. Output has expanded at an average rate of nearly ten percent and total exports at seventeen percent per year. With an estimated one-fifth of the world's population, China now accounts for almost four percent of world merchandise trade and a substantial share of global production (between three and ten percent, depending on whether current official exchange rates or purchasing power parities are used, and on which set of commodity price data is applied to calculate purchasing power) (Michalski, Miller, and Stevens, 1996: p. 7).

China since 1978 became less centralized, less intrusive in regards to economic management, and more open towards foreign involvement and influences in that country. By 1994, China's total foreign trade was worth $237 billion compared to $14.8 billion in 1976. At the same time, the realized foreign investment and loans has risen to $43.2 billion in 1994 from $5 million by 1976. Therefore, China became the world's seventh largest exporter of goods and services by 1994 (Goodman, 1997: p. 28).

Furthermore, China became the second largest recipient of foreign direct investment (FDI) globally as a host country, with the stock of foreign investment worth $96 billion by 1994 (from under $1 billion in 1979) (Findlay and Watson, 1997: p. 113). Foreign funded enterprises accounted for fourteen percent of the total Chinese industrial output and for thirty percent of China's export value, since most exports, which was made up of products assembled from imported parts and components, consisted up to one-half of the value of manufactured goods exports (Findlay and Watson, 1997: p. 113). As Lardy puts it "by the early 1990s, foreign direct investment became the single most important source of external funding" (Lardy, 1994: p. 72).

4. Assessments: Can China's Economic Might Withstand a Setback or More?

As Keith Bradsher puts it, "while China economy is still one-third the size of Japan's, the potential size of its market has made it very hard for companies to say no when Beijing officials demand that they build factories, transfer the latest technology, or adopt Chinese technical standards" (Bradsher, 03/02/2004: p. 1).[3] Indeed, China now has its diplomatic muscle to resist trade and currency concessions that may undermine its competitive edge. Furthermore, part of China's rapid growth rested in its ability to follow Western as well as Japanese methods of production and management styles (Bradsher, 03/02/2004: p.1). Like Japan after the 1960s, China is "scooping up raw materials that it needs for its rapid modernization: liquid natural gas from Indonesia and Australia, iron ore from Australia, rubber and palm oil from Malaysia" (Perlez, 10/18/2003: p. 2).

Although its biggest comparative advantage rested on its immense and low-paid work force, concerns nevertheless arise. Wages in China are no more than 4 percent of wages earned by workers in both the United States and Japan. In addition, workers tend to work up to eleven hours per day and many lived in factory dormitories (Bradsher, 03/02/2004: p. 2). Rural areas fare less well, with much higher rates of poverty and unemployment south and west of China (an estimated $150 million are unemployed). Furthermore, with China lacking the rule of law comparable to that of the United States, labor issues may merge with human rights issues that continue to plague its government.

The biggest issue remains whether China is the next bubble and how vulnerable is it to acute setbacks (a banking failure, an inflationary spiral, or even a temporary economic bust). The issue remains very mordant in nature, for China is experiencing four major risks. *The first risk* involves a series of excesses and frenzy of factory constructions as well as overcapacity and excessive investment in some sectors of the economy (the Business-Cycle risk). *The second risk* consists of speculative inflows of cash and growing volumes of bank loans (the financial risk) (Bradsher, 01/18/2004: p. 1). *The third risk* occurs due to the rapid growth and a persistent imbalance in trade with the United States. In response of the American's moves to impose tariffs on Chinese products, China followed Japan's example by sending official buying missions to the United States (the protectionism risk). The American trade restrictions amounted to very little damages in Chinese shipments to the United States, although the potential for a more significant trade war existed and could've slowed the Chinese economy and the economies of Asia considerably (Bradsher, 01/18/2004: p. 1).[4] *The fourth and final risk* involves a growing incidence of protests, mainly workers and retirees seeking unpaid salaries and wages (the political risk). Despite President Hu Jintao's efforts to restrict some police powers and to allow for a slightly greater openness in Chinese society, human rights issue remains a hot point of contention. However, there are concerns that should the economy loses steam sharply, political instability could follow (Bradsher, 01/18/2004: p. 1).

Clearly, there are causes for concerns, especially with the financial aspect of China's economic well-being. In December 2003, the Central Bank has tried to persuade banks against reckless lending while the government bailed out two of its largest banks. The Central Bank also made efforts to prepare the banks for possible hard times as well as planned stock sales (Bradsher, 01/18/2004: pp. 1-2). The possibility of economic trouble in China is becoming something economists and experts cannot ignore and take lightly. With a GDP growth of 8.5 percent in 2003 despite the SARS outbreak, there is now a general consensus that growth will have to slow, at least as far as investment is concerned. This is especially true with the 9.9 percent growth in 2005, making China the fourth largest economy in the world, behind the United States, Japan, and Germany (Bradsher, 01/25/2006: p. 1). The statistics behind the growth proved staggering in their own rights. China's national economic output reached $2.26 trillion which past that of both France and Great Britain. Secondly, export recorded a 9.6 percent growth in 2005 while consumer spending continues to play more of a vital aspect of China's economic expansion. Lastly, retail sales climbed 12.5 percent, underpinning the strength behind domestic demand (Bradsher, 01/25/2006: p. 2).

However, other than the overheating concerns some experts and economists continue to have, the issues of whether China is too reliant on investment spending and whether too much of that investment involves ill-considered splurges on new industries and the latest equipment linger on (especially in regards to these new factories with overcapacity concerns). Also, although the problems of non-performing loans (NPLs) are not as serious as they were in the past, China is still heavily dependent on continued heavy borrowing by companies to build more factories and apartment buildings, despite their struggles to earn enough profit on their existing facilities to repay previous loans (Bradsher, 01/25/2006: p. 2). Part of the solution to the problems is for China, according to Qu Hongbin, the senior economist for China at HSBC, to rebalance its growth by "shifting away from investment towards consumption" (Bradsher, 01/25/2006: p. 2). What China will do next is an open question, but countries in East Asia and throughout the world will continue to pay very close attention.

D. India: A Source of Economic Emergence for Asia and Beyond

1. Introduction

India, the world's largest democratic nation and the second most populous behind China, has emerged during the course of over fifteen years as a major power after several decades of a closed economy. It was since the late 1980s that India began to open its economy to the global markets particularly through encouraging economic reform and foreign investment. Reforms are still being carried out, as India's new Prime Minister, Manmohan Singh points out that "we will pursue policies that enable our economy to be better integrated with the world economy without hurting the interests of our people" (BBC News: 06/24/2004: pp. 1-3). While Mr. Singh acknowledged the benefits many people in India are enjoying from globalization and economic reforms, he nevertheless confessed that millions of "our citizens are still plagued by illiteracy, disease, want, hunger, and malnutrition" (BBC News: 06/24/2004: pp. 1-3). Yet, India's economic growth and influence are enough to raise a hot issue of outsourcing, with India arguably being the key source of that debate especially in the United States.

2. India's Economic Growth and Concerns

India's GDP growth blossomed to 10.4 percent in the last quarter of 2003, which made it one of the fastest growing economies in the world. The previous quarter recorded an 8.4 percent growth. The blooming nature of the growth was due to the increase of roughly 17 percent of agricultural production, with farming that accounted for a quarter of India's economy (Rai, 2004: p. 1). Although some expressed doubt that the performance of farm output will repeat at the same level this year, there is an acknowledgment that the growth "indicates the underlying strength in the economy and reinforces the theme that India is growing nearly as fast as China," as states Jyotivardhan Jaipuria, head of research at DSP Merrill Lynch. The news raised confidence among investors to the point that they put some $7 billion into Indian stock in 2003: they remain bullish since then (Rai, 2004: p. 1). In 2005, India's GDP grew to 8.1 percent, fueled by broad-based domestic demand growth and consumption growth. Also, gross fixed capital formation grew an estimated 8.5 percent, signaling growing investor confidence (Asian Development Outlook 2006, 2006: p. 158).

Despite the encouraging economic growth, however, concerns persist. As Ramtanu Maitra concedes,

> The Economists concludes the India's economic backwardness has little to do with democracy as such, but has a lot to do with corruption, fiscal mismanagement, a lack of international ambition, and a history of over-protection at home. On the surface, the argument is cogent, but it is also true that corruption in China is similarly high and often, if not always, fiscal mismanagement is another face of corruption (Maitra, 2004: p. 1).

As Maitra points out, India's economic openness during the past decade led to FDI, which remains concentrated in consumer durable sectors. The flows of FDI have been encouraging, but it went into these sectors where it is "quick-yielding and withdrawal is very easy" (Maitra, 2004: p. 1). Economists are now arguing that India should encourage such investment towards infrastructure and India's power industry. The FDI would in turn help rid India of its decrepit infrastructure such as erratic power supply. Furthermore, India's SMEs are reeling under pressure from imports, which make the issue of protectionism paramount in the midst of ongoing reforms. Investments, Maitra determined, are lacking in transmission and maintenance of existing plants as well as in improving India's port system (Maitra, 2004: p. 1). With heavy investments being made towards India's information technology (IT), some economists and Indian policy makers are arguing that India cannot "leapfrog" past technologies into its IT acumen. It is a matter of addressing massive shortfall of infrastructural development, high illiteracy rate, crippling poverty rate, and high unemployment as well as underemployment before continuing to boost IT as a development strategy (Maitra, 2004:

p. 1).

Notwithstanding the concerns that India are still confronting with, reforms are continuing to be among the new government's main priorities. Palaniappan Chidambaram, India's finance minister, emphasized in May of 2004, that economic reforms would continue and that a growth rate of 7 to 8 percent would be targeted (BBC News, 05/28/2004: p. 1). Investors remained unimpressed, for the "Common Minimum Programme", announced on May 27th, is destined to do away with key elements of the previous government's privatization program, especially of state firms. The possibility of a ballooning of the deficit because of increased funding to the rural poor looms large in the minds of investors and some policy makers. The day after the "Common Minimum Programme" was announced, trading shares fell 4.16 percent on Bombay's Sensex index (BBC News, 05/28/2004: p. 1).

II.
The Lessons to be Learned from the Asian Experience

A. Concerning Economic Growth and Sustainability

The first lesson we should learn from the essence of economic growth and sustainability is that the rapid growth of Southeast Asian countries was due by and large to the detailed interventionism of the governments. It was not the intervention that turned the region around as a whole per se. Rather, it was the type of interventionism that mattered critically. The economic growth and development of Japan after the Second World War was in many ways a model for the emerging Southeast Asian countries. As stated before, it was these countries that began to realize the need for economic growth as the absolute necessity towards prosperity in veins similar to Japan and the West. In order to engage in global trade successfully, a developing country must first look inwardly in a realistic fashion and determine the elements needed to build a nation towards prosperity.

The second lesson is that the importance of governmental interference in countries in East Asia and Southeast Asia rested in the "bottoms-up" approach. The first step towards economic prosperity was to deal with the issues facing the population (such as education, land, health, and income). The governments of the region wasted no time in eradicating inequalities in regards to educational obtainability, income distribution, health accessibility, and the availability of land. During the ISI stage, the governments made further investments towards education, training, and health. The efficient usage of resources, labor pooling, and knowledge spillovers were highly encouraged by the governments of the region. Industrial protectionism was meant to last until industries gained enough production experience to compete in world markets. In essence, it was the social bargain between the governments, the business leaders, and the population that made growth and prosperity possible; the bargain that embraced free trade with the need to the population to enjoy and benefit the fruits of economic blossomings. Furthermore, the peoples' participation in political matters was also an important proponent for economic growth.

The third lesson is that notwithstanding the criticisms against ISI outlined in Chapter One, this strategy successfully paved the way for EOI. As we have seen in the learning curves (Figure 1.1), as firms gained further experience in production, their production costs decreases. Therefore, these firms accumulate the capacity to emulate firms already with the advantage in production and trade. As the countries in the Asia-Pacific region shifted towards EOI, these firms, especially SMBs, were ready to compete globally. Seeing the potential for further economic expansionism, the United States, Japan, and Europe bestowed Southeast Asia with FDI, portfolio investments, economic aid, technological transfers, and ideas. Therefore, Southeast Asian countries became principal exporters from textiles, clothing, and shoes and to higher value-added goods such as electronics. As their exports increased after the mid-1960, their GDPs rose to levels no fewer than 5 percent on average for the next three decades. The emphasis on savings as the key in financing high rates of investment helped to assure the growth.

B. Concerning the Asian Financial Crisis of 1997-1998

According to Blecker,

> In order to reduce the magnitude of currency fluctuations and lessen destabilizing flows of short-term capital, countries need to adopt appropriate packages of capital controls and transactions taxes, as well as prudential regulations of international investments. Target zones for exchange rates and coordination of macroeconomic policies are also needed to stabilize global financial markets and thus to allow capital flows to achieve their intended benefits of enhancing global efficiency and growth. And while it important to begin thinking about new types of international institutions to regulate global financial markets, a more immediate priority is to reform the IMF in order to make it more responsive to the needs of debtor countries and more concerned with restoring equitable growth rather than bailing out wealthy investors (Blecker, 1999: p. 143).

The first lesson we should learn from the Asian Financial Crisis is that a more tightened monitoring of the financial sector is critical in order: 1) to prevent the re-occurrences of non-performing loans, illiquidity of loans, and the insolvency that plagued the banking systems in East Asia, and 2) to establish a better unit of account that is needed in order for currencies to maintain real, constant values.[5] As stated by Warren Coats:

> An established monetary standard spontaneously persists as a social convention because no trader by himself finds it advantageous to abandon it. If the public are to choose intentionally between standards, they must do so in a setting of constitutional choice. In short, the unit of account is a public good (Coats, 1994: p. 15).

Thus far, countries in East Asia were successful in establishing special agencies in charge of restructuring their banks, purchasing their bad loans to be sold off later, and recapitalizing their banks. Banks mergers and finance companies were also successful, especially in a bid to rationalize the banking industry (Tan, 2000: p. 232).

However, supervision of the banks and finance companies must be tightened to ensure better capital adequacy ratios, management of risk, disclosure of information and transparency, and internal control procedures. Moral hazard and implicit guarantees should be eliminated through better supervision of the financial sector; thus promoting fair-burden sharing and market discipline. Likewise, East Asian countries must make bankruptcy and foreclosure laws more effective. Furthermore, the governments must close down banks endangered by insolvency, with their assets sold, rather than bailing them out with public funds and "defending the indefensible" (Tan, 2000: p. 232).

Having a good system of deposit insurance for financial institutions is crucially important in economies should there are rapid growths in the banking and financial sectors. This system should then: 1) put the burden of resolving failed banks on shareholders and on large, uninsured credits rather than on international institutions or on small depositors and taxpayers, 2) place stiff and uncompromising accountability conditions on economic officials, especially those who believe in rescuing banks simply because they're "too large to fail," and 3) give bank supervisors protection against political pressures to either delay corrective actions or not engage in them at all (Goldstein, 1999: p. 12). Essentially, it is a matter of striking a balance between limiting systemic risk and encouraging disciplined market transactions domestically and worldwide.

As in the banking system, special agencies were created to take over the debts of corporations to be sold at a later date. In return, the firms would get an injection of funds to escape the prospects of insolvency. Mergers of firms, or their subsidiaries, are encouraged in order to rationalize the corporate sector. *However, firms that are facing insolvency with little hope of recovery should be allowed to close down.* Because bankruptcy laws are inadequate, creditors are faced with difficulties to force insolvent firms into bankruptcy. *Furthermore, firms should stop borrowing foreign funds on short-term maturities for investments in long-term projects.* This mismatch between short-term maturities and investment projects caused cash flow problems for borrowers (Tan, 2000: pp. 234 and 259).

The IMF, according to Goldstein, should encourage emerging countries to maintain comprehensive registers of their creditors. And creditors should in turn be encouraged to create standing committees that could help coordinate future debt reschedulings. In dealing with moral hazard at the national level, the IMF should persuade emerging countries to put forth sensible deposit insurance reform in their financial systems. At the international level, the IMF should provide emergency assistance only if there's a good prospect of resolving the applicant country's underlying debt and balance of payments problems (Goldstein, 199: p. 13). Too large of an aid especially from the IMF increases moral hazard, because, as we've seen in the past, large rescue packages allowed private creditors to escape from bad lending decisions at relatively little costs and consequences (Goldstein, 1999: p. 12).

The second lesson, taking on from where the first lesson leaves off, is that banks collectively are a special source of vulnerability. Banks are important in developing countries as a source of financial intermediation services. For that reason, bank capital requirements, according to Eichengreen, "must be related to the source of their funding as well as the riskiness of their loans and more generally for regulating the flow of short-term foreign funds into the banking system" (Eichengreen, 1999: p. 168). In the end, Asia did the opposite, using the banking system as an instrument of industrial policy and conduit for the transfer of foreign funds rather than using it as an exemplar of sound financial policies.

The third lesson is that East Asia today must stimulate aggregate demand. The collapse of the banking and corporate sectors led to a significant decline in aggregate demand, which contributed to the recession that plagued these East Asian countries. Investments in plant and equipment were not likely due to high interest rates and the reluctance of banks to engage in further lending. Therefore, consumers have little incentive to spend, and more reasons to save. A rise in unemployment and the decline in sale prices meant that the government revenues began to fall substantially, prompting large cuts in public sector spending. Stimulating aggregate demand would help to restore consumer confidence, which is crucial to any recovery process since consumption expenditure accounts for 50 to 74 percent of GDP in most Southeast and East Asian countries (Tan, 2000: pp. 234-235).

Related to the need for stimulating aggregate demand is the importance of *investor confidence restoration.* Investment spending is an integral part of aggregate demand and, therefore, it must rise significantly should recovery take full swing. One way to induce the rise of investment expenditure is to reduce the cost of investment. This reduction could be accomplished by reducing the interest rate, rehabilitating the banking system, and decreasing (or suspending) various government charges. However, the prospects for economic and financial recovery must be strong and promising if the measures are likely to have a significant impact on investment spending (Tan, 2000: pp. 234-235).

The fourth, more striking lesson to be learned from the Crisis, however, is that strong economic fundamentals are not enough to protect a country from the financial panics that often accompany a crisis. Singapore, Hong Kong, Taiwan, and to some extent, Malaysia, were bestowed with huge foreign reserves, little or no foreign debt, current account surpluses, relatively strong banking systems, and sound monetary and fiscal policies. However, they did not escape from the financial panic that adversely affected the Asia-Pacific region (Tan, 2000: p. 256). Furthermore, *large current account deficits are not benign.* The way in which deficits shall be dealt with is to make sure that returns of foreign funds are balanced against risks in the form of sudden curtailment of foreign lending and the need to eliminate that deficit immediately (Eichengreen, 1999: p. 167).

In addition, as in the case of Thailand, financial liberalizations were done prematurely, without proper and adequate preparations. While capital flows were liberalized, it was done while the fixed exchange rate was maintained. The policy tested international confidence in its ability to maintain the fixed exchange rate: speculative attacks against the currency became a daily economic ritual (Tan, 2000: pp. 256-257). This predicament brings about the *fifth lesson,* which is that *developing countries, with few exceptions, should move toward greater exchange rate flexibility.* The greater the flexibility, the greater the incentives for banks and corporations to hedge their foreign exposures, which in turn, will give them better positions to cope with financial turbulence should it occur (Eichengreen, 1999: p. 168). Asia was simply under-prepared for the currency depreciations that occurred in a very short span of time. The IMF, according to Goldstein, should encourage emerging economies to adopt and maintain a currency regime of managed floating (Goldstein, 1999: p. 106). Basket pegging, as some experts suggest, may not be a bad idea should sudden, extensive shocks should occur.

The sixth lesson is that East Asian and Southeast Asian countries were also guilty of their over-reliance of short-term foreign capital flows relative to foreign reserves. There were mismatches of short-term foreign liabilities and foreign assets, which led to financial difficulties once massive withdrawal of foreign capital took place; in other words, with short-term capital flows, their short maturities make it easier for investors to run as soon as trouble hits. Furthermore, foreign liabilities were not hedged against foreign exchange risk, especially during sudden currency depreciation. What made matters worse, however, was that large inflows of foreign capital were invested in speculative assets such as property, shares, or industries where there was already global excess supply. The asset bubbles began to burst, and the poor profitability from industrial investments resulted in many borrowers unable to service their foreign loans. Once domestic currencies began to float, only to depreciate rapidly, the local currency costs of repaying loans denominated in foreign currencies were simply too huge for firms to even remain solvent (Tan, 2000: pp. 258-259). Simply put, the dependency on short-term funding, with short-term funding denominated in foreign currency, is risky business for the aforementioned reasons (Eichengreen, 1999: pp. 167-168).

In other words, as far as capital flows are concerned, avoiding too much of a good thing is, well, a good thing. Capital flow, as Morris Goldstein puts it, has been beneficial to the world economy because:

> It has loosened the constraints imposed by self-financing and improved the overall productivity of investment on a global scale. This finances development and raises living standards in borrowing countries while providing savers in lending countries with the opportunity to earn a better return on their money. It has permitted both borrowers and investors to obtain better diversification against shocks to their domestic economies. It has helped foster the transfer of best-practice production processes (Goldstein, 1999: p. 8)

However, capital flows bring with them risks, namely volatility. As seen in Asia and Latin America (like Mexico) as far as the boom and bust cycles of such flows are concerned, when capital flows are very large and occur at a pace that exceeds the domestic capacity to supervise the financial sector and to build a credit culture, subsequent banking crisis tends to emerge. Moreover, a sudden stop or reversal in private capital flows can "turn liquidity problems into solvency problems, induce large cuts in spending that bring on recession, and spread crisis considerably beyond their origin" (Goldstein, 1999: p. 9). Therefore, the IMF should, according to Goldstein, advise the emerging countries to follow the Chilean example by imposing holding-period taxes on short-term inflows until their ability to intermediate such flows is stronger and more ideal (providing of course that the measures are transparent and not impeding the entry of foreign financial institutions) (Goldstein, 1999: p. 10).

The seventh lesson we should learn from the Crisis is that strong and coherent political leadership is vital for the country's economic, political, and social well-beings. A financial crisis must be looked upon beyond economic terms, because what the Asian experience in particular has taught us is that a crisis carries with it significant political, social, and security dimensions (Goldstein, 1999: p. 32). The leadership should strive to be decisive and consistent in their policies without being influenced by special-interest firms. Leadership should be able to eliminate and prevent crony capitalism and moral hazard. There were few checks and balances on the abuse of managerial power particularly at the governmental level. Partially due to crony capitalism, there were few regulations requiring firms to disclose adequate information about their operations, adhere to proper accounting standards, or to institute prudent financial control procedures. Crony capitalism played a huge, if not, a decisive role in poor investment decisions and risky financing arrangements (Tan, 2000: pp. 259-261). Leaders should also be able to recognize that better regulation of the economy is not only beneficial to nations worldwide, but also practical and absolutely necessary. Therefore, generating support for and ownership of reforms is of vital importance, not only for countries from within that are engaging in or at least contemplating reforms, but also for countries abroad that have the desire to improve their economic pictures and the overall global economic landscape.

The eighth lesson is that the IMF must continue to improve its surveillance capacity and enhance its contributions to the management and resolution of a crisis, for in the past, the IMF as with the World Bank, were simply doing too much. The key word here is continue, for since the IMF began to work on the Turkish financial crisis of 2000, the conditionalities represented a better understanding of the scope of Turkey's problem. The IMF ceased being aggressive and opted for fuller collaboration with the Turkish financial officers in reversing the effects of the Turkish financial crisis. In regards to East Asia and South East Asia, there is every reason to believe that the IMF will modify its efforts in crisis management and resolution in ways that would be deemed both realistic and practical. As with the World Bank, the IMF should just simply return to the basics. It should reform its lending policies in order to limit the level of moral hazards so prevalent in years past. Furthermore, the IMF ought to concentrate more on encouraging and assisting in crisis prevention while focusing on leaner agenda on monetary, fiscal, and exchange rate policies as well as of banking and financial sector scrutiny and reform. The more detailed structural reforms and the social aspects of economic development should be left to the World Bank and other international organizations that have the requisite expertise in those areas. Furthermore, the World Bank should do more in designing social safety nets (Goldstein, 1999: pp. 18-19). This is important as poverty and pension plans are highly viable issues especially in more advanced developed economies. Also, to counter systemic threats as effectively as possible, the global community will need quick access to adequately and securely funded international backup facilities that can aid victims of contagion. This would supplement existing credit lines (Goldstein, 1999: p. 17).

The final, more far-reaching and far-seeing lesson is that there will be financial surprises in the future. It is simply not always the question of whether financial crises can be prevented or predicted, but rather what mechanisms can be created or improved to at least alleviate the severity of them. As what Asia demonstrated, moral hazard is not the answer, nor is just standing by and letting nature run its course. Instead, a new international financial architecture must be created with a renewed sense of shared urgency, commitment, vision, courage, and unshakable insightfulness. Goldstein puts it in another way by stating that

> While this report concentrates on the financial architecture and on the role of the IMF, it is well to remind ourselves that financial stability is not an end in itself but rather a means to broadly shared global prosperity and that it is a fantasy to believe that financial stability can be maintained without attention to the social aspects of development (Goldstein, 1999: p. 19)

III.
Notes

1. Japan's corporations such as Fujitsu and Hitachi altogether eliminated 31,400 jobs worldwide by 2001 and closed factories in countries of Southeast Asia, including Malaysia and Singapore: the countries Japan had long associations with before and after the 1985 Plaza Accord (Arnold, 2001: p. 1).
2. In 2003, Japan's economy grew by 7 percent, its fastest rate in thirteen years. However, deflation remained a huge problem and was eating into corporate profits while increasing companies' debts (BBC News, 02/18/2004: p. 1). Although the Japanese economy is showing improvement after a decade of stagnation, the issue of whether the economy is reaching a true turning point remains an open question.
3. Whereas Japan profited handsomely from selling videotape recorders two decades ago, China is beginning to dominate in the production of the next generation DVD technology, with BBK Electronics Corporation started by licensing technology from Sony. As Keith Bradsher puts it, "China has both licensed technology and used the attraction of its potentially huge market to lure foreign investment" (Bradsher, 03/02/2004: p. 3).
4. The trade war and its effects on China and its Asian neighbors are especially important because countries of East Asia are increasingly sending components to China for final assembly and reshipment to the United States and beyond.
5. An unit of account is the unit in which the medium of exchange and other assets are denominated and in which other values and prices are expressed (Coats, 1994: p. 3).

Chapter Eight
Epilogue
A Final School of Thought: Taking Stock in a Vision With & Beyond the Lessons

I.
Introduction

> A politics of sustainable globalization needs more than just the correct picture of what is happening in the world. It also needs the right balance of policies. Specifically, it demands a new social bargain between workers, financiers, and governments that will make for sustainable globalization. What is needed instead of either of these extremes [let the market rule everywhere versus the paternalism of the welfare state] is a new social compact that embraces free markets but also ensures that they benefit, and are tolerable for, as many people as possible. You stabilize globalization by democratizing globalization-by making it work for more and more people all the time (Friedman, 2000: p. 424).

From the start of Southeast Asia's economic development and sustainability, the countries in the region, as with Japan and now China, were successful in mending the need to embrace free markets with the needs of the people to acquire opportunities, equitable education and health, as well as training. This applied to much of the global community since the early 1960s as witnessed not only in Asia, but also in the Americas, in Europe, and in parts of Africa. The leaders during that era were visionary in their buildings and re-buildings of their respective countries; the visions that were bold yet burning, illuminating, and ultimately inspirational (reflect for a moment that vitality President Kennedy exerted during his unfortunately short tenure). Asia was in a sense unique and a trailblazer because as it was successful in addressing the needs of their populace before embarking on global trade and investments, it remained traditionalist in its reliance on family and the community. And as foreign investors made their imprints on the economies of East Asian countries, people continue to benefit through their governments' encouragements of savings, rising earnings, more job opportunities, greater and more diverse skills, and knowledge sharing.

There continues to be a globalization in Southeast Asia, for it is experiencing a rapid, though uneven, acceleration of the movement of people from rural areas and agricultural lifestyles to urban areas and urban lifestyles, the attributes of the latter that includes global fashion, food, markets, and entertainment trends. There is a globalization of another kind; that is, the interlink between nation states and the global markets. Once Southeast Asia took the necessary steps in its ISI stage, it readied itself to participate in the global markets, which continues to be made up of investors, consumers, and even speculators. To some extent, countries in East Asia continue to be protectionistic in nature, but their economic outlooks became far-reaching and visionary since the decades of the 1960s.

In the end, however, the countries, particularly in Southeast Asia, diverted from the right balance of policies after the mid-1980s: their collective sense of vision is not as illuminous and inspirational as it was generations ago. Economic sustainability was simply no longer profound, as mismanagement, practicality, opportunism, and short cuts replaced idealism, proper risk-taking, accountability, and exuberance to worrisome results. While there were pluses in getting into the globalization system, there were also minuses. Countries that engaged themselves in economic openness, particularly through deregulation and privatization, found themselves vulnerable to external forces (primarily because they were ill-prepared in dealing with them). Nations, especially those with strong economic fundamentals like Singapore, Taiwan, Australia, New Zealand, and to some extent, Malaysia, weathered those vulnerabilities with success. Others, like Indonesia, Mexico, Argentina, Russia, Thailand, and to a large extent, Brazil, did not. It wasn't really the matter of openness per se, but the policies associated with it and its timing. For instance, Argentina, once a top economic performer in the world at various points of the last century, decided to peg its currency to the American dollar in the mid-1990s at the time when the rise of unemployment and inequality in wealth was beginning to take shape.

The Argentina example is not totally irrelevant with the purpose and scope of this book. Rather, its policy making shows some parallelisms with the kind of policies the Pacific region began to make since the 1980s. When a country pegs its currency to a foreign currency, typically called dollarization, it is essentially abandoning its own currency for that of another. It can be an attractive option, for it means lower transaction costs and inflation, greater openness and transparency in the government sectors, and elimination of exchange rate risk.

However, dollarization brings with it problems. For one thing, pegging causes lesser flexibility in the country's decision making surrounding monetary and exchange rate policies and seignorage (money earned through its printing) is lost. Secondly, pegged rates become problematic when they become immensely overvalued (either because the country's inflation rate remains higher than that of its trading partners or because the foreign currency to which the country's currency is pegged rises up and drag it up against other currencies (Goldstein, 1999: p. 14). Therefore, for instance, should the dollar strengthens, a foreign currency pegged to it suffers, for it becomes overvalued, subject to speculations, and demand growth consequently weakens, which was the case during and after the mid-1990s.

This was especially the case with countries that had low levels of international reserves (which sometimes caused them to raise interest rates to make assets denominated in its currency more attractive, thus defending the pegging). But high interest rates slow economic growth and the economic fundamentals, like, for instance, strong trade, good fiscal balance, and low unemployment, weaken. Argentina did not fully peg its currency to the dollar, but it was left with little flexibility in dealing with the contagion effects of the 1994-1995 Mexican Crisis, which was characterized by severe outflows of capital, lower prices in the stock markets, as well as depreciation of its currency in foreign exchange markets. Argentina's poverty rate reached about fifty percent in 2002.

The issue of pegging is something of a Catch-22 because there's really no way to get out of it gracefully (a government wants economic growth with low inflation and yet remains, in some ways not by choice, highly dependant on the performance of a currency being dollarized). As Morris Goldstein puts it, "when the overvaluation is small, there is apt to be little political support for upsetting the applecart with a change in the pegged rate, and by the time the overvaluation has become large and obvious, it is often too late to avoid a crisis" (Goldstein, 1999: pp. 14-15). The overvaluation was modest in Asia because the economic fundamentals remained fairly strong in some respects. However, the countries of the Pacific region were made more vulnerable because of weak banking systems, highly leveraged corporations, large current account deficits, as well as sharply fall in export growth (Goldstein, 1999: p. 15).

To further the argument against pegging, especially in connection to Asia, critics contend that dollarization does not necessarily yield to greater systemic stability. A key complaint with the $G\text{-}_3$ exchange rate regime is that:

> with over fifty percent swings in the yen/dollar rate during the 1990s, with the depreciation of the dollar in the first half of the decade and then appreciating vis-à-vis the yen from 1995 to 1997-put the competitiveness of the Asian crisis economies on a yo-yo course that contributed significantly to their boom-bust cycle; that the gyrations of the yen added substantially to Japan's economic instability; and that the rise of the dollar has stoked the huge and rising US trade deficit (Goldstein, 1999: p. 57).[1]

The second argument, though more general in nature, is that high short-run variability of $G\text{-}_3$ exchange rates has discouraged international investment and trade, resulting in costly hedging and plant location decisions. The latter is especially true even after the Crisis. Furthermore, the current system, according to the critics, has generated large and persistent exchange rate misalignments that have caused significant resource misallocation as well as fanning protectionist pressures. Furthermore, in the absence of announced exchange rate targets, stabilizing speculation and more effective international economic policy coordination has been impeded (Goldstein, 1999: p. 57). However, not everyone agree with those assessments. To them, the Asian Crisis was primarily about financial-sector weaknesses and excessive borrowings by financial institutions and corporations. On the other hand, in conjunction with the case against pegging to the

G_{3} exchange rates (particularly to the dollar), there are calls, from John Williamson among others, for the emerging countries (like Malaysia) to engage in basket pegging so as to soften the sharpness of the volatility of a particular host currency. Thailand had the right idea before, although it engaged in the basket pegging with the dollar that had too much weight and influence.

While the Argentina example spells out the type of risk associating with globalization, it is worth noting that a lack of a balance Friedman was referring to served also as a chief vulnerability factor when explaining an economic crisis and its aftermath. Malaysia, for example, also pegged its currency to the dollar, but did not suffer the Crisis as severe as Argentina. But while countries like Indonesia and Argentina benefited from the series of deregulation and privatization policies during the 1980s and early 1990s, the balance of right policies in maintaining and enhancing upon such benefits were no longer balanced. Argentina was crippled in particular by constant changes in economic ministers during much of the 1990s while it took some time for Malaysia's leaders to put their heads together for ideal policy responses to the Crisis.

The concept of the social bargain is very important because it is one of the key cornerstones of the global model (the other being the relationship between business and the government). The financial crisis, as Haggard points out:

> accelerated changes that were already undermining the implicit social contract of the pre-crisis model of growth with equality. The Crisis made clear that the next generation of poor people could not necessarily count on unremitting growth to lift them out of poverty, and also that the achievements of the nascent working and middle classes were more fragile than thought. With the aging of populations, urbanization, and more open economies, and the recurring risk of financial shocks, the holes in the social safety net became more apparent, leading to new insecurities. Ideally a new contract would continue to address the problems of poverty alleviation that was so effectively managed through high growth. But at the same time, it would begin to address the insecurities faced by the growing urban working and middle classes (Haggard, 2000: p. 230).

Haggard's point is well worth taking, for job security is not much of a norm as it was a generation ago. With outsourcing becoming a more prominent political and economic issue as we speak, the questions of how to create and keep jobs and opportunities, how to maintain pension plans, how to maintain and improve research and development, how to keep companies and corporations from going under, and how to engage in responsible yet visionary sound economic well-being yield no easy answer. Thus, creating a new social bargain will be trickier than many would thought as we are living in a different age, with technology making things more possible than any of us could've foreseen. Even ideas and technology need support, for they can't exist alone. As pointed out by

Friedman, "ideas and technology don't just win and spread on their own. Good ideas and technologies also need a strong power that promotes those ideas by example and protects those ideas by winning the battlefield" (Friedman, 2000: p. 444). However, there is a problem with that as well. As Catherine Crier argues, and convincingly so, is that:

> we have come to expect everything from the law and very little from ourselves. We do not trust one another to be honest or fair. Subjective decisions are suspect. We want things measured objectively and reduced to writing. The most minute decisions or tasks are governed by rules that conveniently replace judgment, reason, and innovation. Yet all the statutes in the world cannot insure we have good cops or teachers or politicians" (Crier, 2002: p. 4).

As you can see, the problems in reforming the global financial system through reforming ourselves run much deeper. The rule of law is crucially important, but it is that rule of law that goes beyond the formulaics in order to encompass the farsightedness for the benefits of the greatest amount of people as possible.

Deindustrialization, a concept of manufacturing giving way to the service sector adds to the overall problem. Wealth inequalities are expanding not just within a nation, but between nations, as debt accumulates to record numbers. Loans throughout the years are increasingly becoming a way out for a number of countries, only to find out that they are in deeper holes than before. Noting that the debt crises have revealed serious weaknesses in the international financial architecture, departing U.N. Secretary-General Kofi Annan's moving speech on June 12th, 2004, supplicated the global community for the need of a renewed social bargain. As Annan states:

> Developing countries have recognized that they have the primary responsibility for their own development. Donor countries and agencies....are gradually ceding ownership over programs and projects. I urge you to continue along this path of reform. Building democratic institutions is essential, as are popular participation in decision making and the protection of women's rights. The most vulnerable members of society should also have a special claim on your attention, and I hope that even as you strive for fiscal prudence you will also ensure that the necessary social investments and safety nets are put in place (CNN.com, 06/12/2004: p. 1).[2]

While Annan remains cautionary yet hopeful, Friedman is chillingly prophetic. As he puts it, "global financial crises will be the norm in this coming era. With the speed of change going on today, and with so many countries in different stages of adjustment to this new globalization system, crises will be endemic" (Friedman, 2000: p. 441).

II.
The Way Forward

A. The Hope Remains, the Initiatives Needed

1. Creating a Better Economic System in Asia and Beyond

However, despite Friedman's claim, the question remains whether there is hope for a better regional and global financial picture in a world today that seems to go on in various directions? A short answer is yes, but a much longer answer requires further analysis in the state of our world today and where we shall go tomorrow, for clearly, this is beyond Asia. To Eichengreen, preventing a crisis or its impact is a matter of creating better mechanism to contain it. This must be done by eliminating alternatives and proposals for the sake of crafting a practical agenda for reforms. This is because, as Eichengreen points out, *"certain proposals will not, by themselves, significantly improve the way crises are prevented, anticipated, and managed"* (Eichengreen, 1999: p. 79). Thus, disclosure and discipline as solutions to all problems are not enough. What is needed is full information, the scope of that which would allow leaders to identify problems, curtail their lending, and avoid problems in their balance sheets. This is because disciplining the market cannot work without information, for information serves as "the cornerstone of accountability at both the corporate and government levels" (Haggard, 2000: p. 229).

In dealing with market disciplining in the age of rapid and never-ending information flow, the *first key step* is to improve the transparency of relations between politicians and their financial supporters. The *second key step* is that in regulating the private sector, proceedings must take place in initiating and maintaining support from political coalitions willing to check private power and hold themselves "accountable for their relationships with private actors" (Haggard, 2000: p. 229). However, improving the information environment will carry its own limitations, for, as Eichengreen argues, "it is unrealistic to expect too much of such an initiative" (Eichengreen, 1999: p. 80). In our new era, information will be vital in the ongoing economic transformations, as defined in the *New Economy* to be discussed later in this chapter.

Thomas Friedman's position is quite different from Eichengreen's, though both viewpoints can, and should, *be complemented in fixing the global financial architecture for the sake of the long-term.* To Friedman, while financial crises are here to stay, solutions are needed to lessen their impacts. *First,* in a case of an emergency, the IMF, the G-7, and the major world central banks shall be able to inject capital into markets to prevent system-threatening meltdowns (Friedman, 2000: p. 442). *Secondly,* every investor involved with an emerging market should be prevailed upon to ascertain whether it is developing the operating system and software to properly allocate capital and generate the incomes needed to pay back its lenders. *Thirdly,* the international community must make sure that the IMF, investors, and banks are constantly pressing for more accurate and timely data on how an economy is developing and where capital (especially short-term capital) is flowing. *Lastly,* banking and financial regulation must be vigilant enough to detect and diffuse problems as early as possible (Friedman, 2000: p. 442).

Ameliorating corporate governance is inescapably linked with reforming the global financial system. The OECD, through drafting the principles of sound corporate governance, understood this well. The principles include: 1) guaranteeing shareholders' rights, 2) guaranteeing the equitable treatment of all shareholders, whether they are minority or foreign, 3) guaranteeing that the board exercises effective monitoring of management, 4) ensuring transparency and full disclosure, and 5) recognizing the role of other shareholders in the firm, including workers and suppliers (Haggard, 2000: pp. 227-228). This should be done by not only placing greater emphasis on financial regulation, but also by changing incentives. Southeast Asia and much of the global community engaged in changing incentives through external (trade) liberalization since the 1980s, though, unfortunately, at the expense of prudent and consistent financial regulation and discipline. Liberalization is important for it prevents collusion. However, such a strategy shall, as Haggard aptly points out, "be complemented by a strengthening of competition policy and antitrust law, including a shift from reliance on administrative enforcement, which remains vulnerable to capture, to judicial enforcement that can encourage monitoring by affected parties" (Haggard, 2000: p. 228). This is something the then New York Attorney General now the state's Governor Elliot Spitzer understands all too well, as he continues with his crusade to clean up the market after the Enron tragedy.

However, the strategy carries another important component, namely for government to support the restructuring of corporate debt in exchange for commitment to principles of good corporate governance and operational restructuring, using the government's short-run advantage as a bank shareholder as leverage (Haggard, 2000: p. 229). This component required creative yet far-reaching negotiations; the kind of bargaining that can even make the altering of loan contracts to include majority-voting, sharing, and non-acceleration clauses more possible (Eichengreen, 1999: p. 67). Not only will it discourage maverick investors from resorting to lawsuits and other methods of obstructing settlements that would be beneficial to the debtors and creditors, but it would allow governments to obtain forbearance from creditors by getting them to roll-over maturing loans instead of forcing disruptive defaults (Eichengreen, 1999: pp. 67-68).[3]

2. Creating a New Social Contract

The issue of a social contract is worth revisiting, because the changes in the dynamics of our societies requires a refocusing and renewed commitment in maintaining and nurturing economic growths. The social contract will be more complex, as job demands change, new technologies are introduced, financial shocks are bound to recur, and the population that is becoming older yet more well-informed and educated. The contract is intrinsically linked with the new economy of the Twenty-first century and beyond, for the welfare of the peoples would influence not just economic growth per se, but its sustainability and the ability to wither the affects of future shocks and crises. Thus, the right set of policies must be set forth and initiated for the contract, and ultimately the economies worldwide, to be successful.

Formulating a social contract poses riddles as well as problems, for there are a number of approaches a government is confronted with for the sake of its national economic well-being. Each approach has its benefits and potentials as well as limitations. *One approach* is what Haggard calls a "conservative reaction" approach, which entails a traditional reliance on family and community in Asia. Governments in Malaysia and Thailand, in particular, argued that high economic growth stemmed from harnessing work, discipline, and responsibility at the individual level. This is linked to the overall Asian culture of hard work and sacrifice even before the economic growths of the late 1950s and beyond. The social welfare programs contradict the roots of past success based on "productivity-enhancing investments in health, education, and performance-based small credit programs" (Haggard, 2000: p. 230).

However, the limitations of this approach is that low-cost employment, particularly in manufacturing and services, may be overly relied upon should large real devaluations and the consequent fall in unit labor costs occur. Exchange rate adjustments are designed to promote expenditure switching. However, with abundance of labor-producing economies in Asia and abroad, relying on real wage adjustments as a solution to problems in manufacturing and services can be self-defeating in the long run, especially since countries like India, Singapore, and increasingly China are becoming knowledge-intensive economies. Besides, such an approach may do more in terms of masking the weaknesses in the quality of the workforce rather than upgrading it, as was the case in Thailand (Haggard, 2000: pp. 230-231).

The second approach leans towards social welfare, which is characterized by providing safety nets to the more vulnerable. While the benefits rest in providing health care, job training, and some buffer from further severity of poverty, it is argued that any extension of safety net programs would adversely affect recovery in the short-run and competitiveness in the long run. Furthermore, the viability of the welfare state option can be dubious in situations where there's little in terms of strong, unified labor movements and social democratic parties (Haggard, 2000: pp. 230-231). The Southeast Asian region by in large have no such political forces, though Indonesia's recent presidential election may generate hope and at least cautious optimism in that regard.

The third approach combines the aforementioned growth strategy of the past with the new requirements of those vulnerable to external shocks. In formulating a social contract using this approach, political debates are likely to revolve around five central, interrelated policy areas, namely: the provision of social insurance, the reform of industrial relations and labor market issues, decentralization, education, and poverty (Haggard, 2000: p. 231).

In regards to social insurance programs, which include unemployment benefits, health insurance, and pensions, the question remains how much support will they receive, if any. The question persists especially since household spending remains high in the region and middle-income Asian countries, at least for the most part, continue to exercise sound fiscal policy (Haggard, 2000: p. 232). Moreover, a country's present condition, its future goals and its past performances will influence the degree and level in which social insurance programs will even be considered. Singapore already has this system well in place. But, countries that are more traditionally based, like the Philippines, Thailand, and Indonesia, are likely to be the slowest in adapting to a social insurance system of any kind. This is because not only there's a lack of strong encompassing unions or strong democratic parties, the emphasis is place more on the ethics of personal responsibility rather than on re-distributive objectives (Haggard, 2000: p. 232). Countries that are more developed, such as Malaysia and South Korea, are likely to design the social insurance system. This is because, for one thing, a substantial portion of the workforce is in the formal sector. Moreover, as in Malaysia, emphasis is being made in improving the design and administration of public works programs and to have them institutionalized so as to respond to future crises (Haggard, 2000: p. 232). Therefore, a preventive element behind the insurance system is quite apparent in the overall scheme in improving the economies in various countries of the region. However, as with Indonesia under a new leadership but with old, chronic problems such as high unemployment and poverty rates as well as corruption, it may not far-fetched in foreseeing the country becoming not only democratized, but initiating an social insurance of any type as part of its goals in improving its economy.

In regards to reforming industrial relations and tackling labor market issues as well as decentralization, a new set of priorities and policies should at least be considered. In the past, the traditional social bargain in East Asia rested on an authoritarian approach to labor relations, where unions were either repressed or controlled by the government. However, with the population becoming more educated and democratically inclined, with more women entering both labor and politics in particular, the governments in East Asia should find ways in initiating new approaches to labor relations as the economy is becoming more complex and technically inclined. A key step in doing so entails governments to cease controlling unions for the sake of allowing unions to form, engaging in collective bargaining, as well as allowing and settling strikes (providing that the unions will be organized and transparent) (Haggard, 2000: p. 233). In regards to decentralization, the matter remains not only administrative in scope, but also in achieving a national level of democratization in order to form responsible, accountable governments, organizations, unions, and institutions (Haggard, 2000: pp. 234-235). Thus, decentralization would improve efficiency and effectiveness especially in education.

Tackling labor market issues is important for a number of reasons. *First,* In the case of Southeast Asia and beyond (especially in the United States and parts of Europe), employment growth rates have been far lower in recent years in comparison to high output and productivity growth rates. *Secondly,* income/expenditure inequality (a variable tightly linked to the distribution of labor earnings) has increased between rural and urban areas in countries like India and Indonesia. The low wage growth of those at the bottom of the distribution over a period of high economic growth tends to spell out a slow pace of poverty reduction (Felipe & Hasan, 2006: pp. 1-2). *Third,* employment in the informal sector is either on the rise or is remaining persistent.[4] There are two dimensions to this phenomenon. One dimension is agricultural employment, which remains a significant share of total employment in a number of countries especially in Asia. The other dimension is that many jobs that are being generated outside agriculture remain in the informal sector, which is expanding in fast-growing transition economies like China and Vietnam. *Lastly,* the nature of employment in the formal sector is changing (as mentioned before). Formal sector employment is becoming increasingly non-synonymous with regular contracts that entail benefits and job security. In the Philippines, for example, the proportion of non-regular workers in total employment rose from about 20 percent in 1991 to 28 percent in 1997 (Felipe & Hasan, 2006: pp. 3-4). With the economies becoming increasingly globalized, transitional-type employment is becoming more prevalent especially in the United States where about one in five Americans are temp workers (as opposed to about one in ten in the 1980s). The prevalence of outsourcing fits compelling in the changing dynamics of labor markets worldwide.

The outsourcing phenomenon is one of the factors behind the changing dynamics. The effective global supply of labor has increased rapidly driven in part by the integration of China, India, and former soviet satellite nations. Yet, the surge of the global labor force has not been accompanied by a surge in capital for investment. Consequently, there has been a steep reduction in the effective global capital-labor ratio from $53,500 in 1990 to $37,600 in 2000 (Felipe & Hasan, 2006: p. 5). This trend poses worries because:

> the decline in the available capital per worker globally combined with the fact that capital is more mobile than labor has generated anxiety at being able to attract the now more relatively limited pool of available capital and appears to have eroded the bargaining power or workers virtually everywhere (Felipe & Hasan, 2006: p. 5).

The second factor behind the dynamics is that "while the relative labor abundance of developing countries would suggest the use of more labor-intensive techniques of production in their formal industry and service sectors, in reality the formal sectors of developing countries are not very different from those of industrial countries in terms of capital intensity" (Felipe & Hasan, 2006: p. 6).This is problematic because given the supply of labor available, the more capital intensive the techniques would require less employment for any given rate of investment. In short, overly capital-intensive techniques will yield higher unemployment rate. Furthermore, the introduction of such techniques can raise the demand for skilled workers disproportionately (a problem since such workers are of short supply in developing countries). As a result, a sharp increase in wages earned by skilled workers will occur, and income disparities will become even greater (Felipe & Hasan, 2006: p. 6). Moreover, the employment of these skilled workers may not be permanent and even if it is contractual in nature, the level of benefits and stability will not be the same as with full-fledged employees of companies of the formal sectors.

In terms of generating productive employment, Singapore and Thailand has been demonstrating convincingly over the years that increasing public investments in rural infrastructure and provision of agriculture extension services are vital not just for raising productivity in agriculture, but for maintaining if not enhancing economic growth. This is key, because increased productivity on the farm will also benefit non-farm sectors as well (which will raise demand for the output of the non-farm sector) (Felipe & Hasan, 2006: p. 7). However, the buck doesn't stop here. Jobs in the formal sector must be promoted more rigorously by governments throughout much of the world. This should be done by setting up policies that would promote diversification of production activities (whether traditional or not) into new areas, facilitate restructuring of existing activities, and foster coordination between public and private entities. The governments should strategically and with coordination, engage in the development of non-traditional activities: the activities where the underlying costs and opportunities are not known from the start and surface only when such activities start. Likewise, export push, either through lower wages or higher productivity, should continue to be exercised rigorously. Ideally, export push through high productivity should be pursued, providing that productivity is improved through introduction of competition policies as well as education and training (Felipe & Hasan, 2006: pp. 7-8).

And reforming education is also a key essential when formulating a social contract. While support for primary and secondary education will remain, even in the event of a financial crisis, questions remain on the tertiary (collegiate) level. As Haggard points out, "the key principle for a post-crisis social contract on higher education should be to channel public spending on universities primarily into research and other public goods while avoiding across-the-board support, which can contribute to overbuilt, inefficient public university system" (Haggard, 2000: p. 234). Once again, the goal behind such a reformation remains preventive in outlook, for misguided spending on college education can potentially drain human and administrative resources to disastrous results.

Addressing poverty is no less a crucial component behind formulating a social contract. As seen in a country like Indonesia, poverty causes low morale and the programs design to alleviate it run the risk of inducing moral hazard (an idea that programs design to help the poor have the potential of "making them come back for more"). Furthermore, such programs collectively may end up as a source of patronage and corruption among local politicians. The solution includes making the programs well-defined and far-reaching as much as possible while appealing to the poor for the sake of having them stay involved, which was what former President Megawati tried to do during her tenure in Indonesia. But appealing to the poor is not enough, for a road map is needed in order to give a country a clearer picture in terms of where it is, where it is going, and how. In the end, Megawati's road map into the future remained ill-defined.

B. The New Economy

The New Economy, as Catherine Mann and Daniel Rosen describe it, is

> all about transformation. The definition of the New Economy stipulates that structural policy reforms make networked technologies immensely valuable for generating productivity. The outcome of this mix of policy and technology is transformation in the way markets, firms and individuals operate and make decisions. The transformation is toward more productive use of scarce resources, be they money, inputs like steel, lumber or water, or hours of labor. This is important and challenging for policymakers, in part because adjusting to a new way of doing things often entails displacement of old ways of doing things-displacement of people and vested corporate interests that is (Mann and Rosen, 2001: p. 3).

Thus, the transformation is all about continuity for the sake of growth and productivity; the continuity in the significant changes in the activities of firms, governments and persons. The four policy domains critical to supporting the New Economy environment of transformation, higher productivity growth, and economic well-being include: 1) fiscal policy and the fiscal activities of government, 2) trade and cross-border investment policies, 3) pro-competitive market policy and legal environment, and 4) banking and financial market policy (Mann and Rosen, 2001: pp. 4-5). The domains are worthy of focus because: a) specific structural policies are needed to achieve the knowledge-based economy (KBE) characteristics and subsequent New Economy outcome, b) increased complexity, dynamism, and synergies among structural policies in the New Economy suggest that these policies are better addressed together rather than separately, and c) the forces of the New Economy affect how structural policies work to transform an economy, thus warranting a fresh review of those policies (Mann and Rosen, 2001: p. 5).

1. On the Question of Fiscal Policy and Fiscal Activities of Government

Governmental agencies should build on the elements of e-APEC, the E-government teams that are comprised of foreign, domestic, and government entities that can bring productivity as well as enhancing information and communications technologies (ICTs). However, careful spending and investment are of paramount importance. As Mann and Rosen point out:

> High return government spending in areas where the market fails are even more critical, given the need to support transformation in the New Economy, because the productivity gains to be achieved are greater. Conversely, low return government spending on economic intervention where no market failure exists stymies transformation, and must be very critically assessed given the increased opportunity costs of that spending (Mann and Rosen, 2001: p. 8).

Careful spending is important because it enhances fiscal balances, allows for lowering of taxes, allows increased spending on social needs, and frees up human talent previously absorbed into uncompetitive enterprises. Furthermore, economies pursuing the New Economy should quantify the extent and nature of tax evasion (Mann and Rosen, 2001: p. 8).

2. On the Question of Trade and Cross-border Investment

Throughout the 1980s, various countries in East Asia and Latin America engaged in liberalization policies with mixed results. Assuming that liberalization and reforms will be done correctly and with discipline, then APEC in particular can prevent the widening of the productivity-related digital divide in the region. Moreover collective liberalization should be accompanied by multilateral trade rounds for the climate of reforms to be more viable, realistic, yet ideal. Unlike liberalization of the 1980s and 1990s, liberalization of today and beyond must be bestowed with complete commitments by all involved. And so, as Mann and

Rosen states, "the APEC forum should extend the institutionalization of transparency, monitoring, and assessment of commitments which would support further liberalization" (Mann and Rosen, 2001: p. 6).

However, the issue of bilateralism in trade is becoming more of a viable one. As explained throughout this book, the integration of Southeast Asia as a region into the global economy has been largely driven by market forces, particularly by FDI and the related rise on intra-industry trade. Moreover, notwithstanding the effects of the Asian Financial Crisis, Asia benefited from global trade since the 1950s beginning with Japan. Incomes rose, poverty fell, savings over consumption was a norm (even when people began buying more during that period), and growths of exports and imports has outpaced income growth. The employment picture before 1997 was favorable as women participated more than ever before.

In recent years, however, countries in Asia and in other regions are increasingly leaning toward preferential trade agreements and on a bilateral basis (ADO 2006, 2006: p. 267). Part of the reason for this trend is the frustration with the slow and halting speed of multilateral trade negotiations conducted under the auspices of the WTO (where the environment tends to be diverse and complex). Bilateralism is becoming more attractive because it allows "like-minded" countries to make more progress on a wider range of issues in less time. Also, bilateral trade agreements are increasingly being looked upon as comparative strategies for broad-based trade liberalization (ADO 2006, 2006: p. 275).

But, other than the assertions that they are inherently discriminatory and that they place third parties, which do not qualify under the rules of origin, at a disadvantage (a common argument), there are other problems in using that approach. There's a risk that the rules of origin, a series of laws and regulations that determine the economy origin of goods and products, would confer preferences while complicating investment and trade decisions. *Secondly*, bilateralism could jeopardize multilateral trade agreements as countries refocus their energies on reaching reciprocal deals, often to the exclusion of others. *Thirdly*, although bilateralism coexists with high most-favored nation (MFN) tariffs, high administered protection through, for instance, the use of antidumping measures could result (ADO 2006, 2006: p. 280).[5] *Lastly*, countries with less bargaining power are proned to be more harmed by bilateral arrangements than by multilateralism.

If bilateral trade arrangements are pursued any further, deepening integration should be the angle in pursuing them for the sake of, as Michael Plummer puts it, possibly presenting additional opportunities to those currently accommodated within the multilateral framework (ADO 2006, 2006: p. 290). This goes hand-in-hand with Mann and Rosen's aforementioned argument for reforms to be multilateral in nature in the new economical and technological age. To Plummer, this integration approach to bilateralism should entail: 1) wide coverage of goods with few exclusions, 2) wide coverage of services and coverage of all modes of service delivery, 3) rules of origin that are simple, consistent, and transparent, 4) even-handed and transparent customs procedures, 5) clear and simple codes surrounding technical barriers to trade, 6) open competition and non-discrimination among members for government procurement and as little discrimination on nonmembers as possible, 7) nondiscriminatory enforcement of intellectual property rights, 8) establishment of dispute-settlement provisions that would be fair, transparent, and timely, and 9) laws that protect foreign investors from expropriation or unwarranted actions against their interests (ADO 2006, 2006: p. 290).

The key here is to not allow bilateralism to be too much two-sided. By engaging in deep integration, which entails reducing trade costs through behind-the-border reforms while improving trade efficiency, countries would benefit more than in traditional preferential trade agreements (PTAs). The Doha Development Agenda of the WTO was exploring means to ensure that bilateral and regional trade agreements will be consistent with WTO's principles such as transparency and fair trade (ADO 2006, 2006: p. 296). The Doha Talks in discussing the feasibility of the Agenda collapsed in the summer of 2006. Although this alone does not spell the end of multilateralism, the failed talks was a serious blow to what the WTO was trying to achieve. But, Evan Davis put this matter into perspective when he states that over 50 percent of world trade is already occurring under bilateral or regional deals (Davis, 07/25/2006: p. 3).

3. On the Question of Pro-Competitive Market Policy and Legal Regime

The New Economy depends on transformation, transparency, and greater dispersion of information. As seen in the previous subsection, full information is key if problems are to be identified and its sources effectively dealt with. While Eichengreen reminds us not to expect too much from reforming the way information are given, the general consensus is that such a reform is critical particularly in economies that are becoming increasingly knowledge-based. Therefore, legal regimes and competition policies are of importance should corrupt, unfair, or anti-competitive practices not overshadow the benefits of the New Economy. According to Mann and Rosen, two related endeavors should be undertaken. *First,* competition policy regimes must work internationally for the network benefits of the New Economy to avail. APEC should discuss how its Principles to Enhance Competition Policy and Regulatory Reform operate in the marketplace of the New Economy where more transactions cross international borders (Mann and Rosen, 2001: p. 7). *Secondly,* economies pursuing reforms should look at international forums such as the United Nations Commission of International Trade Law (UNCITRAL), Organization for Economic Cooperation and Development (OECD), and The Hague as models and for their legal precedent and legislative language (Mann and Rosen, 2001: p. 7). In short, the overall climate of the "rule of law" must be supported, but that rule of law that goes beyond the formulaic and the window-dressing (as alluded by Catherine Crier).

4. On the Question of Banking and Financial Market Policy

As seen in the events leading up to the Asian Financial Crisis, poor supervisory oversight and lack of financial skills undermine the conduct and performance of the financial system as a whole. Therefore, to prevent the re-occurrence of the problem, economies should develop on-going relationships with established supervisory training and exchange mechanisms (Mann and Rosen, 2001: p. 7). Non-bank financial markets such as bond, stock, and venture that are thin will perplex the New Economy. Therefore, transparent and complete public listing requirements along with strong accounting standards will help deepen and strengthen the financial markets not only in Asia, but worldwide. Likewise, liberating barriers to cross-border financial transactions and institutions should be at least considered (Mann and Rosen, 2001: p. 7).

C. The Signs of the Public's Re-awakening

Although there exists some resistance to change (examine France's racial and ethnic problems especially in relations to job opportunities and standards of living), there are signs that people throughout much of the world want a new direction for better prospects for the future. What happened in Thailand and even in places like Hungary was no accident or a coincidence.[6] The public, mostly in urban areas, grew weary on the developments of the Thai government, especially of Thaksin's Shin Corp deal. While many would deem the public's outcry of such a deal an overreaction (especially when considering Thailand's admirable economic recovery under Thaksin's leadership in the aftermath of the Crisis of 1997-1998), the Thaksin debacle does spell out something of great importance: public's awareness and growing resiliency. With new leadership emerging in parts of Asia, Africa, and even in the Americas, it is quite obvious that much of the global population is demanding change within their governments and beyond. Experts such as Eichengreen are still calling for a new global financial restructuring to spur economic growth while engaging in policies to prevent to financial clashes of the 1990s (at least as far as severity is concerned).

People like myself are increasingly calling for that as well. We are calling for mechanisms to help ensure better discipline, transparency, accountability, foresight, and policies to build a more promising global community. What's happening in Southeast Asia in terms of the graying of the population, insurance, medical expense and pension concerns, infrastructural and poverty issues, as well as leadership that in some ways lack the long-term vision for growth and sustainability, are the concerns pervasive throughout much of the world. Grandparents are having troubles caring for their parents while many students struggle to cope with the changing markets while tuition affordability is becoming increasingly out of reach. With the population becoming more educated and well-aware with current events and developments surrounding us, the governments are now dealing with new challenges in not just simply "keep sweeping matters under the rug." The popularity of Lyndon H. LaRouche, Jr., American controversial economist and statesman, stems from the public's desire and, to an extent at least, the sense of urgency in finding answers to not only why things are occurring in the world today, but also what shall be done to reverse the tumultuous period from the 1990s well throughout the first years of this century. Whether that re-awakening will last for long (say, for a generation or more) is not easy to say. What is for certain, however, is that plenty of lessons must be learned from this period to prevent future crises and mismanagements. But we, the people, have the capacity to reverse the disorderly effects of the past decade such as, for instance, electing ideal leadership with insights for the future and then help such leadership bring those insights to fuller fruition. It will not be easy, but slowly and unevenly so, many of us are beginning to learn those lessons of the past. I realized that by the people I've spoken with, including a barber at a barber shop several years ago in a struggling neighborhood in Washington DC, who knew a thing or two about globalization and what was wrong with it. What's fundamentally the problem, however, is that lack of organic coherency among us to conjure up the clear picture of the happenings of the past and present and what must be done in response. It's a matter of going outside the box for something more far-reaching and far-seeing.

III.
Some Final Thoughts

The key to the New Economy is that transformation of activities will yield higher productivity and economic well-being. A set of strong structural policies are critical for robust human resources development (or, as mentioned throughout this book, efficient labor pooling) to take shape. As Mann and Rosen argue,

> Without good structural policies, skilled and flexible people will migrate to environments where their abilities are allowed to shine. Without good structural policies that create a robust domestic environment, domestic firms will see little value in investing in human resources development. Without good structural policies that underpin solid economic growth, the government will be starved for financial resources to support human resource development. Thus, human resource development and human resource deployment depend on the structural policy fundamentals that create a dynamic environment (Mann and Rosen, 2001: p. 12).

This argument goes hand-in-hand with the social bargain argument of Friedman. The OECD, for example, supports the notion that the fundamentals such as macroeconomic stability, openness and competition, as well as economic and social institutions remain strong and are working (Mann and Rosen, 2001: p. 12). These aforementioned structural policies are more effective when addressed together, for these policies are inter-related. The governments of the future should be efficient and effective, *but not excessive in its intervention.* The New Economy is meant to be comprehensive in goals and in scope, which is why looking at and grouping economic, financial, and social issues into a bigger picture is critical for a viable yet feasible "road map": the map that envisions the state of a country, a region, and the world a generation later that yields not only hope, but promise, optimism, excitability, and a fuller sense of destiny.

The Doha collapse and its implications do not mean that reforming global trade and the global financial structure cannot be done despite the ongoing bilateral trends. It's simply a new challenge in creating the road maps at national and international levels to create even more longevity in prosperity while preventing as much as possible the future economic and financial crises like ones witnessed in the past decade alone. The road ahead is murky at best although there's a growing recognition that building, rebuilding, and engaging in prudent yet preventive measures against cronyism is a must for the sake of re-building, growth, and re-growth. There's a growing consensus that the economic and social leap forwards must be envisioned, planned, and maintained. Otherwise, Asia, the Americas, and ultimately our global community will enter into an economic, political, and social abyss in nature and in scope never before seen. In the post Bretton Woods era, the Asian Financial Crisis of 1997-1998 was simply yet in essence, the tip of the iceberg.

IV.
Notes

1. The G-3 exchange rate regime consists of the dollar, the yen, and the euro.
2. Annan's speech was made at a conference in Sao Paolo, Brazil to mark the Fortieth Anniversary of the Group of 77. The name "Group of 77" remains despite its current membership of 132 participating nations (CNN.com, 06/12/2004: p. 1).
3. A roll-over means that a loan is periodically re-priced at an agreed spread over the appropriate, currently prevailing rate.
4. The informal sector is characterized by: 1) production that is typically carried out with very little capital, 2) production methods that are traditional, and 3) productivity levels and earnings that are correspondingly low (Felipe and Hasan, 2006: p. 3).
5. A MFN tariffs is a tariff level that a member of the GATT/WTO charges on a good to other members),
6. The Hungarian riots in the latter half of 2006 stemmed from Prime Minister Ferenc Gyurcsany's admission that he and his government lied about the extent of their success in their first four years in office in order to win April 2006 re-election. The economic accomplishments were especially exaggerated.
   Source: The BBC News. "Hungary's Troubled PM Vows to Stay." Great Britain: BBC News, 20 Sept. 2006: p. 1. http://news.bbc.co.uk/2/hi/europe/5363138.stm.

The Bibliography

Arnold, Wayne. "Japan's Electronics Slump Takes a Toll on Southeast Asia." New York, NY: *New York Times*, 1 September 2001: 1-4. www.nytimes.com/2001/09/01/business/worldbusiness/01ELEC.html

Arphasil, Prakarn. "Financial Liberalization and Financial Crisis: The Case of Thailand." *Financial Big Bang in Asia.* Masayoshi Tsurumi, editor. Singapore: Ashgate Publishing, 2001: 167-190.

Asia-Pacific Economic Cooperation (APEC). "About APEC." 35 Heng Mui Keng Terrace, Singapore: *APEC*, downloaded 27 June 2004: 1-2. www.apec.org/apec/about_apec.html

Asian Development Outlook 2006. *Developing Asia and the World: Subregional Summaries: Malaysia.* Manilla, The Philippines: The Asian Development Bank, 2006: 31.

Asian Development Outlook 2006. *Foreword.* Manilla, The Philippines: The Asian Development Bank, 2006: iii.

Asian Development Outlook 2006. *Economic Trends and Prospects in Developing Asia: India.* Manilla, The Philippines: The Asian Development Bank, 2006: 158-167.

Asian Development Outlook 2003. *Economic Trends and Prospects in Developing Asia: Indonesia.* Manilla, The Philippines: The Asian Development Bank, 2003: 68-74.

Asian Development Outlook 2005. *Economic Trends and Prospects in Developing Asia:Indonesia.* Manilla, The Philippines: The Asian Development Bank, 2005: 95-99.

Asian Development Outlook 2006. *Economic Trends and Prospects in Developing Asia: Indonesia.* Manilla, The Philippines: The Asian Development Bank, 2006: 198-203.

Asian Development Outlook 2003. *Economic Trends and Prospects in Developing Asia:Malaysia.* Manilla, The Philippines: The Asian Development Bank, 2003: 78-81.

Asian Development Outlook 2005. *Economic Trends and Prospects in Developing Asia: Malaysia.* Manilla, The Philippines: The Asian Development Bank, 2005: 103-107.

Asian Development Outlook 2006. *Economic Trends and Prospects in Developing Asia: Malaysia.* Manilla, The Philippines: The Asian Development Bank, 2006: 208-212.

Asian Development Outlook 2003. *Economic Trends and Prospects in Developing Asia: Singapore.* Manilla, The Philippines: The Asian Development Bank, 2003: 89-92.

Asian Development Outlook 2005. *Economic Trends and Prospects in Developing Asia: Singapore.* Manilla, The Philippines: The Asian Development Bank, 2005: 114-117.

Asian Development Outlook 2006. *Economic Trends and Prospects in Developing Asia: Singapore.* Manilla, The Philippines: The Asian Development Bank, 2006: 220-223.

Asian Development Outlook 2003. *Economic Trends and Prospects in Developing Asia: Taipei, China.* Manilla, The Philippines: The Asian Development Bank, 2003: 60-63.

Asian Development Outlook 2005. *Economic Trends and Prospects in Developing Asia: Taipei, China.* Manilla, The Philippines: The Asian Development Bank, 2005: 86-89.

Asian Development Outlook 2006. *Economic Trends and Prospects in Developing Asia: Taipei, China.* Manilla, The Philippines: The Asian Development Bank, 2006: 137-140.

Asian Development Outlook 2003. *Economic Trends and Prospects in Developing Asia: Thailand.* Manilla, The Philippines: The Asian Development Bank, 2003: 93-97.

Asian Development Outlook 2005. *Economic Trends and Prospects in Developing Asia: Thailand.* Manilla, The Philippines: The Asian Development Bank, 2005: 118-121.

Asian Development Outlook 2006. *Economic Trends and Prospects in Developing Asia: Thailand.* Manilla, The Philippines: The Asian Development Bank, 2006: 225-229.

Asian Development Outlook 2005. *Export or Domestic Demand-Led Growth in Developing Asia?* Manilla, The Philippines: The Asian Development Bank, 2005: 40-62.

Asian Development Outlook 2006. *Routes for Asia's Trade.* Manilla, The Philippines: The Asian Development Bank, 2003: 267-302.

Associated Press. "Poll Shows Runoff in Indonesia Election." *New York Times*, 6 July 2004: 1-3.
www.nytimes.com/aponline/international/AP-Indonesia-Election.html

Athukorala, Prema-Chandra. "Swimming Against the Tide: Crisis Management in Malaysia." *Southeast Asia's Economic Crisis: Origins, Lessons, and the Way Forward.* H.W. Arndt & Hal Hill, editors. New York: St. Martin's Press, 1999: 28-40.

Bank Negara (Central Bank of Malaysia). *Annual Report 2004 (press release).* Kuala Lumpur, Malaysia: *Bank Negara*, 2005: 1-21.
www.mida.gov.my/beta/pdf/BNMAnnual2004.pdf

Basle Committee on Bank Supervision. "Capital Requirements and Bank Behaviour: The Impact of the Basle Accord." Working Papers, April 1999. Basle, Switzerland: *The Bank of International Settlements*, 1999: 1-64.
www.bis.org/publ/bcbs_wp01.pdf

BBC News. "Asia's Growth Picks up Pace." Great Britain: *BBC News*, 11 December 2003: 1-2.
news.bbc.co.uk/1/hi/business/3309237.stm

BBC News. "Bird Flu Kills Thai Boy of Five." Great Britain: *BBC News*, 9 December 2005: 1-2.
news.bbc.co.uk/2/hi/asia-pacific/4512422.stm

BBC News. "Country Profile: Indonesia." Great Britain: *BBC News*, 2 June 2004: 1-5.
news.bbc.co.uk/1/hi/world/asia-pacific/country_profiles/1260544.stm

BBC News. "Export-led Growth Spurt for Japan." Great Britain: *BBC News*, 18 February 2004: 1-3.
news.bbc.co.uk/1/hi/business/3498783.stm

BBC News. "Hungary's Troubled PM Vows to Stay." Great Britain: *BBC News*, 20 September 2006: 1.
news.bbc.co.uk/2/hi/europe/5363138.stm

BBC News. "India Finance Boss Defends Policy." Great Britain: *BBC News*, 28 May 2004: 1-2.
news.bbc.co.uk/1/hi/business/3756755.stm

BBC News. "India PM Promises Public Reform." Great Britain: *BBC News*, 24 June 2004: 1-3.
news.bbc.co.uk/1/hi/world/south_asia/3835871.stm

BBC News. "Indonesia Beats Forecasts." Great Britain: *BBC News*, 17 Febraury 2003: 1-3.
news.bbc.co.uk/2/hi/business/2771755.stm

BBC News. "Indonesia Leader Being Sworn In." Great Britain: *BBC News*, 20 October 2004: 1-3.
news.bbc.co.uk/1/hi/world/asia-pacific/3756870.stm

BBC News. "Indonesia to Expel Terrorism Expert." Great Britain: *BBC News*, 2 June 2004: 1-2.
news.bbc.co.uk/1/hi/world/asia-pacific/3768521.stm

BBC News. "Major Party Endorses Wiranto Bid." Great Britain: *BBC News*, 26 May 2004: 1-2.
news.bbc.co.uk/1/hi/world/asia-pacific/3749077.stm

BBC News. "Minister Quits over Thaksin Deal." Great Britain: *BBC News*, 3 February 2006: 1-2
news.bbc.co.uk/2/hi/asia-pacific/4676352.stm

BBC News. "Singapore 'Cheapest for Business." Great Britain: *BBC News*, 21 March 2006: 1-3
news.bbc.co.uk/2/hi/business/4830158.stm

BBC News. "Singapore Falls Into Recession." Great Britain: *BBC News*, 10 July 2001: 1-2.
news.bbc.co.uk/1/hi/business/1431658.stm

BBC News. "Singapore to Give Shares to Citizens." Great Britain: *BBC News*, 20 August 2001: 1-3.
news.bbc.co.uk/1/hi/business/1500468.stm

BBC News. "Singapore Aims to Boost Economy." Great Britain: *BBC News*, 12 October 2001: 1-3.
news.bbc.co.uk/1/hi/business/1594867.stm

BBC News. "Singapore's Economic Growth Slows." Great Britain: *BBC News*, 10 April 2006: 1
news.bbc.co.uk/2/hi/business/4894908.stm

BBC News. "Singapore Enjoys 'Healthy Growth'." Great Britain: *BBC News*, 3 January 2007: 1-2
news.bbc.co.uk/2/hi/business/6227001.stm

BBC News. "Singapore Reports Steady Growth." Great Britain: *BBC News*, 10 October 2005: 1-2.
news.bbc.co.uk/1/hi/business/4325638.stm

BBC News. "Taiwan's Economy Worsens." Great Britain: *BBC News*, 23 July 2001: 1-3
news.bbc.co.uk/1/hi/business/1452767.stm

BBC News. "Taiwan Beats Recession." Great Britain: *BBC News*, 17 May 2002: 1-3.
news.bbc.co.uk/1/hi/business/2030941.stm

BBC News. "Thai Court Calls for Resignations." Great Britain: *BBC News*, 9 May 2006: 1-2.
www.news.bbc.co.uk/2/hi/asia-pacific/4753157.stm

BBC News. "Thai PM Hints at Stepping Down." Great Britain: *BBC News*, 15 March 2006: 1-3.
news.bbc.co.uk/2/hi/asia-pacific/4807758.stm

BBC News. "Thai PM Sells Mobile Firm Stake."Great Britain: *BBC News*, 23 January 2006: 1-2.
news.bbc.co.uk/2/hi/business/4638380.stm

BBC News. "Thai Rulers to Tackle Corruption." Great Britain: *BBC News*, 24 September 2006: 1-2.
news.bbc.co.uk/2/hi/asia-pacific/5367394.stm

BBC News. "Thailand to Build India Ties." Great Britain: *BBC News*, 26 November 2001: 1-4.
news.bbc.co.uk/1/hi/world/south_asia/1676262.stm

BBC News. "Thailand's Economy Grows by 6.7%." Great Britain: *BBC News*, 8 March 2004: 1-2.
news.bbc.co.uk/1/hi/business/3543945.stm

BBC News. "World Trade Growth Picks Up Speed." Great Britain: *BBC News*, 5 April 2004: 1-3.
news.bbc.co.uk/1/hi/business/3601757.stm

BBC World Service. "International Investors Wait to See the Shape of Thailand's New Government." Great Britain: *BBC News*, 8 January 2001: 1-3.
www.bbc.co.uk/worldservice/business/highlights/010108_thailand.shtml

BBC World Service. "Special Series: The Asian Economy-The Bleak World Bank forecast for Indonesia's Poor." Great Britain: *BBC News*, 29 February 2000: 1-4.
www.bbc.co.uk/worldservice/asiapacific/eastasiatoday/ea_archive/indonesiaecon.shtml.

BBC World Service. "Special Series: The Asian Economy-The Reality Behind Thailand's New Glowing Financial Figures." Great Britain: *BBC News*, 28 February 2000: 1-3. www.bbc.co.uk/worldservice/asiapacific/eastasiatoday/ea_archive/thailandecon.shtml.

BBC World Service. "Special Series: The Asian Economy-Malaysia's Economic Recovery." Great Britain: *BBC News*, 28 Febraury 2000: 1-3. www.bbc.co.uk/worldservice/asiapacific/eastasiatoday/ea_archive/econ.shtml.

Beinart, Peter. *The Good Fight: Why Liberals-and Only Liberals-Can Win the War on Terror and Make America Great Again.* New York, NY: Harper Collins Publishers, 2006.

Blecker, Robert A. *Taming Global Finance: A Better Architecture for Growth and Equity.* Washington, DC: Economic Policy Institute, 1999.

Bradsher, Keith. "Chinese Economy Becomes 4th Largest in the World." New York, NY: *New York Times*, 25 January 2006: 1-4. www.nytimes.com/2006/01/25/business/worldbusiness/26yuancnd.html?

Bradsher, Keith. "Is China the Next Bubble?" New York, NY: *New York Times*, 18 January 2004: 1-6. www.nytimes.com/2004/01/18/business/yourmoney/18china.html?hp

Bradsher, Keith. "Like Japan in the 1980s, China Poses Big Economic Challenge." New York, NY: *New York Times*, 2 March 2004: 1-4. www.nytimes.com/2004/03/02/business/worldbusiness/02YUAN.html?

Brown, Colin. "Indonesia: the changing balance of commercial power?" Sheridan, Kyoto, ed. *Emerging Economic Systems in Asia: A Political & Economic Survey*. St. Leonards, Australia: Allen & Unwin, 1998: 180-207.

Central Intelligence Agency (CIA). "The World Factbook: Indonesia" Washington, DC: *CIA*, 2006: 1-14. www.cia.gov/cia/publications/factbook/geos/id.html#Econ

Chin, Kok Fay and K.S. Jomo. "Financial Reform and Crisis in Malaysia." *Financial Big Bang in Asia.* Masayoshi Tsurumi, editor. Singapore: Ashgate, 2001: 225-250.

Cho, George. *The Malaysian Economy.* London: Routledge, 1990.

Chowdhury, Anis."Malaysia in Transition." Abu N.M. Wahid, ed. *The ASEAN Region in Transition: A Socioeconomic Perspective* .Sidney: Ashgate Publishing Ltd., 1997: 43-65.

Claessens, Stijn and Thomas Glaessner. *Are Financial Sector Weaknesses Undermining the East Asian Miracle.* Washington DC: The World Bank, 1997.

CNN.com. "Annan: World has Become 'More Unequal" United States: *Cable News Network*, 12 June 2004: 1 www.cnn.com/2004/WORLD/americas/06/12/annan.un/index.html

CNN.com. "ASEAN Looks for Money Swap Consensus." United States: *Cable News Network*, 4 April 2001: 1-3. www.cnn.com/2001/BUSINESS/asia/04/04/asean.swaps/

CNN.com. "ASEAN to form EU-style Trade Bloc." United States: *Cable News Network*, 7 October 2003: 1-3. www.cnn.com/2003/WORLD/asiapcf/southeast/10/07/asean/index.html

CNN.com. "Thai Protesters Hit Shopping Areas." United States: *Cable News Network*, 26 March 2006: 1-3. www.cnn.com/2006/WORLD/asiapcf/03/25/thailand.thaksin.ap/index.html

CNN.com. "Thailand's Thaksin Back in Charge." United States: *Cable News Network*, 23 May 2006: 1-3. www.cnn.com/2006/WORLD/asiapcf/05/22/thailand.thaksin.ap/index.html

Coats, Warren. *In Search of a Monetary Anchor: A 'New' Monetary Standard.* San Francisco: An International Center for Economic Growth Publication/ICS Press, 1994.

Cole, David C. and Betty F. Slade. *Building a Modern Financial System: The Indonesian Experience.* Cambridge: Cambridge University Press, 1996.

Crier, Catherine. *The Case Against Lawyers.* New York, NY: Broadway Books, 2002.

Das, Dilip K. "An Introduction to the Regional Economy."*Emerging Growth Pole: The Asia-Pacific Economy.* Dilip K. Das, editor. London: Prentice Hall, 1997: 44.

Davis, Evan. "The Death of the WTO's Doha Talks." Great Britain: *BBC News*, 25 July 2006: 1-6. news.bbc.co.uk/2/hi/business/5215318.stm

Djiwandono, J. Soedradjad. "Causes and Implications of the Asian Crisis: An Indonesian View."*The Asian Financial Crisis: Origins, Implications, and Solutions.* Hunter, William C., George G. Kaufman, & Thomas H. Krueger editors. London: Kluwer Academic Press, 1999: 115-126.

Doner, Richard F & Ansil Ramsay. "Thailand: From Economic Miracle to Economic Crisis."*Asian Contagion: The Causes and Consequences of a Financial Crisis.* Jackson, Karl D. editor. Colorado: Westview Press, 1999: 171-207.

Economist.com. "Country Briefings, Thailand: Factsheet." London: *The Economists*, 2006: 1-4. www.economist.com/countries/Thailand/profile.cfm?folder=Profile-FactSheet

Eichengreen, Barry. *Toward a New International Financial Architecture: A Practical Post-Asia Agenda.* Washington, DC: Institute for International Economics, 1999.

Embassy of the Republic of Indonesia. "News and Views". London, Great Britain: *The Embassy of the Republic of Indonesia*, 2003: 1-4. www.indonesianembassy.org.uk/nnv_2003_12_29.html

Felipe, Jesus and Rana Hasan."The Challenge of Job Creation in Asia." Economics and Research Department (ERD) Policy Brief, Series no. 44. Manilla, The Philippines: The Asian Development Bank, 04/2006: 1-13.

Findlay, Christopher and Andrew Watson. "Economic Growth and trade dependency in China." *China Rising: Nationalism and Interdependence.* David S. G. Goodman and Gerald Segal, editors. London: Routledge, 1997: 107-133.

Fiscal Policy Office and the Office of Industrial Economics, Bangkok, Thailand. "Thailand: The Road to Recovery." *Asian Corporate Recovery: Findings from Firm-Level Surveys in Five Countries.* Dominique Dwor-Frecaut, Francis Colaco, and Mary Hallward-Driemeier, editors. Washington, DC: The World Bank, 2000: 219-238.

Flatters, Frank. "Thailand and the Crisis: Roots, Recovery, and Long-Run Competiveness." *The Asian Financial Crisis: Lessons for a Resilient Asia.* Wing Thye Woo, Jeffrey Sachs, and Klaus Schwab, editors. Cambridge, Massachusetts: The MIT Press, 2000: 257-274.

Friedman, Thomas L. *The Lexus and the Olive Tree.* New York: Farrar, Straus, & Giroux, 2000.

Glick, Reuven. "Thoughts on the Origins of the Asian Crisis: Impulses and Propagation Mechanisms." *The Asian Financial Crisis: Origins, Implications, and Solutions.* Hunter, William C., George G. Kaufman, & Thomas H. Krueger editors. London: Kluwer Academic Press, 1999: 33-64.

Godement, Francois. *The Downsizing of Asia.* London: Routledge, 1999.

Goldstein, Morris. *Safeguarding Prosperity in a Global Financial System: The Future International Financial Architecture.* An Independent Task Force Report Sponsored by the Council on Foreign Relations & published by the Institute for International Economics (IIE). Carla A. Hill & Peter G. Peterson, Co-Chairs and Morris Goldstein, Project Director. New York, NY: Council on Foreign Relations, Inc., 1999.

Gomez, Edmund Terence & Jomo K.S. *Malaysia's Political Economy: Politics, Patronage, and Profits.* New York: Cambridge University Press, 1999.

Goodman, David S.G., "How Open is Chinese society?" *China Rising: Nationalism and Interdependence.* Ed. David S.G. Goodman and Gerald Segal. London: Routledge, 1997: 27-52.

Grenville, Stephen. "Capital Flows and Crisis." *The Asian Financial Crisis and the Architecture of Global Finance.* Gregory W. Noble and John Ravenhill, editors. Cambridge: Cambridge University Press, 2000: 36-56.

Guerin, Bill. "Indonesia's Economy: Everything But Money." Hong Kong, China: *The Asia Times Online, Ltd.*, 2003: 1-3. www.atimes.com/atimes/printN.html

Guerin, Bill. "Indonesia: Economy Key in Presidential Run-In." Hong Kong, China: *The Asia Times Online, Ltd.*, 8 June 2004: 1-4. www.atimes.com/atimes/printN.html

Guitian, Manuel. "Lessons for the International Financial System." *The Asian Financial Crisis: Origins, Implications, and Solutions.* Hunter, William C., George G. Kaufman, & Thomas H. Krueger editors. London: Kluwer Academic Press, 1999: 461-466.

Gwynne, Robert N., Thomas Klak, and Denise J.B. Shaw. *Alternative Capitalism: Geographies of Emerging Regions.* London, Great Britain: Arnold Publishers, 2003.

Haggard, Stephan. *The Political Economy of the Asian Financial Crisis.* Washington, DC: The Institute of International Economics, 2000.

Haggard, Stephan & Andrew MacIntyre. "The Political Economy of the Asian Financial Crisis: Korea and Thailand Compared." *The Asian Financial Crisis and the Architecture of Global Finance.* Gregory W. Noble and John Ravenhill, editors. Cambridge: Cambridge University Press, 2000: pp. 57-79.

Hahnel, Robin. *Panic Rules: Everything You Need to Know About the Global Economy.* South End Press, Cambridge MA, 1999.

Hamilton-Hart, Natasha. "Indonesia: Reforming the Institutions of Financial Governance." *The Asian Financial Crisis and the Architecture of Global Finance.* Gregory W. Noble and John Ravenhill, editors. Cambridge: Cambridge University Press, 2000: 108-131.

Hanna, Don. "Restructuring Asia's Financial System." *The Asian Financial Crisis: Lessons for a Resilient Asia.* Wing Thye Woo, Jeffrey Sachs, and Klaus Schwab, editors. Cambridge, Massachusetts: The MIT Press, 2000: 45-70.

Harvey, Rachel. "Indonesia's Packed Election Year." Great Britain: *BBC News*, 19 January 2004: 1-3.
news.bbc.co.uk/1/hi/world/asia-pacific/3402449.stm

Harvey, Rachel. "Profile: Susilo Bambang Yudhoyono." Great Britain: *BBC News*, 18 May 2004: 1-3.
news.bbc.co.uk/1/hi/world/asia-pacific/3725301.stm

Harvie, Charles. "The Financial Crisis In Indonesia: The Role of Good Governance." *The Causes and Impact of the Asian Financial Crisis.* Great Britain: MacMillan Press, Ltd., 2000: 95-132.

Hausmann, Ricardo. "Should There Be Five Currencies or One-Hundred and Five." *Foreign Policy* Fall, 1999: 65-79.

Hoa, Tran Van. "Causes of and Prescriptions for the Asian Financial Crisis." *The Causes and Impact of the Asian Financial Crisis.* Tran Van Hoa and Charles Harvie editors. Great Britain: MacMillan Press, Ltd., 2000: 11-25.

Hwang, Y Dolly. *The Rise of a New World Economic Power: Postwar Taiwan.* New York: Greenwood Press, 1991.

Iwasaki, Yoshihiro. "Whither Thailand." *The Asian Financial Crisis: Origins, Implications, and Solutions.* Hunter, William C., George G. Kaufman, & Thomas H. Krueger editors. London: Kluwer Academic Press, 1999: 193-205.

Jackson, Karl D. "Introduction: The Roots of the Crisis." *Asian Contagion: The Causes and Consequences of a Financial Crisis.* Jackson, Karl D. editor. Colorado: Westview Press, 1999: 1-28.

Khan, Habibullah. "A Brief Assessment of Singapore's Economic Miracle." Abu N.M. Wahid, ed. *The ASEAN Region in Transition: A Socioeconomic Perspective.* Sidney: Ashgate Publishing Ltd., 1997: 87-108.

Krugman, Paul R. *The Return of Depression Economics.* London: W.W. Norton and Company, 2000.

Krugman, Paul R. and Maurice Obstfeld. *International Economics: Theory & Policy.* 5th Edition. New York: Addison-Wesley, 2000.

Krugman, Paul R. "What Happened to Asia?" Massachusetts: Massachusetts Institute of Technology (MIT), January of 1998: 1-11.
web.mit.edu/krugman/www/DISINTER.html

Lardy, Nicholas R., *China in the World Economy.* Washington, DC: Institute for International Economics, 1994.

Lauridsen, Laurids S. "Thailand: Causes, Conduct, Consequences." *Tigers in Trouble: Financial Governance, Liberalisation and Crises in East Asia.* Jomo K.S. editor. Hong Kong: Hong Kong University Press, 1998: 137-161.

Lee, Tsun-Siou. "Economic Development and Financial System Reform in Taiwan." *Financial Big Bang in Asia.* Masayoshi Tsurumi, editor. Singapore: Ashgate, 2001: 89-105.

Maitra, Ramtanu. "Why India's Economy Lags Behind China's." Hong Kong, China: *The Asia Times Online, Ltd.*, 27 June 2003: 1-4.
www.atimes.com/atimes/South_Asia/EF27Df04.html

Malaysian Industrial Development Authority (MIDA). "Performance of the Manufacturing and Related Services Sectors 2005." Malaysia: *MIDA*, 16 February 2006: 1-149.
www.mida.gov.my/beta/pdf/Performance%20of%20the%20Manufacturing%20and%20Related%20Services%20Sectors%20in%202005.pdf

Malaysian Institute of Economic Research. *Short-Term Outlook - Executive Summary.* Malaysia: *MIER*, April 20th, 2004: 1.
www.mier.org.my/sterm.shtml

Mann, Catherine & Daniel Rosen. "The New Economy & APEC." Singapore: The APEC Secretariat, 2001.

McFarlane, Bruce. " The ASEAN Economies: Growth and Change in Newly Emerging Socio-Economic Systems." Sheridan, Kyoko, ed. *Emerging Economic Systems in Asia: A Political & Economic Survey.* Australia: Allen & Unwin, 1998. 119-143.

McLeod, Ross H. "Indonesia's Crisis and Future Prospects." *Asian Contagion: The Causes and Consequences of a Financial Crisis.* Jackson, Karl D. ed. Colorado: Westview Press, 1999: 209-240.

Michalski, Wolfgang, Riel Miller, and Barrie Stevens. *China in the Twenty-first Century: An Overview of the Long-term Issues.* Paris Cedex, France: Organization For Economic Cooperation and Development, 1996: 7-36.

Montes, Manuel F. and Muhammad Ali Abdusalamov. "Indonesia: Reaping the Market." *Tigers in Trouble: Financial Governance, Liberalisation and Crises in East Asia.* Jomo K.S. editor. Hong Kong: Hong Kong University Press, 1998: 162-180.

MSNBC.com. "Embattled Thai PM Hands Over Power to Deputy: Move Follows Two Months of Protests Calling for Thaksin's Resignation." New York, NY: *NBC News*, 04/05/2006: 1-5. www.msnbc.msn.com/id/12128723/from/RSS/

Murray, Geoffrey & Audrey Perrera. *Singapore: The Global City State.* New York: St. Martin's Press, 1996.

Mydans, Seth & Thomas Fuller. "With Premier at U.N., Thai Military Stages Coup." New York, NY: *New York Times*, 20 September 2006: 1-5. www.nytimes.com/2006/09/20/world/asia/20thaicnd.html?hp&ex=1158724800&en=f076b8d685fd69d1&ei=5094&partner=homepage

National Development Planning Agency (BAPPENAS). "Indonesia: The Impact of the Economic Crisis on Industry Performance." *Asian Corporate Recovery: Findings from Firm-Level Surveys in Five Countries.* Dominique Dwor-Frecaut, Francis Colaco, and Mary Hallward-Driemeier, editors. Washington, DC: The World Bank, 2000: 141-158.

Naughton, Tony. "Taiwan: An Island State with Economic Insulation?" *The Causes and Impact of the Asian Financial Crisis.* Tran Van Hoa and Charles Harvie, editors. London: MacMillan Press Ltd., 2000: 160-172.

Neher, Clark D. *Southeast Asia in the New International Era.* San Francisco: Westview Press, 1991.

New York Times. "Thai Court Says Vote Was Unconstitutional." From Reuters. New York, NY: *New York Times*, 8 May 2006: 1 www.nytimes.com/reuters/world/international-thailand-court-ruling.html?hp&ex=1147147200&en=a8d81ecd9320c217&ei=5094&partner=homepage

Nidhiprabha, Bhanupong. "The Debt-Deflation Episode in Thailand." *Southeast Asia's Economic Crisis: Origins, Lessons, and the Way Forward.* H.W. Arndt & Hal Hill, editors. New York: St. Martin's Press, 1999: 67-80.

Noble, Gregory W. and John Ravenhill. "The Good, the Bad, and the Ugly? Korea, Taiwan, and the Asian Financial Crisis." *The Asian Financial Crisis and the Architecture of Global Finance.* Gregory W. Noble and John Ravenhill, editors. Cambridge: Cambridge University Press, 2000: 80-107.

Organization for Economic Development and Cooperation (OECD). "ADB-OECD to Host Conference on Combating Corruption in Asia-Pacific." Paris Cedex, France: *The OECD*, 28 November 2003: 1-2. www.oecd.org/daf/ASIAcom

Organization for Economic Development and Cooperation (OECD). "Fourth ADB-OECD Anti-Corruption for Asia and the Pacific: Kuala Lumpur (3-5 December 2003)." Paris Cedex, France: *The OECD*, 2 October 2003: 1-2. www.oecd.org/documentprint/0,2744,en_2649_34857_15712016_1_1_1_1,00.html

Perkins, Dwight Heald and Wing Thye Woo. "Malaysia: Adjusting to Deep Integration with the World Economy." *The Asian Financial Crisis: Lessons for a Resilient Asia.* Wing Thye Woo, Jeffrey Sachs, and Klaus Schwab, editors. Cambridge, Massachusetts: The MIT Press, 2000: 227-255.

Perlez, Jane. "Asian Leaders Find China a More Cordial Neighbor." New York, NY: *New York Times*, 18 October 2003: 1-3. www.nytimes.com/2003/10/18/international/asia/18CHIN.html?

Perlez, Jane. "Mahathir, Malaysia's Autocratic Modernizer, Steps Down." New York, NY: *New York Times*, 1 November 2003: 1-3. www.nytimes.com/2003/11/01/international/asia/01MALA.html?

Perlez, Jane. "Saying Farewell to an Indonesia She Knew Too Well." *New York Times*, 19 June 2004: 1-3. www.nytimes.com/2004/06/19/international/asia/09jone.html?8hpib

Phongpaichit, Pasuk. "Japan's Investment and Local Capital in ASEAN since 1985. Shoichi Yamashita, ed. *Transfer of Japanese Technology and Management to the ASEAN Countries.* Tokyo: University of Tokyo Press, 1991: 3-22.

Pugel, Thomas A. and Peter H. Lindert. *International Economics.* 11th Edition. London: McGraw Hill, 2000.

Radelet, Steven C. & Wing Thye Woo. "Indonesia: A Troubled Beginning." *The Asian Financial Crisis: Lessons for a Resilient Asia.* Wing Thye Woo, Jeffrey Sachs, and Klaus Schwab, editors. Cambridge, Massachusetts: The MIT Press, 2000: 165-184.

Rai, Saritha. "India's Economy Soared by Ten Percent in Last Quarter of 2003." New York, NY: *New York Times*, 1 April 2004: W1.

REUTERS. "Former General Yudhoyono Wins Indonesia Poll." *New York Times*, 4 October 2004: 1-3. www.nytimes.com/reuters/international/international-indonesia-election.html

Robins, Fred. "Taiwan's Economic Success." Sheridan, Kyoto, ed. *Emerging Economic Systems in Asia: A Political & Economic Survey.* St. Leonards, Australia: Allen & Unwin, 1998: 45-69.

Robins, Fred. "Asia's 1997 Crash: Its Character, Causes, and Consequences." *The East Asian Development Model: Economic Growth, Institutional Failure, and the Aftermath of the Crisis.* Frank-Jurgen Richter editor. London: MacMillan Press, Ltd., 2000: 17-52.

Ryan, Orla. "Asia Still Scarred by Crisis." Great Britain: *BBC News*, 2 July 2002: 1-5.
www.news.bbc.co.uk/1/hi/business/2077575.stm

Sachs, Jeffrey & Felipe Larrain. "Why Dollarization is More Straitjacket than Salvation." *Foreign Policy,* Fall 1999: 80-93.

Sadli, Mohammad. "The Indonesian Crisis." *Southeast Asia's Economic Crisis: Origins, Lessons, and the Way Forward.* H.W. Arndt & Hal Hill, editors. New York: St. Martin's Press, 1999: 16-27.

Saler, Thomas D., *All About Global Investing.*
New York: John Wiley & Sons, Inc., 1996

Sarel, Michael. "Growth in East Asia: What We Can and What We Cannot Infer." *Development and Underdevelopment: The Political Economy of Global Inequality.* Mitchell A. Seligson & John T. Passe-Smith, editors. London: Lynne Rienner Publishers, 1998: pp. 408-419.

Sing, Lim Hua. *Japan's Role in Asia. 2nd Edition.*
Singapore: Times Media Private Ltd., 1999.

Solomon, Robert. *Money on the Move: The Revolution in the International Finance Since 1980.* Princeton, New Jersey: Princeton University Press, 1999.

Stiglitz, Joseph E. *Economics.* 2nd Edition. New York: W.W. Norton & Company, 1997.

Tan, Gerald. *The Asian Currency Crisis.* Singapore: Times Academic Press, 2000.

Tejima, Shigeki. "Foreign Direct Investment by Japanese Firms in the Asia-Pacific Region." *Emerging Growth Pole: The Asia-Pacific Economy.* Dilip K. Das, editor. London: Prentice Hall, 1997: 130.

Thong, Gregory T.S., "Foundations of Human Resources Management Practice in Japanese Companies in Malaysia." Shoichi Yamashita, ed. *Transfer of Japanese Technology and Management to the ASEAN Countries.* Tokyo: University of Tokyo Press, 1991: 135-149.

Weaver, James H., Michael T. Rock, & Kenneth Kusterer. *Achieving Broad-Based Sustainable Development: Governance, Environment, and Growth with Equity.* West Hartford, Connecticut: Kumarian Press, 1997.

Williamson, John. "The Case for a Common Basket Peg for East Asia Currencies." Washington, DC: *The Institute for International Economics*, 1996: 1-13.
www.iie.com/publications/papers/paper.cfm?ResearchID=280

Wong-Anan, Nopporn. "Thailand Sets Election Rerun for October 15." (Printer friendly version). London, Great Britain: *Reuters*, 30 May 2006: 1-2.
today.reuters.com/news/newsArticle.aspx?type=worldNews&
storyID=2006-05-30T093633Z_01_BKK249003_RTRUKOC_0_US-
THAILAND.xml&pageNumber=0&imageid=&cap=&sz=13&
WTModLoc=NewsArt-C1-ArticlePage2

Yamashita, Shoichi. "Economic Development of the ASEAN Countries and the Role of Japanese Direct Investment." Shoichi Yamashita, ed. *Transfer of Japanese Technology and Management to the ASEAN Countries*. Tokyo: University of Tokyo Press, 1991: 23-54.

Yoshihara, Kunio. *Japanese Investment in Southeast Asia* Honolulu: The University Press of Hawaii, 1978.

The Index

~

~

About the Author

David A. Hollingsworth is currently an assistant editor/intern for the Center for International Relations, a Forum based in Arlington, Virginia. He writes op-ed pieces for the Center surrounding issues and developments that shape our global community. A graduate from both American University and the State University of New York at Buffalo, Mr. Hollingsworth wrote extensively on economic development matters particularly of Asia and Latin America and ways in which to foster future developments while taking steps to prevent crises in magnitudes like those witnessed in the 1990s. Furthermore, Mr. Hollingsworth possesses a considerable legal experience which helps sharpen his analysis on pertinent and sometimes pressing issues. Although born and raised in New York City, Mr. Hollingsworth currently resides in Washington, DC.